Withdrawn

The
Little Bookstore
of Big Stone Gap

Center Point
Large Print

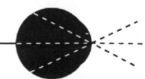

**This Large Print Book carries the
Seal of Approval of N.A.V.H.**

The
Little Bookstore
of Big Stone Gap

a memoir of friendship, community,
and the uncommon pleasure
of a good book

Wendy Welch

CENTER POINT LARGE PRINT
THORNDIKE, MAINE

This Center Point Large Print edition
is published in the year 2012 by arrangement with
St. Martin's Press.

Copyright © 2012 by Wendy Welch.

The text of this Large Print edition is unabridged.
In other aspects, this book may vary
from the original edition.
Printed in the United States of America
on permanent paper.
Set in 16-point Times New Roman type.

ISBN: 978-1-61173-583-3

Library of Congress Cataloging-in-Publication Data

Welch, Wendy.
  The little bookstore of Big Stone Gap : a memoir of friendship,·
community, and the uncommon pleasure of a good book / Wendy Welch.
    p. cm.
  Originally published: New York : St. Martin's Press, 2012.
  ISBN 978-1-61173-583-3 (library binding : alk. paper)
    1. Bookstores—Virginia. 2. Antiquarian booksellers—Virginia.
    3. Married people—Employment. 4. Book collectors. I. Title.
Z478.3.V57W45 2012b
381'.4500209755—dc23
                                                        2012029961

If you have ever walked away from doing something "important" to do something better, this book is dedicated to you.

It's also dedicated to everyone who loves books.

CONTENTS

Author's Note

This is a true story. I've changed some names and identifying details, created composites, and altered a few elements of the timeline to make events easier to understand. I hope the people who find themselves described here enjoy reliving the moments, and I hope the rest of you enjoy reading about all the silly things we did.

When you sell a person a book you don't just sell twelve ounces of paper and ink and glue—you sell a whole new life. Love and friendship and humor and ships at sea by night—there's all heaven and earth in a book, a real book.

—Christopher Morley,
The Haunted Bookshop

Prologue

Let me live in a house by the side of the
  road
Where the race of men go by—
The men who are good and the men who
  are bad,
As good and as bad as I.
I would not sit in the scorner's seat
Nor hurl the cynic's ban—
Let me live in a house by the side of the
  road
And be a friend to man.

—Sam Foss,
"The House by the Side of the Road,"
from *Dreams in Homespun*

THREE A.M. SLEEP WAS GONE. My mind whirled with boxes to unpack, items to find.

Sliding from under the cat curled on my chest— she opened one eye and indicated displeasure—I crept toward the stairs. From behind came a soft *whump* as our Labrador gained the mattress, made peace with the cat, and claimed the sleep that eluded me.

Downstairs, an electric kettle sat next to the tea chest on an otherwise empty counter, testament to my Scottish husband's priorities. I made a mug of raspberry tea and wandered into the large front room. The cavernous house, walls lined with empty bookshelves, stretched into dark nothingness, waiting. In the middle of the room my laptop rested on an old mission table, the only other furniture. Both looked dwarfed and out of place.

I could relate. Since arriving in Big Stone Gap, Virginia, Jack and I had been living as gracefully as fish astride mopeds. On something dangerously close to a whim, we became the broke and terrified owners of a five-bedroom, three-bath-with-one-working Edwardian mansion, complete with squeaky hardwood floors and a leaking roof. Under the influence of salsa and sangria, we'd decided to turn this house into a used book store, or die trying.

Probably the latter, I thought, watching the Internet fire up against the blue-gray darkness. *What are we doing here, anyway? This is the kind of town you see in true crime documentaries, where the bodies are never found because the locals don't tell.*

Jack had just yesterday erected a gigantic sign in four-hundred-point type, announcing USED BOOK STORE OPENING SOON. That pretty much cemented our status as "those new weirdos in the old Meade house." Passersby who stopped to read the sign made encouraging comments along the lines of, "A bookstore? You're nuts!"

For which were we nuts, I wanted to ask: For pretending we'd never heard of iPads, e-books, and Kindles? For thinking a town coping with its own dying coal industry would support a new business? Believing the downturned economy would swing upward soon? Hoping that the old guard in a notoriously insular region might welcome new kids onto the block? Or, our worst nightmare, for all of the above?

Headlights swung in a wide arc outside, startling me from doom-laden reverie. A siren emitted a single *whoop* amid a sudden blue flash. *Must be pulling over a drunk driver,* I thought. Our would-be bookstore sat along the top of a T-intersection. A police SUV hovered in its junction as a spotlight lit the front room. Curtainless floor-to-ceiling windows left us naked to outside eyes, but why were the police investigating at three in the morning?

The Bronco drove around the corner and tried to enter a grass driveway at the side yard. The chain-link fence—a priority because of our born-to-ramble dogs—had gone up as soon as we moved in, closing off that drive. Now the SUV stopped inches from the mesh; if a vehicle could look frustrated, this one did. It turned and chugged back around the corner, pulling up at our curb.

The driver's door opened. Running a hand over my tangled mass of red hair, I belted Jack's bathrobe tighter and opened the front door.

Or tried to. It was original to this 1903 monstrosity we now owned, so I managed to turn the brass lock, but the warped wooden frame stuck. A keyhole sat below the knob, looking smug. Was the door locked? Where was that key? Had we found it yet? I tugged again. Nothing.

A short, squat shadow came striding up the stairs. *This is how people get shot!* I thought, envisioning the officer's view from the other side—a dark body mass struggling with an object just out of sight. I waved in an "I come in peace" sort of way.

The policeman put a hand to his holster.

"Hang on!" I called through the glass. "The door won't open!" I gave a mighty tug and the knob fell into my hand as the door flew wide, throwing me off balance; raspberry tea sloshed onto the floor and the bathrobe belt slackened. Slipping the doorknob into a pocket, tightening my grip on the mug, and tossing hair from my eyes, I stepped barefoot onto the porch to say, "Good morning, Officer."

His eyes swept over hair, robe, mug, feet. "Do you live here?"

No, I'm a burglar; the tea is for cover. Tempting though it was, commonsense pistons fired in time, and instead I replied, "Yes, sir."

"Mmm." He pushed his gun, hovering an alarming two inches from its holster, back into place.

"My husband and I just bought this house."

"What for?"

Because we're nuts. "We're opening a bookstore."

"A bookstore? You're nuts!" He slapped his thigh in gleeful emphasis.

"So I believe. Were you pulling someone over for drunk driving?" *Why are we having this conversation in the middle of the night?*

The officer stared as if I truly were insane. "What? This is an official safety check. I figured burglars since I saw movement and light."

And they put up signs and erected a chain-link fence? Aloud I replied, "Nope, just harmless little Jack and Wendy. I had insomnia and came down to use the computer. But I saw you in the intersection when your siren . . . um, blipped."

The officer averted his gaze, rocking on the balls of his feet. "Oh. Yeah. I hit the wrong button."

Okay, that was endearing, so we stood on the porch and talked into the dark. Grundy, as he introduced himself, planned to retire in six months. His brother, a successful surgeon, owned a place in the Florida Keys, a palatial home of seven bedrooms, cathedral ceilings, and a sauna, to which Grundy had yet to be invited. Grundy attended church every Sunday, was a member of the Kiwanis club, voted in all civic elections, but it was his brother who had millions, and if you asked Grundy it was down to insurance fraud.

"Ain't that the way of it?" my new friend lamented. "Me in public service, him getting rich."

Grundy knew the elderly women who'd shared the house before us. "Looked in on 'em from time to time," he said, eyebrows wiggling in a way it seemed wise not to explore. After the former owner went to a nursing home, her friend had been evicted without ceremony. "Got the lawyer's letter at noon, she was out on the street by four."

I emitted a sympathetic noise.

"Don't feel sorry for *her*. Con artist of the first water. Probably owes money to everybody from here to the state line."

"Oh," I said.

"Since they left, I usually drive up in the yard, check the house, make sure everything's all right. Couldn't do that tonight. Fence in the way." He squinted at me in an accusing manner.

"We have a black Lab, Zora. She's a good watchdog." *Asleep, upstairs.* "And Bert, our terrier, is a total yipster. Barks at everything." *Also sound asleep.*

He nodded, apparently relieved that his duties had passed to qualified personnel.

By the time Grundy shook my hand farewell,

dawn had slipped its early promises into the sky. He started for the steps, then looked back. "Y'know, it's great y'all are putting in a bookstore. Not a lot to do around here. I'll come see you after I retire. I like Westerns."

It felt good, that tossed-off tacit approval. Like being given the key to the city. Town. Village. Front door.

As I turned toward the house, a brief *whoop* sounded and a blue flash lit the intersection. Grundy rolled down his window. "Gol durn it!" he called with a smiling shrug, then lifted his hat in salute and drove into the sunrise.

The front door wouldn't lock, but so what? Grundy watched over us as we slept.

Upstairs, my husband opened one dozy eye and watched me trick our Labrador off the mattress with the doorknob. "Is that from the front door?" Jack asked as Zora, realizing she'd been had, dropped the brass ball with a sarcastic clunk and padded into the hallway, followed by a sleepy Bert.

"We now know someone in this town." I gave him a brief rundown of meeting Grundy.

Jack shook his head, eyes closed. "We're going to fit right in here," he said, and pushed his face into the pillow.

Dear Lord, I hope so, I prayed silently into the graying light.

CHAPTER 1
How to Be Attacked by Your Heart's Desire

Ever since happiness heard your name, it has been running through the streets trying to find you.

—Hafiz of Persia

PEOPLE TALK ABOUT FOLLOWING THEIR bliss, but if you're stubborn, unobservant sods like Jack and me, your bliss pretty much has to beat you over the head until you see things in a new light. By the time Jack and I met, some twelve years before the bookstore in Big Stone Gap entered our lives, we had between us lived in eight countries and visited more than forty; the first five years of our marriage were spent in Jack's native Scotland as cheerful workaholics with pretensions to vagabond artistry. His salary as a college department head and mine for directing an arts nonprofit afforded us fulfilling lives of music, story, friends, and travel throughout the British Isles and the States.

Since we'd married late in Jack's life, the second time for him and the first for me, an awareness of our age difference (twenty years) kept an easy balance going. The undertow of time's river reminded us to be happy with each other while we had the chance. With this in mind, we slid our day jobs between hop-away weekends performing stories and songs at festivals, fairs, and conferences. At first, Jack sang and I told stories, but as the years rolled by, his song introductions got longer and I sang more ballads until we were pretty much both doing both.

Driving home from these road trips tired and happy, Jack and I often engaged in casual banter about what we'd do "someday" when we gave up the weekend warrior routine. Such conversations revolved around a recurring theme:

"Someday we'll give up this madness, settle down, and run a nice bookstore," I'd say.

"A used book store, with a café that serves locally grown food," he'd agree.

"It will have incredibly beautiful hardwood floors that squeak when you walk across them."

"Lots of big windows to let in the sunlight, as it will of course face south."

"In a town with tree-lined streets, where there's lots of foot traffic so people walk in on impulse. Everyone will love us as colorful local characters. You can wear a baggy Mr. Rogers sweater and push your glasses up your nose and talk about

Scotland, and I can teach at the nearby university and write the great American novel."

"It will have high ceilings with old-fashioned wooden fans." Jack liked to stick to physical descriptions.

"And a unicorn in the garden." Two can play at that game.

"Of course! It will keep the elephants company." My husband is a go-with-the-flow kind of guy.

Mile after road-weary mile, we created castle-in-the-clouds daydreams about the used book store we would run "someday." When the five-thousand-square-foot personification of this idle pastime appeared without warning at a most inconvenient moment, it didn't so much enter as take over our lives.

We didn't arrive in Big Stone intending to run a used book store, and in fact we almost passed up the chance when presented with it. Two years before we moved to Virginia, we had left the United Kingdom for the States so I could take a position in the Snake Pit. (That's not its real name, in case you were wondering.) That move landed me in a high-power game of snakes and ladders in a government agency—except we played with all snakes and no ladders. In this "bite or be bitten" ethos, it really didn't matter what was true; it mattered whether you could bite harder than you were bitten—and that you never questioned why biting was the preferred method of communication.

Freedom might be another word for nothing left to lose, or the moment when common sense blossoms through the mud. One fine day I woke up seeing clearly for the first time in two years. A willing entrant into the Snake Pit—because the job looked exciting and as though it offered chances to do good in the world—I'd become instead just another biter. No, thank you; life is not about who gets the biggest chunk of someone else's flesh.

Unless you're a zombie.

I talked to a lawyer, gave two weeks' notice, and walked away. Almost everyone has experienced a Snake Pit at some point in their lives—more's the pity. Bad as our Pit was, Jack and I were fortunate. We owned our house and don't eat much, so we could call it quits. That's a luxury many people stuck in horrible situations—from minimum wage to white collar—don't share. Sensitive humans doing a job they hate to keep food on the family table or a kid in school deserve major honor. If you're in that position, kudos for sticking it out. God grant you an exit ramp soon, and forbearance until it appears.

For Jack and me, exiting Pitsville seemed like a bad cliché: midlife crisis meets crisis of conscience. The Fourteenth Dalai Lama expressed sympathy for anyone who "lives as if he is never going to die, and then dies having never really lived." C. S. Lewis said almost the same thing in *The Screwtape Letters*, that people who suddenly wake up in the middle of some "important" activity and ask themselves, "am I enjoying this?" rarely answer yes, yet spend their lives doing the same things anyway.

Living in a world with no moral center had thrown us into an off-kilter limbo. We longed to return to a gentle life with friendly people who had less to prove and more honesty in how they proved it. So when I was offered a low-profile job running educational programs in the tiny southwestern Virginia town of Big Stone Gap, we packed our bags and shook the venom from our shoes.

Big Stone (as the locals call it) is nestled in the mountains of central Appalachia, in what locals call the Coalfields. The town had been on its way to becoming the Chicago of the South in the early 1900s, until the coal boom went bust. Now it was just another dot on the map, full of coal miners and retirees, with an embattled downtown and a Walmart up by the four-lane. Football games and high school reunions were the biggest local events.

A nice gentle job in The Gap (its other nickname) seemed a good situation in a pleasant place; we could hang out for a year enjoying life in the slow lane without getting too attached. I'm from central Appalachia, Jack from Scotland. Mountains and rural living are some of the ties that bind us.

While helping us look for housing cheap enough to be realistic yet cozy enough to be comfortable,

Debbie, the affable local realtor, discovered we liked old houses. Her company had just acquired one she hadn't yet seen, so we stopped and explored it together, just to take a break.

That's how the Bookstore ensnared us. Edith Schaeffer, who with her husband cofounded a Christian commune called L'Abri, once wrote, "The thing about real life is that important events don't announce themselves. Trumpets don't blow . . . Usually something that is going to change your whole life is a memory before you can stop and be impressed about it."

That about sums it up.

The five-bedroom 1903 Edwardian sat near two intersections, and edged a neighborhood of sturdy brick homes and leafy bungalows. Parking spaces dotted the front curb. The place felt snug and cozy the moment we walked in, despite its voluminous size.

"Squeaky floors," my husband said with a frown, rubbing one rubber sole across the scarred hardwood.

"The pocket doors stick," Debbie observed, sneezing as she wrestled oak panels from their hiding places amid a shower of dust.

"That's a lot of windows for somebody to wash." I pointed at the floor-to-ceiling panes adorning three open-plan rooms, stretched across the southern-facing house front.

Rickety wooden fans hung from high ceilings,

wires exposed. The second-floor parlor, with its peeling wallpaper, overlooked the town's tree-lined ancillary street one block from where it intersected the main road. The ghost of cat pee wafted from the oak staircase, which boasted exquisite copper corner pieces dulled by neglect. My husband and I stared at each other with lust in our eyes, thanked Debbie-the-Realtor for the impromptu visit, and left her making notes of things to fix before the house could be put on the market.

From the Edwardian mansion, Jack and I headed to Little Mexico, a signature Big Stone Gap restaurant. Little Mexico sits at the top of a hill next to Walmart, and the parking lot offers magnificent views of the surrounding mountains. The season's flowering power—rhododendron pink, mountain laurel white, cornflower purple—displayed its full glory in the midday sun. Inside, we dipped tortilla chips into fiery salsa and eyed each other through sangria glasses.

We had no money. We'd bought a house in the Snake Pit with cash when we first came over from Scotland, but the economy had just tanked while the housing market crashed amid escalating horror stories; no way would we be able to sell that house quickly. Thus we couldn't afford to buy without getting a mortgage, and given the nose-diving economy and the limited appeal my esoteric PhD in ethnography had in the job market, that didn't seem wise. We needed to just park ourselves quietly for a year and regroup. It was madness to even think along unicorn-in-the-garden lines. No, the word "bookstore" would not come out of my mouth.

Jack crunched a corn chip. "That big white house would have made a perfect bookstore, had it been in a bigger town."

I knew it! "Oh, did you think so?"

My husband of ten years smiled. "I knew that's what you were thinking. Debbie said the population is 5,400. That's not enough people to support a bookstore, and anyway we won't be here that long."

"Yep," I agreed. "Stupid to get entangled in something like that now, when we're so tired and, you know, off balance."

"Aye. Not to mention, we don't have enough money."

"Or energy. Pity to see something so nice and not be able to take advantage of it, but the timing is so wrong. We need a sure thing. I'll handle this job for a year or two, and you can find some relaxing retirement project."

Jack waited a beat, then said thoughtfully, "But if we were to stay a wee while longer, there is a college nearby where you might teach . . . well, not that we're thinking of long-term plans now."

My heartbeat accelerated. "No, not that we're thinking long-term."

"We'll set up a bookstore someday."

"Mhmm. Someday."

We crunched in silence, and then Jack drew his sword and slew the dragon. "What if someday is today?"

Not even a gentle *pop* resounded as the cork flew from our bottled-up lives. But the waitstaff seemed startled when I leaned across the table, stomach grazing the chip basket, and kissed my best friend long and hard on the lips.

CHAPTER 2
No Longer Renting the Space Inside My Skin

Oh the water is wide, I can't cross o'er.
Neither have I wings to fly.
Build me a boat that will carry two,
And both shall row, my love and I.
                              —Scottish folk song

THE INK WASN'T DRY ON my signature before I regretted the impulsive, made-with-the-heart-not-the-head decision to buy that house at the side of the road. Sure, we've all heard the Dr. Phil chatter: follow your bliss and the money will follow.

Yeah, right. Anybody out there still unaware that life does not always resemble a Hallmark commercial? Bank accounts are amazing reality checks—no pun intended.

The Edwardian wanted structural fixing, while our minuscule savings needed cash injections, not drainage. Buying that big white elephant would be driving on the wrong side of the money highway. A house back at the Snake Pit waited to be sold in the tanking real estate market. The word "recession" loomed in nightly news stories. The quiet little position I'd come to town for was not PhD level, and a couple of staff members already wondered openly what I was doing there. (The job was with the same type of state organization as the toxic one I'd fled had been, which those with the foresight God gave mayflies might call a dumb move. We would call it that, and many other things besides, in the coming months.) I had defended my doctoral dissertation just as the economy—along with university hiring—was drying up. The possible safety net of something opening at one of the two area colleges, should my day job go away, was not a strong bet. A safety net that lacks enough strength to catch you really isn't much of a safety net, is it?

Stacked against all that, we had two very important things going for us: we believed in ourselves and each other, and we were desperate. We craved returning to a sweet, happy, slow life. A lot of money wasn't important—just enough to eat, sleep, and stay warm through the winter. All we asked was to contribute something to a community and derive pleasure from doing so—plus health insurance.

Necessity may be the mother of invention, but desperation is her very pushy pimp. Jack and I had a long talk that afternoon as the waitstaff, convinced we were crazy and in need of gentle humoring, brought basket after basket of chips and salsa. (To this day, when gripped by intense emotions, I crave fried salt.) At one point I described living in the Snake Pit as "renting the space inside my own skin." A phrase that had been haunting me for weeks. I'd never said it out loud before. Trapped in all those hidden agendas, putting a foot right proved impossible.

Let two mild examples suffice. In one instance, a volunteer begged an employee organizing a very large and important event for a specific assignment, got it, and then left the task undone, while bragging to another person that he'd never intended to do the work; instead he fired off an e-mail to the organizer's boss, telling the (notoriously uninvolved and oblivious) senior official how angry he felt that such an important task had been neglected. Another time, a supervisor told me to send a certain answer to a "concerned citizen's" question, copied to the supervisor. When the concerned citizen e-mailed again, the supervisor e-mailed him directly that I had given incorrect information, and he would speak to me about it.

Just another day in the Snake Pit. Watch your back, and if you have any energy left over, do your job.

My husband looked me in the eye. "We're not going to live like that anymore."

Jack does not make promises lightly; I started to feel a little safer.

A little. It's hard to explain, but the Pit had been my dream job until it revealed its horrors. A perceived opportunity to do positive things had ended in literal nightmares. Now here Jack and I were, just two months later, talking about another dream we'd cherished for a long time. I didn't see how I could survive if it too went rotten.

I said as much to Jack. He looked at me with those keen hazel eyes, and covered my hand—trembling around my glass—with both of his. "We just left a maze of moral weirdness," he said. "It's got you confused. Think a minute, love. How can something be rotten when it has you, me, sincerity, and books at its center?" he asked.

Put that way . . .

Passivity eddied away as we took up oars and began to row—hard. We could do this; we could open a bookstore inside that house, live upstairs, and just see how things went for a year, then reassess. Maybe then we would go back to doing gigs full-time, or the fairy godmother of decent, honest living would visit us some other way.

Now might be a good time to point out that all this soul-searching took place before the Edwardian even hit the real estate market. Impatient little souls we were, but once dreaming became an option again, waiting five more minutes felt impossible. If we waited, I'd lose my nerve and go back to triple-guessing every move and how it could be perceived—a nasty habit I'd picked up in you-know-where.

Jack, who knows me very well, took no chances. Seeking out Debbie straight from the restaurant, he explained our plan.

"A bookstore!? You're nuts!" she said, and helped us use our house in Pitsville as collateral for buying the big, beautiful, scary home five minutes after it went on the market. We moved in upstairs an hour after signing papers at the lawyer's office. That night, even before we had bedroom furniture, Jack took two hundred dollars from savings and bought lumber, hammer, and nails. The next morning he dug through the boxes filling our front room—*our* front room!—to find his tools, and installed bookshelves downstairs amid the rubble and chaos. Subliminally, I think we considered filling the space with shelves symbolic. Like Dr. Seuss's Whos in Whoville, each hammer blow shouted, "We are here, we are here, we are here!"

Books to put on those shelves had to wait awhile, since we were flat broke and living out of cardboard-box furniture. Lacking funds to collect ours in a rental truck—we'd just shoved clothes and anything small enough to fit in boxes into our car and fled—we planned to make do for a month or so until we had a little money saved up. In fact, moving in above the shop-to-be was the only thing making the store financially possible in our present circumstances. Although I'd like to say we were clued in enough to understand the accompanying tax breaks of living where one works, we planned to live upstairs because it required no additional cash outlay and offered sufficient space for two humans, two dogs, and two cats. Living overhead kept us from having financial overhead, which was what saved us in later months. God looks after fools and little children.

News spread quickly about the incomers who had bought the old Meade place and planned to reside above some kind of shop. The only people living above shops in Big Stone were shift workers in low-paying jobs, invisible in rented flats (apartments to you) over main-street businesses they didn't work in or own. Now the owners of a business were going to live above it?

A small town's rumor mill activates quickly. In a place with perhaps six shops on its main street, where the Walmart didn't have electric doors yet, we became the story of the week. Locals stopped by, asking if we really planned to live atop—as the story grew—a bed-and-breakfast, consignment clothing store, massage parlor, or Scientology reading room. Jack erected a USED BOOK STORE OPENING SOON sign on the lawn almost as soon as we moved into the house, as much for self-defense as information. The curious and concerned stopped on the sidewalk, pointing as they passed. Their comments pretty much boiled down to "A bookstore?! You're nuts!"

Yet new and interesting friends also began gathering, including several invisible shift workers who loved reading. James, a miner disabled after an accident, staffed gas pumps by day and wrote poetry by night; he would later become a founding member of the store's writing group. Dave, fortysomething and as excited as a little boy, appeared on our porch one day, asking if we were really starting a bookstore. Newly diagnosed with epilepsy, he'd been let go from a burger place when the seizures started—no severance, no insurance, and no job prospects.

"I love to read," he said as his brother sat behind the wheel of a big red pickup, drumming his fingers on the dashboard and occasionally honking. "I can't drive; they took my license away 'cause of the seizures. Bud drives me when he can, but he don't like reading. I'll be back after you're open. When'd you say that'll be? And all the books are gonna be half price?"

The enthusiasm of Dave and James renewed our flagging energy. Soon we were even hunting for ways to join in community activities. When we could spare a minute, we looked around for places to visit, people to meet. One of the fastest ways to make friends turned out to be volunteering at the outdoor drama. Big Stone Gap has nurtured many writers, including John Fox, Jr., author of *The Trail of the Lonesome Pine*. In the 1970s, Fox's novel became a musical, kind of a folk opera, staged each July and August. Barbara Polly, the original female lead, still organizes Big Stone's annual summer run of what is now the longest-running outdoor drama in America. Jack and I did the preshow music one night, and at intermission a tall, dark-haired woman walked up to us and drawled, in a voice so Southern it fairly wafted magnolia blossom perfume, "Say somethin' else."

"Excuse me?" Jack said, startled but polite, and the lady, hand to her forehead, feigned a swoon.

"Whew!" she exclaimed, turning to me. "His accent's makin' my toes curl. I'm meltin' faster than butter on hot toast."

That's how we met Isabel, who became one of our staunchest friends. (And yes, she acts like that all the time. If you come to Big Stone, I'll introduce you.)

We also met Tony, a local pastor, and his wife, Becky. He'd been conned into selling the popcorn, and when Jack bought some, Tony said, "Hey, you're the new couple trying to start a bookstore, right? Poor souls. Well, good luck with that. Got a church yet?"

Word had apparently gone out that we were shopping for a church. More precisely, my Quaker husband said on our first Sunday morning in town, "Find a place we can go when we're not at a

Friends meeting, and let me know when you do." Then he rolled over and went back to sleep. The Society of Friends, aka Quakers, met a good two-hour drive away, so we planned to attend once a month there and find a church home in Big Stone Gap the rest of the time. Off I set on this mission, wearing a skirt and a smile.

Three churches sat just up the street from our store, and two more down. It's a Southern small town. We have four hairdressers, three museums, two nail salons, and fifty-six churches within a two-mile radius.

Spoiled for choice, I started with the Methodists, a mere four blocks up the road: great music, but they pledged allegiance to the American flag as part of the service. While I support both the United States and Christianity, mixing them promotes an unexamined assumption that makes Jack, a Christian who was not then American, nervous. Ixnay on the Methodists—although I met a lot of very nice individuals who shook hands and said, "So you're half of that bookstore couple! When's it open?" (An improvement over "You're nuts!") This was also my first meeting with David and Heather, a sweet couple down the street who frequented the shop once it opened. Heather later became an integral part of our pinch-hitting support staff.

The Baptists came next. Pledge as part of service. Bless you; next.

Another nearby church's sermon suggested—how

can I put this? that God was not only American, but male, white, and a fan of a particular football team. I really don't consider myself picky when it comes to churches, but a few weeks later, I still hadn't found anything plausible for Jack. Then someone at my day job suggested, "Y'all should try the one at the end of your block. It's full of weirdos and artistic types like you."

Uh, thanks.

We went, and they seemed like nice folks, so we went back, and word went 'round town that the New Couple had settled into a church. Pastors and lay ministers stopped calling.

In the Artists and Weirdos congregation, we met Teri and Gary. Teri is the town chiropractor. She and her professional-drummer husband parent a growing menagerie of some of the smartest, best-adjusted children ever. Teri and Gary wanted the bookshop to succeed for the sake of their kids, but we had no idea when we met them how helpful they would soon become.

Mark and Elizabeth also introduced themselves, then a moment later someone referred to her as Dr. Cooperstein.

"Oh, you have a doctorate?" I asked. "Where do you teach?" She gave me an odd look and said she directed the local hospital's emergency room. I was about to apologize when the minister's wife said, "Hey, that's right. You're a doctor, too."

Elizabeth beamed at me. "Oh! Where do you

practice? Would you like to visit the hospital?"

By the time we'd finished sorting my "phud" degree from her "mud," we were laughing and friends.

"I guess we all assume other people are what we are," Elizabeth said as her teenaged son, utterly disgusted at middle-aged women laughing and carrying on this way, edged out the door to wait on the porch.

In retrospect, many foundations for long-term friendships were laid during that church hunt. And between the church crowds, drama night team, and book enthusiasts who stopped by to see what we were up to, the bookstore-to-be carved out what looked like an accepted space for itself, and fairly quickly. It made us feel good, that so many locals really seemed excited about a bookshop coming to town; in the history annals of Big Stone, no bookstore had been recorded since its incorporation in the late 1800s.

For the rest of the townsfolk, seeing us gear up must have been like watching old people run a marathon—admiring their spirit while questioning their grasp on reality. Residents called us sweet, brave, and other pleasant code words for "lunatic" in an intriguing "glad you're here, sorry you won't be staying" sort of way.

That "won't be staying" remark came up pretty often, but we attributed it to a bad economy and the stereotypes people held about the education levels and reading habits of Coalfields Appalachia's residents. We figured people were assuming Big Stone lacked the population or interest to support a store, but just look at all the people already stopping by to ask us about it and wish us well! More than a dozen! How heartening!

It would be some time before we began to understand how naive and unprepared we were to run a business in a small town.

Jack and I worked hard getting the store ready, and drove each other crazy doing it. My husband's generally laid-back approach to life is simple. If a problem exists, the buzzer will get louder or someone will start shouting; everything else is small stuff. I am more the type who, leafing through a magazine in the dentist's office, will read an article about plastics containing carcinogens and call home.

"Jack, empty the fridge and see if we have any plastic containers in there. If we do, dump the food out behind the back garden. Don't give it to the dogs, and remember not to put cooked food in the compost pile. I'll stop on my way home and buy glass storage sets. While you're emptying the fridge, you might want to go ahead and scrub the vegetable drawer; I noticed a smell yesterday."

People often characterize my beloved as "long-suffering." He refers to living with me as "exciting." Meshing *"Aaggghhh"* and "ahhhhhh" life approaches creates a strong balance when we manage it, and since we like each other, we usually do manage it.

So it was no surprise to Jack when I sat down one day (soon after we scraped together enough cash to go get our furniture and thus had chairs again) to pencil the closest thing we ever had to a plan for opening: a list scribbled on the back of an envelope.

Find Location (check)
Get books
Name store
Build bookshelves (check)
Learn to use cash register or something
     like that (find cash register)
Establish how to run a trade credit system
Publicity
Cat, optional (check and mate)*

*We have two cats. Get it? Oh, never mind.

Five years later, I found this list in a drawer and laughed. Besides revealing my housekeeping limitations, it seemed surprisingly comprehensive for someone making it up as she went along. Adding a degree in family therapy, plus lifetime supplies of hand sanitizer, patience, Goo Gone, pencils, packing tape, and humor—not necessarily in that order—would have been wise. Other than that, the envelope pretty much covered it. That's how you run a used book store. (Dogs may be substituted for cats if well behaved.)

The day I made the list, Jack poured himself a Scotch and we took the easiest item first. Our shop sat across the street from the amphitheater where the outdoor drama of Fox's novel ran, so our name needed to celebrate his *The Trail of the Lonesome Pine* legacy.

After less thought and more alcohol than should have been put into it, we came up with Tales of the Lonesome Pine Used Books, Music and Internet Café, which seemed to cover everything— although we later learned it wouldn't fit in the phone book advertisement. As we met other business owners, it became evident that the Lonesome Pine moniker could get even better exposure. With a bottle of wine one night, we had a good time renaming several businesses around town. For some reason, friends who helped create the list wish to remain anonymous, but Ms. Polly the drama director loved it:

The liquor store	Ales of the Lonesome Pine
The local gym	Whales of the Lonesome Pine
The car dealership	Deals of the Lonesome Pine
The post office–cum– federal courthouse	Mails and Jails of the Lonesome Pine

The pharmacy	Ails of the Lonesome Pine
The farmers' market	Kales of the Lonesome Pine
The school museum	Fails of the Lonesome Pine
And the pet grooming service that actually did use the idea	Tails of the Lonesome Pine

In a small town, we make our own fun. Beats people making fun of us.

Okay, back to that envelope checklist. What next? Well, maybe getting in some books so we could sell them?

Jack wanted something else first. "A mission statement."

"A what? Are we on a mission here, babe?"

"I come from a business college background, and I need a mission statement," he insisted, stroking his white goatee. (He does that beard thing when he wants to look wise.) So Jack drafted a mission statement and we hung it on the wall:

Tales of the Lonesome Pine Used Books, Music and Internet Café Mission Statement

1. We believe in providing quality books, music, crafts, and service at a fair price.
2. We believe in making a fair profit.

3. We believe in shop hours that balance the wishes of our customers with our need for a life.
4. We believe in assisting and advising customers to the best of our ability; we believe everyone is fallible.
5. We believe in being responsible members of our community.
6. We believe that a used book store is neither a new book store nor a garage sale; that it is a hard way to make a living; that it is a kind of sacred trust; and that it should be friendly and fun for customers and us.

The mission statement provides balance on days when we can't remember why we thought owning a business/living in a small town/being married to each other would be fun. Usually we don't have trouble recalling any of that, but in those early days of naïveté and enthusiasm, plenty of marriage-and-resolve-testing times lay ahead.

CHAPTER 3
Mommy, Where Do Books Come From?

*Sometimes the questions are complicated
and the answers are simple.*
—Dr. Seuss (aka Theodore Geisel)
as quoted in *Looking Tall by Standing
Next to Short People & Other
Techniques for Managing a Law Firm*
by H. Edward Wesemann

WE BOUGHT THE HOUSE IN July and planned to open shop in October; a quick turnaround meant the place could start paying us back for its purchase. Since we didn't have any investment capital, without remorse or pity we culled our personal library for inventory. From a life lived in the Arts and Academia, Jack and I owned a few thousand books, some of them rather obscure and wonderful. Husband and wife looked each other in the eye and swore it went downstairs to the shop if: we had owned it more than three years but not read it; if we had read it but never reread it (even if we intended to someday); or if we'd never used it in research.

I write scholarly articles and Jack records weekly programs for public radio, besides running an annual tour to Scotland and Ireland for folkies; these facets of our lives require some research. As traditional performers, we sometimes taught at folkie meccas like the John C. Campbell Folk School and Swannanoa Gathering, so if we'd cracked open the spines even once for such purposes, the books stayed. But we dispatched without mercy favorites, gifts, and "important reads" we had intended to get around to someday. Even works autographed by writer friends went in. (If you're reading this Jane, Theresa, et al., we're sorry!)

Before you think too badly of our ruthlessness, stop and consider. Love expressed through a thoughtfully chosen book lingers, along with the memory of its imparted wisdom. Giving up the physical item doesn't sever anything. As for that beloved childhood copy of *Charlotte's Web*, where do Fern and Wilbur live: on the page, or in your heart?

When Jack and I began culling our collective books, we learned a lot about each other's previous lives. Bookshelf anthropology can be fascinating; how many times have you scanned a friend or associate's bookcases to discover similar—or disquietingly dissimilar—tastes? I used to ferret out kindred spirits in the Snake Pit that way. A volunteer working with one of our music programs came in one morning and said, "Hey, you've got *Ethnomimesis* in your bookcase! I loved his interpretation of identity versus ego, how songwriters singing about issues to prove they're rebels just parrot popular opinion. So ironic!"

I practically leapt over my desk to embrace her, then took her to lunch.

Jack certainly enjoyed culling my books. "As near as I can tell, dearest, your life consists of making bizarre items for bazaars—or planning to—and reading boring ethnographic tomes," he said, chucking *Crocheted Finger Puppets* atop Vladimir Propp's *Morphology of the Folk Tale* in the "for bookshop inventory" pile.

"I have squandered my academic existence learning how to analyze someone's speech, discern their underlying biases, pick up on geographic background, and detect hidden agendas while missing the point of everything they had to say," I answered, waiting until Jack bent over another box before surreptitiously removing *Puppets* from the shop pile and stashing it under some laundry. "Being an ethnographer is a noble profession, but it tends to encourage people to turn over rocks looking for hidden meanings, instead of just listening."

Jack winked at me. "I know, dear. I live with

you." He stood, stretched, stepped behind me, and pulled *Puppets* from its hiding place. "You spend a great deal of time analyzing inner voices while crafting things from wool."

"Oh, good one," I responded, dashing to the bathroom and retrieving Jack's copy of *Positively 4th Street* from where he'd stashed it beneath the ancient claw-foot tub. I tossed it lightly against my palms, eyes narrowed. Without a word, my husband set *Crocheted Finger Puppets* on my "keep" shelf, and I handed over *Positively 4th Street*. We understand each other so well.

About fifteen hundred volumes went downstairs, even after all the wheeling, dealing, and ferreting out of hiding places. (For days, I encountered Jack's books lying atop cabinets and stuffed behind house-repair projects. He never found mine because I hid them in my yarn stash.) Having our personal collection in the shop not only made us instant inventory experts, but it turned the whole enterprise into something like an adoption agency. We felt a vested interest in seeing the little guys go to good homes. Once the bookstore opened, our friend Neva Bryan, an author herself, bought a book autographed by one of my writer friends. Neva glowed over her find, while I was happy because My Friend the Book went to live with My Friend the Writer; they would appreciate and look after each other.

But Neva and the rest of our customers waited

in the future (we hoped) as we prepared for the Grand Opening—which wasn't looking too grand, in all honesty. The books from our personal cull barely filled half of one room's shelves, yet three rooms waited. It didn't feel cozy or full of promise, more barren and tomblike. Lacking money to buy more, we tried laying the books flat, end to end. That took up shelf space, but it pretty much looked like a book morgue.

Surveying the scene of our crime novels, we took stock of, well . . . the stock. Closing the door on the back room full of empty bookcases helped, but that glorious, open-plan, long front suite with its oak columns and sweet, sticky pocket doors, where we dreamed of patrons edging along overstuffed shelves, remained a veritable cavern with nothing in it but books lying sideways. The word "ridiculous" hovered in the background. Even those with no retail skills whatsoever (namely, us) could see our meager stock foretold doom.

One evening I came down the wooden stair with its beautiful copper corner pieces, which I planned to shine back to perfection someday after we got the shop ready, and beheld my beloved sitting at the bottom. Shoulders slumped, chin resting in hands, he sat with an empty whiskey glass at his knee. We didn't have money for extras; Jack dipping into his water-of-life reserve meant things were bad.

I sat down beside him and together we surveyed the emptiness that embodied our leaped-before-looking stupidity.

Jack sighed. "Perhaps I shouldn't have installed quite so many sleepbuilts at the start. We could have put in some more furniture, armchairs, that sort of thing." (Jack called his shelf design "sleepbuilts," because they were super-easy to make, and he'd built so many that he could do one in his sleep. I called them that because the saw and Jack's snoring produced a similar sound.)

"Where would we have gotten money for armchairs?" I asked. We had already put our personal couch downstairs in one of the front rooms and broken up our dining set, its table holding the shop's coffee and tea service, chairs spread across the store. Upstairs we had our bedroom furniture, a couple of plastic four-drawer units, and a lot of cardboard boxes.

Jack shrugged. "I'm not too old to search skips." *Search skips* is Scottish for Dumpster diving. Sounds better in Scots, doesn't it?

Now, you should know that Jack is just an inch or two taller than I am. If you chose to describe me as "cozily round," or even use Alexander McCall Smith's tactful "traditionally built," that would be a fair cop. Jack, however, is lean muscle in a compact package. Wiry, they calls it in the Old World. He can carry three two-by-fours with ease, yet not see over the edge of a Dumpster standing on tiptoe. The image of my beloved swimming up to his eyebrows in pizza boxes and old diapers made me giggle. Where there's giggling, there's hope. Hope coupled with hard work can trump even stupidity. Yes, we'd been silly in our failure to plan, but in the month since we had committed to a bookstore, as we'd built shelves and sifted books, the shop had moved from an antidote to the Snake Pit to having its own meaning. *Le bookshop, c'est moi.* Or us, in this case.

We'd gone from the rather selfish need to heal ourselves, to providing something a whole bunch of nice people had taken the time to tell us they looked forward to having. Locals strolled up the sidewalk, stopped us in the grocery store, chatted after church about when we would be open, said how nice it was to have a bookstore coming to town. They liked that they were getting a bookshop! It felt so good to be wanted.

Staring at the book morgue, I knew the men and women who had come by to ask about our opening looked forward to what we represented: a simultaneous intellectual, emotional, and economic investment in the Coalfields of central Appalachia—not to mention access to books, glorious, cheap, preloved books. So as God was our witness they were going to get the world's greatest—well, friendliest, nicest, whatever—bookstore. We would not be defeated by low stock

51

numbers—not yet, anyway. Rallying, I said, "Don't worry, love. Even though we're in a bit of a bind here, I have a way forward."

My husband cast a suspicious eye toward me, knowing that when I said not to worry, he probably should. But I continued with an expansive wave at the dead books, "Clearly we need more inventory."

"Clearly we're out of money, Wendy." The recent furniture fetch in a rented U-Haul, coupled with the three rooms of newly made shelving, had drained my day job's modest paychecks. We'd been eating Crock-Pot chili or mac and cheese interspersed with some old army rations a friend from my Snake Pit days had given us. I don't know exactly why she gave us that box of twelve MREs (meals ready to eat)—perhaps she felt bad when I walked away and didn't want to see us starve—but let me just say, food that can't spoil doesn't taste good.

"The solution is obvious," I went on. "And I am the perfect person to implement it."

Jack closed his hazel eyes as if in pain. "Just tell me."

I kissed his brow. "At great personal sacrifice, dear, I will give up my Saturday mornings to go garage-sale-ing, and will return with boxes of book bargains." With that, I rose from my seat on the stairs, wiped my hands of the ubiquitous coal dust, and made an internal commitment to get that slump out of my beloved's shoulders.

Having been a graduate student for ten years, I was intimately familiar with yard sales. I consider myself adept at spotting bargains and think browsing sales is fun, but had been avoiding them since we were rapidly approaching the point where we couldn't afford air, let alone amenities. We cut our own hair and changed our car's oil, so I didn't want to be tempted to spend even small amounts of money on nonessentials. But now, a lifelong addiction had become a business skill. No way were our dreams dying without a fight. The people who'd stopped and talked to us, who'd told us they were counting on us to open (and then not close six months later) could not be disappointed. The readers of the world—okay, the Appalachian Coalfields—were waiting.

Yeah, it was overblown self-aggrandizement, but every once in a while, that really works to stop a self-pity party.

Soon I was at play in the field of the books, with apologies to Peter Matthiessen. (For those of you unfamiliar with *At Play in the Fields of the Lord*, his novel about sincere yet bungling missionaries living fish-out-of-water lives in the jungle, it's a wonderful, thought-provoking read.) Buying from yard sales is one of the least expensive yet most time-consuming ways of getting stock. Time is money—especially when you haven't got any money. All through July, I swept onto front lawns offering ten cents per for every title they had.

My weekend hunts quickly and inexpensively gathered an impressive collection of battered Jackie Collins novels and Farrah Fawcett detox diets, hardback Danielle Steels and ten-year-old batches of Harlequin romances. I didn't know what I was doing. Fortunately, it wasn't costing much.

The shelves grew fat on these unsellable space-takers until I wised up. From e-mailing other bookstore owners, reading Internet advice, seeing what sold on eBay, and restarting my common sense after so many years in graduate school, I soon learned to bypass vintage sets of Better Home and Gardens cookbooks with Volume 2 missing, or Reader's Digest Condensed Books. (In case you're interested, those are why Atlantis sank.) Amid aerobic workout handbooks and treatises on U.S. foreign policy during the Cold War, regional reading interests soon emerged: coal, country music, Christian romances, and every description of horror novel. The Coalfields population would prove complex in its reading habits.

Booksellers need to have common sense. Title by title, sale by sale, I began to work out that if *everybody* had old Stephen King paperbacks, maybe we didn't need them for our shop. If Harlequins were a dime a dozen, why would people buy them from us for a dollar? You know the old saying: "You're not a real [insert profession here] until you learn to say no." Even at ten cents a title, I had to learn to say no. Two life coaches aided me in this process: the books—silent on the tables and cement driveways, testimony to what had been popular last year—and the people hosting the sales, who almost always had specific questions about what we would stock once they found out about the bookstore.

Never missing an opportunity to let others know about our new place, I chatted up sale-holders at almost every venue. They were quick to ask, "Will you carry Westerns/true crime/science fiction and fantasy?" In this way, I got to know the area's real reading tastes, not just what people wanted to jettison in their driveway for a dime.

Learning to recognize diamonds among dross became that summer's lesson. It took a few weeks, but one memorable day I left a garage display of overpriced Anne Rice hardbacks to find a collection of prayer shawl pattern books on the same lawn for a quarter each. Rice wasn't so popular once Stephenie Meyer sucked the life-blood from the vampire market, but pattern books command serious cash in secondhand shops. It was a nice little moment, realizing I now knew which were more useful.

Book valuing is a lot like car pricing: once you drive the new vehicle off the lot, resale plummets. Bestsellers at twenty-seven dollars new flood the used market once the first wave of readers tosses them aside. Classic literature is like a vintage MGB; it proves well worth having years later, but is easy to find and hence not that expensive as rarities go. What enthusiasts really want is an MGA, the model made just before MGBs; far fewer exist; they are older, hence harder to find in good shape; and they are hunted by those who know what they're doing.

Taking the car analogy back to the book world, aficionados have for the most part read *Dollmaker* by Harriette Arnow, but *Hunter's Horn* is a lesser-known work by this famous author. That combination of obscurity and renown creates good prospecting territory. I picked up *Horn* for fifty cents at a thrift store one afternoon and listed it on an Internet bookseller site at nine dollars in "acceptable" condition. It sold the next morning.

Giddy with success at an 850 percent markup, Jack and I congratulated ourselves for turning a profit before opening day. I had yet to learn this euphoria's counterbalance, that those "big markups" were few, far between, and—as gas money goes—not that big. We were too green in the business to understand yet that we wouldn't score "buy low, sell high" hits every day.

Common sense can be a hard-slog commodity. We tried hard to hang on to ours in the early months. Jack and I had always been adept at calling each other on moments when one of us lost reasoning ability and began to dream too big, but euphoria is as addictive as any drug. We wanted to be happy. We wanted to do good. So we did stupid things—like assuming rare books were just lying around waiting for smart people like us to find them—and never examined the condescending superiority of our assumptions.

An old joke has two economists walking along a road. One looks down and says to the other, "There's a one-hundred-dollar bill in the ditch." The other economist doesn't even look. "No, there isn't. If there were, someone would have gotten it by now."

That's rather like book prospecting: a juxtaposition of what seems to be in front of your eyes balanced against everything you know (and have spent nights on the Net researching) about books, authors, current reading trends, classic literature, and physical book conditions. It's a small wonder some people in the used book business resort to scanners, those handheld devices that read bar codes and spit out their going market value. Still, call me old-fashioned, but I have no respect, professional or otherwise, for those nasty book prospectors found at library sales. With precious few exceptions, they scoop anything promising into a pile and check bar codes like automatons, then leave their discards in unsorted heaps where those who would have liked to find them can't. My mama didn't raise me to be a rude machine.

I have always wanted to walk up to those kids

and smack the scanners out of their hands. "It's a *book,* son, a *book.* That means it's valuable in and of itself, because it's about *ideas.* Have you read *Light in August*? Do you know the difference between Sylvia Plath and Iris Johansen? Now put that thing down and read something!" My secret fantasy, revealed.

Some dedicated souls do beat the book fields' bushes for a living, but it parallels prospecting for gold in terms of economic stability; over the long haul, the search costs more than the nuggets garner. As with anyone trolling for treasure, some days turned out lucky for me, others mucky. Mining for books burned a lot of gas, not to mention precious weekends. With little enough time during the week to help Jack prepare the shop, I spent weekends running around to sales, sometimes scoring, sometimes wasting hours that could have been spent on the house. We didn't even have curtains upstairs yet. I did not want to end up like one of those poor oddball rare book dealers people avoid at parties, who mutters to herself as she loads her plate with free food.

I often visited sales with Fiona, another member of the Church of Artists and Weirdos up the street. True to type, she is artistic. A transplant from Europe many years ago, Fiona runs a pottery and weaving studio on the town's main street, and her designs command international respect. Not quite five feet tall, she sports a pixie cut of magnolia-blossom white hair. Her smiling eyes hint at mischief bobbing just beneath the surface. I couldn't say what it is about her—her pixielike figure, baby face, or charming upper-class British accent—but sellers knock themselves out to throw discounts at this happy-go-lucky grandmother.

Her daughter, who owns a farm nearby, told us some of the stories. Once Fiona walked up to a Christmas tree lot and, being told the price, said, "Oh, I don't think so." As she turned to go, the man said, "Never mind, ma'am, I'll give you one." A car salesman followed her across a lot one afternoon, discounting a Mazda down to practically nothing. Fiona hadn't been shopping for a car, just taking a shortcut. "It's weird," her daughter Kirsty concluded, "but I didn't inherit that gene. So I always take her with me when I buy livestock."

Fiona's powers came into their own at yard sales. "That bureau is five dollars? How annoying, I've only three dollars left. What a pity." And I would find myself loading the dresser into the back of her SUV while the seller gave her fifty cents in change. Going to sales with Fiona reinforced the age-old adage that little white-haired women can get away with anything. And she got me some really good discounts on boxes of books. Although we believed my garage sale summer was time well spent at the time, in reality I was bringing home quite a bit of what we would later learn to identify as "crap sellers." Still, I was also making friends in the community, chatting up sale-holders, other shoppers, anyone I met on the sidewalk, telling them about our new shop and its October opening.

Even with Fiona by my side throughout August, stock count reached a mere twenty-two hundred. The back-room door remained closed. Across the front rooms, we now resembled a crowded book morgue; the books still lay end to end, but at least they touched each other.

To make matters worse, we didn't just have a dearth of books overall; in one key genre, we had none. Science fiction and fantasy rarely appear at yard sales, for reasons we learned later. With two colleges in the region, that seemed an unwise inventory hole.

Desperation set in, but not the useful kind that spurs invention—more the dark, debilitating variety so familiar from days of yore. Jack said to me, as I moped through the house one day, picking up dead books and putting them down on a different shelf, "You haven't acted so listless in a long while. Not since, er, you know where. Giving up so soon?"

That snapped me out of it, and fast. No more renting the space in our own skins. The book morgue that wanted to be a shop was our problem, waiting for our solution. By hook, crook, or sheer force of will, we would find more books—without going into debt for them.

Don't get the wrong idea: Jack and I were not destitute when we moved to Big Stone. But that "let's make a bookstore" discussion in Little Mexico had not been entirely heart without head. We'd talked at length about how financially insecure running such an enterprise would be. Thumbing our nose at the Snake Pit had been possible only because we had no mortgage or significant debt. That kind of freedom must be carefully guarded, or going into debt "just this once" becomes a lifestyle. So we had sworn, the day we agreed to try the bookstore thing, that we would get the necessary mortgage, but would not borrow a single penny more to finance anything, no matter what. That hefty restriction curtailed some of the simpler ways to get a bookshop going.

Crazy schemes have never been a weak point for us, and blood is thicker than printer's ink. Time to call my sister.

Tracy misspent her youth devouring books about Doc Savage and the slave traders of Gor; laying about our shared bedroom, those paperback covers were . . . interesting. Four years Tracy's junior, I read behind her in a fog of stubborn precociousness until finally assigning science fiction to the same category as coffee—one of those weird things adults liked.

Now those unappealing reads had turned into precious commodities, and I needed my big sister's help. More specifically, I needed her books. Some might consider it a bad sign that I had to call my mother to get Tracy's phone number, but please don't misinterpret or misunderstand: my sister and I are friends but tend not to keep close tabs on each other. After all, isn't that what Thanksgiving is for?

"Hi, Tracy. How's it going?"

"Is everything okay?"

"Sure, sure. Why shouldn't it be?"

"You never call me unless you need something. When you moved to that back-of-beyond place you live in now, you didn't even send me a change of address card."

Accurate, she was.

"Well, you know, we're there for each other when it counts. Right?"

Tracy sighed. "How much?"

Ouch.

She continued, "The last time you said something like that, you had broken your arm and needed a loan for the emergency room visit."

"Hey, I was twenty-two then! I'm older and more financially responsible now."

"Hunh. Mom says your latest harebrained scheme is that you talked Jack into buying some drafty old house and you're trying to start a used book store with no money."

"Exactly. I'm now a responsible business owner in the community. So I was just wondering—"

She interrupted. "When we moved house this

spring, I boxed up all our spare books for you and will bring them down at Thanksgiving. Dennis was not all that excited about having to move boxes of books we weren't going to read again, but I talked him into it. Is that what you were calling about? Mom told you we did that?"

Ah, family. You can count on them, no matter what.

"That is so cool! Thanks, and tell Dennis thanks! But actually, do you remember all those schlocky—I mean, that science fiction and fantasy you used to read, the Star Trek novels and whatnot? Are they in the boxes?"

"Those weren't mine. I gave them back to the friend I borrowed them from, years ago. Why are you interested in—now what was it you used to call them, let me think—'those schlocky near-porn not-worth-starting-fires-with wastes of paper and ink'?"

"Okay, okay. I've changed my mind about a lot of things since then! We haven't got much science fiction in our inventory, and there are two colleges near our store. You just know a bunch of students are gonna be sci-fi and fantasy readers."

"Try eBay."

"We did. They're expensive there. It turns out that people don't sell them at yard sales because they can get more on eBay. So I was hoping you had some, but thanks for the other books."

"If fantasy and science fiction are that popular,

there must be tons of it around. Offer a better deal than eBay, and people will bring them to you instead."

I sighed. "It's kind of a chicken-and-egg thing. We need them before we open, but we can't get the swaps going until we actually have the store running."

"Why not? Ask people to bring their books now and give them credit against when you're officially in business. Issue credit slips. It'll reduce your cash later, but get you books now. And it sounds like you haven't got any money to buy books now."

My sister has always had a way of cutting to the chase.

"Good idea," I said.

"I know. See you at Thanksgiving. By the way, you might want to put this number in your address book." She hung up.

We quickly appropriated Tracy's idea as our own (thanks, Big Sis!), but advertising a prestore swap program still took money. Or ingenuity, and we were short on both at this point. Enter Teri, town chiropractor and another friend from church. Hearing of our plan, she offered unlimited access to her office's photocopier in exchange for book credit once we opened. If it hadn't been for Teri, I really don't know how we would have managed advertising at all.

I designed a flyer with the oh-so-original header

"Calling all bibliophiles: great swap deals!" and traipsed around the nearby towns, hunting down bulletin boards at the Laundromats, drugstores, clinics, and so on. I chatted up bank clerks and dropped in on hairdressers, armed with pushpins, tape, and a smile. By the end of the day, I knew some very important things: the bloke who used to run one of the county's Laundromats got fed up and moved to Kentucky to become a starving artist; the new grandchild of the receptionist at a nearby ear, nose, and throat clinic didn't look anything like his daddy; and the annual Christmas parade was a cliquey stitch-up you could get into only if you knew the right people. In a small town, talking for fun hasn't yet gone out of style.

Then we sat back and waited. Tracy had been right. About a dozen people showed up with stuff; what they pulled from the bowels of their (fortuitously dry) basements proved astonishing. Jack started a ledger recording each person's precredit against opening day, and we spent evenings—lots and lots of evenings—shelving the loot.

A clergyman turned in a puberty-length collection of bikini-clad outer space bimbo paperbacks. He didn't want trade credit. "Just get rid of these painful reminders of high school for me," he said. They sold for an astronomical amount within a month of our opening. I called him back, but he reiterated they were a gift to get us started, so long as his name never got linked to them. He's dead now, God rest his adolescent soul.

Barbara, a book enthusiast who already made a hobby of trading and selling on the Net, brought her stash of mostly Christian fiction, and we hit instant rapport. She offered to take a list of titles and genres we wanted and scour yard sales on our behalf, a task I was only too grateful to hand over to her. Glenn, the happy-go-lucky white-haired actor in local stage productions, appeared with true crime, seeking classics. Mr. Pettry, who was to become one of our regulars, hauled in about two hundred hardback thrillers, all in excellent condition, and proffered a list of others his wife Sylvia wanted.

Garth, town council member, donated how-to tomes on electricity, deck-building, and other manly pursuits. Like the pastor, he had an alternate agenda: "to see the floor of my garage again, just once, before I die." In fact, most people bringing books were donors rather than swappers; they were cleaning house, or just chuffed that a bookstore had come to town and wanted to help it along. Few of that initial ragtag bag team took swap credit.

At the same time, Jack and I got one of our first lessons in how quickly a used book store can become a junk shop. We didn't want to say no to any of these nice people, but what could be done with a six-year collection of *National Geographic* magazines, a selection of 1970s economic textbooks, and yet more Reader's Digest Condensed Books? We stuck them on the shelves and smiled, perhaps suspecting even then what the future held: furtive midnight runs to Dumpsters about town, tossing in stacks of magazines and old textbooks, and scouring the Internet for patterns to make handbags, birdhouses, planters, and shelf brackets from old books. (Although I no longer had a yarn budget, I would have plenty of other crafts to mess about with.)

Actually, that's hindsight talking; at the time we were so relieved that people brought us stuff, refusing anything never really entered our minds. We put every title on the shelf, no matter how old or uninviting. Everybody loved books! Everybody loved all books, all the time! *National Geographic* magazines were beautiful!

We didn't have a clue.

People also came with useful genres, including the science fiction and Westerns we lacked. They got generous swap deals written into the big blue ledger, and left happy—to tell others about us. Word of mouth began to circulate, the best advertising one could ask for.

Many "rural suburbanites" are tucked into the snug hills and hollers that cradle Appalachia's Coalfields; often growing tobacco on their family farm for extra cash, at least one adult commutes to a job in town. Since they didn't live nearby as Dave and company did, this group took a little longer to find us, but as word rippled outward, they also brought in books.

Jack met Larry and Larry's wife, Teddy—he a gentleman farmer, she retired from an illustrious career in Washington, D.C.—when they drove in from their farm one day "to see what all the fuss is about." Jack and Larry struck up an instant and comfortable friendship, and it was Larry who gave us an early understanding of how Big Stone might be different from other small towns in which we'd lived.

While the Gap held the usual collection of doctors, lawyers, and educators, high-powered professionals wielded less real power locally than Old Families. As Larry explained it, "It's not unlike medieval history; sure, it's great to be king, but the Old Families put you on the throne, and they can take you off again. So don't get uppity, because you never know who's friends with an Old Family."

Uppity, we didn't plan on; busy would be enough, if our idea—okay, my sister's idea—worked. And it did. Soon enough, our shop held bags, boxes, milk cartons, and plastic tubs full of stock, glorious stock. With each ragged, tatty plastic sack piled into a corner for sorting, Jack stood straighter. I leaned over boxes and sniffed that heady smell of books: dust, glue, and knowledge, all jumbled together. In our shop. Filling our shelves. Life was good.

Even better, people were talking about us. Friends told friends, and our phone began to ring. We weren't open yet? When would we be? Did we have such and such books, or were we interested in having them brought in for swapping? Life was very good indeed.

Ultimately, we approached the Grand Opening with more than three thousand volumes we hadn't gone into debt for, and a lot of friends we wouldn't have made without the early swaps. Even better, nobody but Jack and I knew how close we'd come to looking like idiots who'd decided on a whim to start a bookstore and made it up as they went along.

CHAPTER 4

Follow Your Ignorance Is Bliss

*All you need is ignorance and confidence,
and then success is sure.*
— Mark Twain (aka Samuel Clemens)
in a letter to his friend, Mrs. Foote,
December 2, 1887

OPENING OUR DOORS JUST THREE months
after buying the Edwardian presented many
challenges, but also kept us from worrying about
stuff; too busy hurling ourselves at an idyllic future
to contemplate some very realistic potential
pitfalls, we just kept smiling and didn't look down.

Yet as the Grand Opening loomed, we got less
sleep and more butterflies in our stomachs as all
those words we weren't saying hatched into
living, fluttering fears. The night before we
opened, lying sleepless and silent in bed, I
rehearsed a litany of things that could go wrong:
no one would come, no one would come, no one
would come. Finally I said into the darkness:
"What if no one comes?"

My husband reached down, picked up Bert (our terrier, asleep on my feet), and placed him in my arms like a teddy bear. Bert blinked, startled and bleary-eyed, as Jack said, "Go to sleep," rolled over, and buried his good ear in the pillow.

I lay there, clutching the bemused Bert until morning.

Opening Day had been chosen to coincide with the annual Home Craft Days held at a nearby college. One of their shuttles stopped across the street from our store. We sneaked out in the wee hours and taped a flyer to the back of the shuttle stop sign: "Waiting for the bus? Why not spend a few minutes with us?" We got extra customers that way, and since we took the sign down as soon as Craft Days ended, the town manager only mentioned casually, a few days later when he happened to be passing by and just popped in for a cup of tea, that not everyone knew posting personal notices on public property was illegal within town limits.

The Grand Opening had that surreal quality of a wedding when it's yours. Is this really happening? Did we actually pull it off? And is that kid sitting in the parked car out front using an e-reader? (We decided we didn't believe in omens. A firm sense of denial can be a dreamer-turned-business-owner's greatest asset.)

The mayor read a proclamation welcoming us to town and establishing our business. Adriana

Trigiani, hometown girl and author of the best-selling Big Stone Gap series of novels, cut the ribbon. A shop full of ceremony attendees clapped; sure, they'd come to see Adri, but still filled our store to standing room only. They looked around. They bought things. We sold so many books that one shelf went bare again—but people were bringing books, too!

Throughout Opening Day we met more of those who would become regulars. Bill Peace is a Korean War veteran; that first morning he entered our shop, turned right with a military click of his heel, and worked his way around the room title by title. It took him an hour and a half. We thought his thoroughness was due to our low inventory, but as the months have rolled into years, Bill keeps that same pattern.

Thelma and Louise showed up as well; to this day, we don't know what their real names are. Cheerful, laugh-a-minute addicts of gruesome crime novels, they made a beeline for our puny little stack of Tess Gerritsen thrillers and bought them all. Like Bill, they would repeat this pattern over the years, moving on to Lisa Jackson and Tami Hoag. I tried to get them started on Sandra Brown, but they had grossness limits.

Michael, a Lutheran lay minister, Eastern European history buff, adjunct college professor, and writer of horror stories—he's a complicated man—planted the seed for a writing group on our opening day, and to our delight agreed to coordinate its monthly meetings when we approached him a few weeks later. This attracted Jenny—born and raised in Big Stone, a sweet-tempered actress in the local theater and the eldest daughter in a family full of characters—who balanced Mike's horror with her romantic stories and insightful poetry. The group quickly collected then aforementioned James, who in addition to poetry wrote guy stuff about trucks, space aliens, and why women were impossible to understand. The four of us would become fast friends—something I didn't know on Opening Day, when Jenny handed over a batch of homemade bran muffins and began browsing.

Jenny wasn't the only one to bring food; Melissa, who owned a shop selling Native American paraphernalia the next town over, brought cookies to wish us well, as did others on subsequent days. Appalachians bring food the way people from other cultures send flowers: to show appreciation, affection, sympathy and solidarity. Mike told me several years later that he went home from Opening Day and told his wife, "Yeah, it's a nice place. I give 'em a year before they close." (He thought there weren't enough readers in town to keep a bookstore in business. He was not the only one: Jenny, James, even Teddy and Larry later admitted that they'd all thought either small-town politics or the small number of readers they thought were in the area would kill us within the year.)

We smiled, poured coffee, smiled, transacted sales, smiled, and bagged books until closing time. That night, in the fading ecstasy of the Grand Opening, Jack and I hid from street view in our upstairs front room, looked out over the main road of our new hometown, and poured ourselves a glass of wine. Jack, who had taught painting and decorating for fifteen years at a Scottish community college, had managed to find time and money to repaper our cozy hideaway in a soft mauve with small flowers sprigged throughout; furnished with our own ancient chest of drawers and a couple of scratchy wing chairs from the thrift store, covered in my crocheted anti-macassars, it felt like the Victorian parlor it resembled. We curled into the yarn-softened seats and recounted the day, savoring each moment in detail. The customers' enthusiasm for the shop's woodwork. The food people had brought, unasked, to welcome us to town. My bright purple house shoes. I'd forgotten to change them before the mayor arrived, and had gone through the ceremony wearing fuzzy slippers—one of the first hints about how easily private and public space could slide into each other. I'd watched Adri notice my shoes and smile before turning away to greet a fan. She was too nice to comment.

When the day's events finally had the flavor

sucked out of them, we prepared for bed. As we brushed our teeth, Jack mused aloud over a comment from the mayor's speech, "something about 'not many people wanting to come here, and we hope you do well.' Hardly the most ringing endorsement for a new business." He spit.

Accustomed to Jack's Scots dourness, I refused to allow him to snatch defeat from the jaws of victory. "She was just welcoming us. C'mon, it was a wonderful day!"

And it had been. We turned off the lamp on the cardboard-box end table, snuggled up with Zora and Bert on our icy feet, and counted blessings: (1) enough savings to get a mortgage on this great location; (2) enough books to at least look like we were serious; (3) a bunch of first-day customers who'd promised to tell all their friends that a bookstore had moved in; (4) the goodwill of a town happy to have said bookstore; and (5) the handyman and crafter woman skills between us to make repairs, rugs, and furniture from scratch, rags, and plywood off-cuts well enough to live upstairs in a cheap-yet-cheerful manner, if not a gracious one.

Not bad for Day One, we thought. It felt like the perfect Hollywood ending. That's the problem with Hollywood. It teaches us to revel in the end of a happy beginning without thinking realistically about what comes next. Cue the timpani and glorious sunset; love conquers all.

Ha.

We should have paid more attention to that odd little phrase stuck in the middle of the mayor's welcoming speech. We should have revisited our fears, spoken that day in Little Mexico, that a population of five thousand was minuscule for a customer pool. But Day One had been a rousing success, and deep in our hearts Jack and I simply could not imagine a life without books and words and the smell of paper, so we resolutely rejected the possibility that our bookstore could flop in short order. Big Stone's enthusiastic welcome gave us hope and a sense of belonging. We believed in our new friends—the swooning Isabel and her sensible, math-teaching husband, William; pragmatic and kindhearted Teri and Gary; Fiona the Garage Sale Queen; writers James, Michael, and Jenny; and Elissa, insurance adjuster by day, and a brilliant freelance photographer who'd shown up to our opening. They were the first of many artists the bookstore would attract, along with informally educated intellectuals looking for serious conversation unleavened by accent assumptions, and all those rural suburbanites out there in the valleys, who just wanted a little light reading at the end of a hard workweek. We basked in the camaraderie and support shown by the region's bibliophiles, and felt well on the way toward a quieter, saner, happier life.

Quiet. Yes, that it would be, in spades.

We opened in October; by Thanksgiving, up to four customers a day trickled through our shop. Our understocked, underadvertised, overstaffed shop. Bill, Thelma and Louise, the writing group, and a few new customers drifted through: just the usual suspects plus just a handful of others.

The dogs Zora and Bert, the cats Val-Kyttie and Beulah, and Jack himself waited to greet the readers we just knew were out there. We had Christmas presents they could buy! Pity they didn't know we were in here. The few who came mostly had credit from before we opened. They used their swap slips immediately, on pretty much the same principle as not buying green bananas after your eightieth birthday. (Why invest in what you might not benefit from?) Without saying anything to us, pretty much everyone in town was assuming we'd close within the year.

Jack and I had figured, based on how much people knew about our church hunt and our opening plans, that everybody showing so much interest in the new kids on the block meant that they'd shop with us, and bring their friends. That, plus the preopening swap buzz, the Opening Day crowd returning with others, good word of mouth from our regulars, and of course the single ad we'd taken out in the local paper, would be enough.

It wasn't.

New customers did appear, saying "James sent me," or "Bill's my uncle," but they came in dribbles rather than droves. It's a wonder we didn't scare them away, since by now we were chasing newcomers out the shop door with our flyers, begging them to put these up at their places of work and to talk about us to their friends.

Meanwhile, everywhere we went—the grocery store, church, out for a walk along the Greenbelt in the blustery wind—people stopped us to ask, "How's the bookstore doing?"

"Great!" we'd smile, teeth gritted. "You should come by and see for yourself!"

They'd give us knowing looks. "Sure, after Christmas. Can't give used books for Christmas, can you? Y'all have a merry one, and we'll come see you in the New Year." Off they'd saunter, the unspoken subtext hanging in the air: *if you're still open.*

After three or four similar encounters, Jack turned to me. "Think they know something we don't?"

"I don't know," I answered, "but don't you suspect that someone has set up a betting pool on how long we'll last? Let's find them and bet against ourselves."

When Fiona's four-and-a-half-year-old grandson walked up to me at church one day, pulled my trouser leg, and said, "So, how's the bookstore doing?" I went straight to Fiona and demanded to know what people were saying. Softhearted

Fiona hemmed and hawed, but finally she admitted that, yes, people were talking about us, all right. Community consensus to bookshop owners: You won't last six months, but bless your hearts for trying, you dear sweet fools.

I confronted Teddy, a woman whose intuitions and insights I trusted. "Why is everybody assuming we're not gonna make it? It's like a self-fulfilling prophecy; they won't shop here because they think we won't be here in a year, and we won't be if they don't shop here."

Teddy smiled but deflected the question. "Why do you think that's what they think?"

I pondered a moment, then began to lay out points. "One, a lot of people probably don't know we're here because we've only advertised in the local paper, and that only circulates in Big Stone. Two, avid readers will be used to buying their books online, so why should they support some new store run by people they don't know? Because as near as I can tell, you're not a Big Stoner unless your grandfather was born here. Three, there's this sort of weirdness in the region; people disparage it even if they're from here. Everyone keeps telling us there aren't enough people who can read to support a bookstore, and that something like half the population graduates from high school. Is that even true?"

Teddy's mouth made a little *moue*. "More like 60 percent. Graduating, that is. Go on."

"Four, even if everybody in town who likes to read did shop with us, that's still a maximum of five thousand people, and not everybody buys a book every day. So if we get half the customers for books in Big Stone, that's just not that many people. And five, if you're not from Big Stone, people seem to think you've come here to do some unspecified evil rather than just, oh, say, open a bookshop? How am I doing so far?"

She smiled. "I think you've hit the low points."

"Okay, so in essence we've got locals who won't shop with us because we're not locals, and we've got the rest who won't shop with us because they think shopping local is beneath them. Now how do we get past any of that?" I asked her, counting on her years of accumulated wisdom in the nation's capital.

Teddy's smile lingered as she leaned across the table and drummed her perfectly manicured fingernails lightly in front of me. "You know what, honey? Most people make a business plan *before* they start."

She had a point.

Teddy was too diplomatic to add that most people also didn't waltz into an area known for being insular and just assume everybody would love and trust them from day one. The shop did have a handful of regular customers, plus a slowly growing list of people discovering us for the first time. Once people found us, they tended to return, and their telling others had been what we'd counted on to grow our customer pool. It wasn't so much that people weren't talking us up, just that this buzz hadn't generated enough volume to keep up with our grocery bill. We needed more customers, faster than public opinion was dragging them in. Well, that, or we needed to eat a lot less. Our word-of-mouth advertising "plan" —more wishful thinking, really—had half succeeded (Jack's take) and half failed (mine; I'm not certain optimist/pessimist couples should be granted marriage licenses).

Of course, among those that did hear about us from local buzz, some would see no reason to change their current routine—which could have been anything from not reading to ordering their books online to driving to Kingsport (a town about forty-five minutes away) to the Books-A-Million. The natural suspicion of a new store before it catches on is somewhat enhanced in a small town, where the "are you from here?" factor adds to reticence. How could we entice readers away from online or out-of-town shopping, and also let interested customers know we were here?

Firing up the computer, I googled "publicize with no money, how to" and soon found a site offering advice to small retailers. What I read chilled my blood. To this day, I am grateful that Jack had no idea that a rule-of-thumb formula existed to compute retail success by population and geography. Had that magic calculation been known that cork-popping day in Little Mexico, we might have drifted downstream a little longer.

My hubby was in the bathroom when I knocked on its heavy wooden door with the news: a bookstore in its inaugural year should expect in dollars about one-fifth the number of the population in its advertising region. A pause followed, and then Jack's voice came, taut as a fiddle string. "Big Stone Gap is a town of five thousand people."

"So the expert opinion is that we'll make a thousand dollars this year, unless we can advertise more widely than town."

Running water muffled his response, but it sounded like "eff the effing experts" and a suggestion of "spit for brains." The door flew open. "Start thinking," Jack ordered.

It's part of our couplehood mojo that I'm the eccentric thinker who creates harebrained schemes, Jack the sensible partner who evaluates their workability. I sat down at the table, stared at "$1,000" written across the top of my notepad, and thought hard.

Although the town housed five thousand, the within-sensible-driving-distance-of-the-store population reached sixty-five thousand across three conjoining counties. They had never heard of us out there and, short of a bullhorn from the car window on some back roads, they weren't likely to. We couldn't afford to drive through every county looking for the Laundromat and clinics that had corkboards to pin up flyers, even if they let us. I had learned the hard way—namely, someone chasing me down, yelling, "You can't post that here!"—that Wise County businesses couldn't post flyers on Lee County bulletin boards. I think it has something to do with the rivalry between high school football teams.

We'd bought one ad in the *Post*, the weekly newspaper covering Big Stone Gap, before opening. And after we opened, one of our most common conversations with people discovering the shop—usually by seeing Jack's sign in our yard or hearing about us from a friend—was:

Them: We had no idea you were here!

Us: Did you see the ad in the paper?

Them: The *Times*? No.

A major newspaper in the region published in nearby Kingsport and covered the rural counties of Southwest Virginia. But we learned this after we had drained our advertising budget with the *Post* ad. Teri and Gary's credit-for-copies swap remained all we could afford for a while.

It is far too tempting for a new business to count on overachieving. Jack and I had done just that, opening on a bloody whim with no idea how little we would make or how long it takes to build clientele. Advice centers around the country warn that 75 percent of small businesses fail in their first three years. All this data swarmed through my head like the horrid beasties from Pandora's mythical box.

But Hope lived in that box, too. And although the story never mentioned her, I'm certain that Hope's little sister, Tenacity, also hung around. She sat on my shoulder that day and together we started on that long-overdue plan to actually run a bookstore.

What did we have to work with? Unlimited photocopies, the qualified good wishes of a small but growing clientele—even if they were taking bets on whether we'd last—a reliable car, and our energetic selves. What did we need? People. People with at least a little bit of discretionary income, who liked to read. Lots of them.

A cunning idea formed. When Jack heard it, he put his head in his hands and sighed.

"Don't you think it could work?" I asked, voice brittle with anxiety.

"Aye, it *will* work. That's what's so bloody annoying; there's no way for me to get out of doing it. I'll fetch my coat."

My devoted spouse spent the slushy gray Saturdays of December standing at the front doors of the Super Walmart two towns over. Serving the three-county population, the big box store shepherded a hefty number of people through its portals each weekend. Two aisles of books bedecked its front central lobe. Anyone buying printed matter in our area did so at Walmart, and those nice readers just needed to know we were here.

We printed bookmarks, five to the page, on Teri's copier, giving hours, location, and trade policy. They were small for two reasons: cost-effectiveness and being able to pocket them if anyone reported Jack's activity. I gambled that people would be curious enough about a book-store not to turn him in to the Wal-guards. It was probably illegal and Jack nearly froze to death, but a thousand bookmarks went out each week-end, and our sales tripled. The phone started ringing with calls like this one:

"Good afternoon. This is the bookstore."

"Hi, that the new bookstore?"

"It is. What can I help you with?"

"I've got like a zillion textbooks from my college days. I was an engineering major. I hate to just chuck them out, but my parents need the space. Would you take them?"

"Sure! What's your name so I can start a credit slip?"

"No, I don't want credit. I live in New Jersey. I'm just down for a funeral; my grandma died."

"Oh, I'm sorry."

"Don't be. She'd been sick for years and hated everybody. So I'll bring these boxes by? My mom's so happy to be clearing out my old room."

That afternoon Tim, a man in his late forties, dumped four boxes of books on the porch, shook our hands, and wished us well. (Tim became one of what Jack calls our "semiannual regulars," people who don't live in town but who always drop in on us when they visit relatives.) Through Tim, we entered the wonderful world of text-book appraisal, a plane of existence akin to the Twilight Zone. What holds value, and why, is a long hard slog of study interspersed with idiosyncrasies, but here's the cheat sheet version if you're interested: history books outdate the day after they're written; math and chemistry hold their value the longest; sociology is a mixed bag; and it doesn't matter what date is on the English anthology, because nobody wants it except the lady with all the cats who lives at the edge of town. That's the skinny on textbooks.

But the gentleman discarding college baggage wasn't the only caller. One snowy January day I answered the phone and a lady said without preamble, "I met a man at Walmart, I guess he was your husband? He's from Ireland."

"Scotland, yes. He—"

"Now listen, he gave me a slip of paper that says there's a bookstore in Big Stone Gap. Is that right?"

"Yes, ma'am. We've just been open a few months. We're—"

"Well, whoda thunk it? Big Stone! Listen, do you have any Danielle Steels?"

"Loads." (Short answers seemed prudent.)

"Well, I'll be right down."

Lulu, the owner of that preemptive voice, slammed through our front door twenty minutes later. A salt-of-the-earth character who rarely lets anyone around her finish a sentence, Lulu would become a fixture in our lives, appearing every few weeks with a friend in tow. She must have introduced twenty people to our shop in the first year alone.

In short, the Walmart caper worked. "Effing experts," said Jack later, reviewing the month's sales figures with satisfaction as he sipped a hot toddy.

So we broke the rules and got away with it, not just via Operation Walmart but by opening a business without capital to keep it going. We got lucky. A couple of years ago, a family started a coffee shop in Wise, a college town near that infamous Walmart. On a main street and near the county courthouse, it looked like a shoo-in, so the family didn't let heavy rents deter them. Throwing wide the doors with enough operating capital for a month, they scraped by happy as clams with their small but steadily increasing profits— prophetic of the stability to come, we all thought, cheering them on as they hit the three-month mark.

And then a winter storm shut down the region. Power stayed off four long days as people huddled in their homes. The family lost everything in the freshly stocked freezer. Unable to cobble together enough money to buy new supplies, they couldn't make their rent and had to give up. Good people, sensible people who might have made it with enough money for another month's inventory, or if the storm hadn't ruined their existing stock.

As Americans, we're always getting told, "Follow your bliss." Sure, but not into blind alleys. Jack and I got lucky, and when we figured out it had been luck, we got busy.

Chapter 5

Holy Grails Full of Frass

The human heart has hidden treasures,
In secret kept, in silence sealed;—
The thoughts, the hopes, the dreams, the
  pleasures,
Whose charms were broken if revealed.
  —Charlotte Brontë, "Evening Solace"

AFTER "THE ADVERTISING PLAN THAT wasn't," we assessed quickly what skills we needed to run a bookshop. There's a British saying, "Start as you mean to go on." We hadn't; we'd let the unexamined belief that desire equaled knowledge guide us. Time for a little reality check.

Many elements of running a shop that sells reading material are common sense; for the rest, there's the Internet. Jack hopped on and read about valuing first editions and repairing damaged books, choosing those first because many people in the early weeks entered the shop with one or the other clutched beneath one arm, asking us to buy them for cash. We didn't know how to respond to such requests, other than the commonsense but not entirely friendly speech I gave once: "I'm sorry, sir, but that book has been chewed at the corner by a mouse, so first edition or not, I won't give you one hundred dollars in trade credit for it."

The first time someone brought a rather handsome hardback to where I sat at the computer and asked if it were a first edition, I had no idea how to tell. With a bright smile, I suggested she browse and I would check "as soon as I finish what I'm doing." Then I googled "first editions" the moment her back was turned.

The Internet proved to be our new best friend in how to value the "rare" old titles, culled from an attic/basement/barn/toolshed/salvage store/dump. People brought them every week, often believing these "holy grails" would net a fortune big enough to finance a child's college education. Sometimes a person just wanted to know the value, but sometimes he wanted to sell his find to us. We never charge to value any book. Put bluntly, valuations usually mean bad news, particularly if the volumes have been stored in heat, damp, or places riddled with varmints.

Among the book lice, molds, mice, household pets, and other living things that devour and damage books, did you know that cockroaches are a top-ten pest? They love print so much that they even poop the written word as "frass." What a nice word for cockroach crap. A book chewed by bugs will sport little oblong balls of frass in whatever color the spine and cover are. Those are feces, but most people who encounter frass don't recognize what yon spots and balls mean. I have seen well-coiffed women in high heels sweep them off with their hands before opening a book.

Unfortunately, Jack and I handle a lot of frass. We opened our store just as the economy tanked, so as the recession deepened, an increasing number of people wanted to sell their holy grails to us.

Thelma and Louise, the aforementioned regular customers and thriller aficionados, showed up one day with a 1940s World Book encyclopedia set, which they hoped to turn into a lifetime supply of Kay Hooper paperbacks. "You know, in the middle of the war, no one knowing who would win, it must be valuable," Thelma said hopefully.

We showed them how many people were trying to jettison similar items on eBay. Thelma and Louise were disappointed, but took it with good humor. Since Christmas was just around the corner, I was getting ready to hold a class in how to make angels from old hardbacks, and they graciously donated their World Books for that— first reserving two volumes for their own use in making personalized angels.

But people came every week bearing encyclo- pedias, 1890s reprints of classics, and book club editions of just about everything, plus books with mold, dog-chewed corners, bugs in the spine, and dead spiders in the pages. We saw them all, and a few ugly things besides. We valued the offerings via AbeBooks, Half.com, and Alibris, Web sites every bookseller knows intimately. We stayed off Amazon itself as long as we could, although they now own AbeBooks.

Occasionally some first editions or otherwise expensive tomes do appear; in those rare instances where someone might really be clutching a holy grail, we suggest they seek real appraisal from an antiques dealer, as we choose not to deal in rare volumes. All this experience soon brought Jack a reputation as an honest and fair expert on antique books, and people began bringing more and more in, knowing we would value them for free.

"That's irony for you," Jack said with a laugh. "Say you don't want to deal in rare books, and people know you won't cheat them."

When I asked if doing so many free consults bothered him, he shook his head. "First, it makes people think we know what we're doing. And second, I'm delighted that we've developed a reputation for honesty. Folks trust us to tell them the truth. Third, it means customers are coming to the shop."

I watched him cope patiently when a persistent individual argued that customers in our shop would indeed pay $450 for a first edition of *Little*

Women, even though we had a paperback copy on the shelf for fifty cents. But it grew hard to let people down gently. The holy grail traffickers either evoked sympathy because they were so nice and hopeful and needy, or provoked annoyance because they fought facts. I became expert at melting away if someone carrying a single volume wrapped in plastic started up our steps. Jack's people skills outstripped mine, I reasoned, hiding upstairs as the familiar refrain began: "I found this in my dad's shed when we were cleaning it out . . ."

One day the door banged opened and Lulu entered, lugging a box. She set it down on the floor with a thump. Bits of dust and straw flew into the air as barnyard ordure wafted.

"Got some real valuable books here," she said with satisfaction. Since Jack was away recording his monthly run of radio programs, I was stuck, and peered into the box. Mouse droppings adorned the top. The corner of one paperback showed teeth marks. Mentally, I armed for combat.

"Great! I'll have a look if you like, but—"

Displaying the largesse of a duchess Lulu gestured that this would be acceptable. Some of the loot looked like it might have once been good stuff: a Langston Hughes children's picture book; a first-edition Hemingway, dust jacket in bad shape. Their barn sojourn had taken its toll. (Let me take this moment to beseech you to store your books well; they want to live in the same climate you do, not too hot or cold, neither too wet nor dry. Treat them as though they are relatives you like, and they will reward you by holding their value and resisting silverfish.)

Lulu wandered the shop speaking loudly to no one in particular as I checked over her books. The Hughes was worth twenty dollars on Half.com, while the Hemingway—which I left in the box because it looked so mangy—was selling for two dollars on AbeBooks. I gave her the good news about Hughes first, intending to soften the blow.

Her face fell. "That all?"

Oh well.

She held out the Hemingway, picking off a piece of mouse poop and dropping it to the floor. From the corner of my eye I saw Beulah trotting over at a brisk pace. "This'll be worth a couple hundred, at least."

Saints preserve us.

I took the book between finger and thumb, laid it on newspaper (not a good idea for a truly valuable hardback, but I hate touching mouse poop) and began to rifle its pages. Beulah jumped into the box of barn offal and started purring. At least one of us was happy.

As I launched into an inane explanation I knew Lulu wouldn't listen to about how book club editions were never worth much, my eyes fell on an unexpected object. Worked so deep into the spine it was almost invisible, an unused stamp showed Ben Franklin's profile facing left on a blue background, surrounded by scrollwork. It had been a long time since my grade-school stamp club days, but adrenaline shot through me, cold and prickly beneath my flesh.

"Gimme a sec, Lulu," I said, sitting back down at the computer.

"Whad'ya find?" she asked.

I pointed to the stamp. She reached to pull it out.

"Don't touch it!" I shrieked, and Beulah leapt from her box and shot into the back room. Lulu yanked her hand back in fright, then skewered me with a reproachful look.

"No need to yell," she muttered, sitting down at the table with her back to me.

Many interesting details about stamps were to come my way that day, including when they were first dated, received glue on their backs, and other fun trivia. Lulu had a stamp inside her mouse-pooped, disgusting book that philately Web sites called a Scott #134. They assigned it a value considerably higher than its 1870s price of one penny; one site suggested two thousand dollars.

Lulu went home a happy camper. I have no idea what she did with that stamp. I just hope she didn't use it on a letter.

From that day forward, I tried to remember to rifle a book's pages before selling it. We have found numerous photos and letters, some dull, some poignant (one from an adoptive mom telling the birth mother she could no longer see her biological son); ancient movie tickets and library notices and raffle sale stubs; funeral prayer cards we gave back to family members, sometimes tracking them across state lines; social security cards for (usually) deceased people; voter registrations for the living; traffic citations; old medical bills; programs for bygone plays, which we gave to local theaters; and money. Two dollars here, one dollar there, and once, to my husband's joy, an English five-pound note. (We find money biannually, so don't get excited.) Probably the oddest thing we've found in a book was a braided lock of hair, wrapped in an advertisement for a woman's wig.

Lulu's stamp became an anomaly—and a cautionary tale—in the usual litany of "Sorry, it isn't worth much," but another important rule about running a bookstore was coming our way. Right after "learn to advertise" and "learn how to discern old books from beat-up ones," was "learn that comeuppances never take long."

Jack's knowledge about first edition and antique book valuing had been acquired on the fly, and of course fast expertise-building gives rise to overconfidence. (To test this theory, ask a college freshman about any historic period of Western civilization on which he's just written a term paper.) Just as we were edging into condescension about all those grubby, falling-apart "rare" books, one special customer taught us to never take anything for granted.

Dubbed Bob the Mad Irishman the minute we met him, he became one of our favorite customers, a fortysomething sweetheart of a guy without the sense God invested in geese. Bob moved here from further south, looking for handyman work. He considered himself the poet laureate of Ireland. The fact that he was neither a published poet nor from Ireland interfered not one iota with this confident self-knowledge.

Jack and I admire those who don't let reality get in their way, so we had a lot of time for Bob. This proved fortunate, because his poems were long and he read us one each time he stopped in. Every visit, Bob brought me a plastic rose from the dollar store. Black hair flopping into crystalline blue eyes, he smiled a crooked smile that showed the dimples in his rugged jawline as he tried to entice my husband to partake from the vodka flask he carried in his pickup. They often sat on the porch together, smoking. It became a ritual: the rose, the flask refusal by me and acceptance by Jack, the poem.

Bob arrived once with a lady in tow, a nice woman I enjoyed meeting. On first glance, she was not a person one expected someone as pretty as Bob to be with. Round and gray, she looked as if she'd experienced a lot of life. She had a cheerful, lined face and discerning eyes. He introduced her as his "assistant." She let that go until he went out on the porch for a cigarette, then set the record straight.

"I let him stay in my spare room. He showed up at the library where I work, looking to get a card, and he couldn't answer any of the questions. No fixed address. No employer. He looked like his dog died. So sad, like a little boy. What the hey, I took him home. Gotta live a little."

She'd gotten the story off him: the girl he adored had taken his diamond and his heart, but the rest of what Bob's lady love needed, she acquired through snorting stuff up her nose. Apparently she inhaled most of his fortune before Bob gave up and left her—and the state.

"I know what he is," the free-spirited librarian said, "but I feel sorry for him and I like the company." So Bob was a kept man.

Besides the roses, sometimes he brought books, but never for credit. Bob wasn't that kind of guy. He said they were gifts for us, given to him by places where he worked on repairs. My personal favorite was the 1890s illustrated book club edition of *The Three Musketeers*: worthless but beautiful, if you catch my drift. But when Bob wanted to own anything from our bookstore, he'd throw fifty-dollar bills on the counter and say, "Let me know when that's used up." It was his way.

Bob must have been coming to the shop the

better part of a year when he brought us four titles he had "picked up working on a house." Among them rested an old Agatha Christie, spine broken almost in half. Jack was away, so we sat on the porch, Bob chain-smoking and taking nips from his flask while I drank a cup of tea.

"I'm having a hard time making ends meet." Bob eyed the smoke ring he'd just made. "The jobs are scattered and my classes are dull, plus I miss a lot while I'm working." Retraining at the community college to enhance his handyman-ing, he'd complained before that he couldn't do both work and school with any modicum of success. "I'm thinking of heading back home, but . . ." He shrugged.

He'd been talking like this a while. I smiled and said he should do what seemed best for him. He read me his latest poem—about Queen Mab's broken dream of love—and we parted.

Months passed and Bob did not reappear, so we figured he went back to his home state to start over. Of course he left no means to get in touch with him. I hadn't even gotten the name or branch of the librarian. His Agatha Christie, *The Mysterious Affair at Styles*, sat around a while. He'd always say, "These are gifts for you and Jack, not for the shop," so we usually took his stuff upstairs. I'd put his *Three Musketeers* in the guest room because it was so pretty.

Kinda bored one day—not that this happens a

lot in the bookstore—I priced some of Bob's gifts on AbeBooks and *Styles* came up $175. When they showed in that price range, especially with a broken spine, usually something had been entered wrong. Double-checking the publisher date and location, sure enough, I'd pulled up a New York 1927 version from Dodd, Mead and Company. The one Bob gave us came from the Bodley Head, London, 1921. My mistake. I corrected it.

The lowest price for Bob's gift of a first edition of Agatha Christie's first novel came up $6,500. Even grubby and with a busted spine, it was listed at $6,500.

The Christie still sits upstairs on a shelf in the corner, waiting for him to stick his head in the door and ply me with roses. We can't sell it. First of all, it's not really ours. (Although we know what Bob would say: "I gave it to you, didn't I?" in that fake Irish brogue.) Second, nobody in our realm of sales wants a beat-up mystery novel worth more than their car. And third, we have this Russian folktale motif idea that as long as his book sits safe and dry and warm in our shop, Bob is somewhere feeling the same. Maybe someday it will glow red to warn us he's in danger. We hope not.

CHAPTER 6
Creating, and Being Created by, Community

What do we live for, if it is not to make life less difficult for each other?
—George Eliot, *Middlemarch*

L EARN TO ADVERTISE" WASN'T JUST a rule we discovered early on, but a steep learning curve that came back again and again as we sought ways to increase our clientele. My dear friend JoAnne Jones, a mentor to many in public relations and fund-raising, taught me a simple message when we worked together on a Red Cross campaign. She always says there's no need for frippery and fancy plans to attract supporters; just be good at what you do, and people will want to support your doings. JoAnne's mantra translated well into our preloved retail world—no point in telling people about ourselves unless we could wow them once they showed up.

We'd stapled flyers onto just about anything that didn't run from us, and pressed them into the hands of customers who probably wished they could run. What else would entice people who didn't already like bookstores—or who liked books but were buying them on the Net—to visit us?

Humans have a natural proclivity to not step outside our comfort zones. Big Stone Gap had never had a bookstore before, let alone a used one; hence people not escorted in by our increasing team of regulars were naturally wary about walking through the door. After all, we were in what looked like a private house, albeit one with a USED BOOKS banner across the ornamental iron fence in the front yard. Despite the huge OPEN sign hanging from our front door's grille —Jack painted the sign onto scrap wood and hung it with two curtain hooks—in our first months a lot of customers still rang the doorbell. Several even asked, "So it's like a library, but you rent the books?" Or, "Once I buy them, can I bring them back?" We needed to get people in the door just to meet us, so they could get comfortable with how the shop worked.

To entice people to drop in, we devised special events featuring music, stories, or crafts. These would play to our natural strengths. As past director of an arts organization back in Scotland, I'm used to making things go, while Jack spent the last forty years playing gigs at festivals, clubs, and coffeehouses. A wide range of interests made creating special events in our own space tantamount to giving unlimited funding to the waif at a candy store. Being slightly less stupid about marketing than when we started, we also looked for ways to hook programs toward selling particular genres of books while enticing new clientele from specific groups of people—senior citizens, young moms, et al.

We wanted to offer outings people would like, but they also needed to be a wee bit different—events that would please local tastes yet not compete with other area programs. Easier said than done, that balancing act between "not the same old, yet not different enough to be threatening," but we figured the Scots-Irish roots of so many in the region would draw participants to a St. Patrick's Day ceilidh.

A ceilidh is a group dance for all ages, with half-time entertainment provided by the participants themselves. We found a team of Scottish social dancers in Northeast Tennessee and contacted their leader, Cynthia West. Her team agreed to teach the steps just for the love of dancing, plus promises of Jack's homemade shortbread.

The first year, the dance attracted twelve participants and was held in the long front rooms of our bookstore; the next year, twenty-four people and four more sets of bookshelves required moving the dance into the Presbyterian church a block down the street, which got Tony, the popcorn-selling pastor we met at the outdoor drama, and his wife, Becky, involved. It's since become a favorite event for some of our favorite customers—like Heather Richards, a former Oxford scholar who weaves her own cloth and cares for her aging mother at home. Heather is a brilliant baker and a gifted fiber artist; we love to see her coming through the bookstore door because she usually brings along "a little something I whipped up this morning." And you should see her dance; she floats on air, light as her meringues.

Heather played a key role in the third St. Pat's ceilidh—the night we now call "Waltzing with Porcupines." The day before the dance, Jack got a call from Mary, a customer who visited the shop sporadically.

"Is it okay if I bring some boys to the dance?" she asked.

Since we usually have a large group of stag women, he said of course. But she persisted.

"I mean younger boys. Three brothers. Their mother, my sister, died last month. I'm trying to get them out to do stuff that might be different, you know, take their mind off things."

Dancing is fun and lively, but is it therapy? Jack nevertheless assured her they would be as welcome as spring rain, and told me about it after he hung up. Odd, we agreed, but whatever.

On dance night, three brown-headed boys in

stair-step sizes arrived. The brothers, aged nine, eleven, and twelve, stood there among the adults, not taking their coats off, looking for all the world like heartbroken porcupines, spines out, smiles in, daring anyone to talk to them. Not one dance did they do in the entire first half.

Scottish ceilidhs have a traditional halftime entertainment of circling the chairs and asking each participant to tell a joke or story, sing a song, play a tune, or do a dance step. The boys sat in the circle, heads down, hands hanging between their knees, radiating boredom and gloom so palpable people kept glancing at them. But Heather knew just what to do; when it was her turn, this most ladylike and accomplished of kitchen goddesses looked away from the boys and told a farting joke, complete with sound effects.

The brothers glanced up.

My turn followed: taking a cue from Heather, I reeled off the scariest, bloodiest, goriest ghost story I knew. The lads sat forward in the hard metal folding chairs. Next in the circle came Grace, the church committee member designated to watch the hall that night, making sure no one smoked or stole communion wafers. Grace, wife of one lawyer and mother of two, is a proper sort of woman who wears her hair short and keeps her trouser creases crisp. She visits our shop to buy British mysteries, to take guitar lessons from Jack, and to solicit for local charities. This pillar of the community hauled out every bad mummy, vampire, and ghost joke she knew, including the old favorite about a clock striking thirteen. The boys shouted the punch lines ahead of her, and Grace—a smart woman in more ways than one—hung her head in shame that she could not defeat them.

The brothers smirked.

Jack looked at Heather, raised his eyebrows in apology or solidarity, and sang,

> *Hark, hark, the pipes are calling*
> *Must have been the beans I ate this morning*
> *Go to the loo, do a [PHTHPBT] down the drain . . .*

If you don't know "The Heinz Baked Beans Song," it is just one example of why British children's rhymes are world-class subversive masterpieces. The song requires everyone to join in on the sound effects, and from Cynthia's posh dance team to Pastor Tony, the adults *PHTHPBT*-ed along with gusto. So did the boys. Loudly. Very loudly. And laughing.

As Heather and I filled water pitchers at the sink a short while later, Mary (the porcupine brothers' aunt) came up behind us and put her arms around Heather in a brief squeeze. "Thanks," she said.

In the second half, we danced Dashing White

Sergeant, requiring a man flanked by two women to face a woman flanked by two men. If you've never seen Dashing White Sergeant, well, the Hokey Pokey is not what it's all about. The three couples circle left, then right, then face each other in a trio. The central person dances with each of his or her flanking "sergeants," then leads them forward and back in a wave pattern. On the second wave, one group arches over while the other trio runs under.

It is an ideal dance for little boys leaning toward mischief.

Short on males, I hauled up two brothers by their sleeves as Jack dragged the third into his line. Having bought some credibility as not-entirely-lame adults, we intended to cash it in and force them to dance. Of course, being preteens, the lads couldn't actually *touch* me, but they agreed to be my partners if I held the ends of their scarves instead of their hands.

My husband and I faced each other across the dance floor, flanked by porcupines, and telegraphed a single thought. *Dance, schmance; this is therapy.*

Poor Cynthia; I doubt in her entire career as a dance teacher she'd ever seen a Scotsman so incapable of performing his own native land's steps. Jack didn't so much execute as murder them; he bungled left, deadpan-dropped right, and spun his partners with such vehemence that they giggled protests. On my side of the line, I played crack the whip at the end of one lad's scarf, and nearly strangled the other by using his jacket shoulders to spin him like a top.

Our sweet and spirited friends, Sigean, form the annual ceilidh's house band (playing bagpipes to banjos) and since the dancers are learning as they go, Tom, Marianne, Frank, Jean, John, Joseph, Matt, and the other musicians who gather to play this annual gig are accustomed to strange things happening. On Waltzing with Porcupines Night, eyeglasses flew into the punchbowl, a shoe got kicked onstage—narrowly missing the uilleann piper—and three brokenhearted boys forgot about cooties or other hardships of life as they grabbed with both hands and spun very hard in hopes of making the grown-ups fall over. Most of us did, at least once.

And when they left, the brothers threw their arms around the musicians and dancers. "See you next year!" they cried.

Gas money for the band: Fifty dollars
Donation for use of the church hall: Fifty dollars
Three little lost boys laughing: Priceless

Sold on special events as a way to get locals to notice us, and encouraged by how our customers ferreted out such interesting people who enjoyed meeting like-minded others, we began asking our customers for more ideas. Lulu turned out to be a retired schoolteacher, so we cajoled her into making us a Science Day one June. She created three hours of cornstarch goop, sink the foil boat with pennies, make your own rocket, and musical instruments made from broken balloons, film canisters, and ink pens. (These sounded like farting cows with intestinal disorders. When the kids who'd descended on the event headed off to various vehicles at the end of the fun, several parents shot us dirty looks over their shoulders.)

But in those first months, when we didn't have a lot of time, money, or leftover energy, we went with activities we knew how to plan. Drawing on Jack's background, our first International Night provided "infotainment" about Scotland with snacks, slides, and a short talk by Jack discussing "stereotypes versus realities." The International Night went over so well that we decided to plan them on a regular basis, and soon got help from our friend Witold Wolny, who heads the international program at a nearby college.

Witold heard about the bookshop after another professor at his college attended the Scottish Night and told him about us. One afternoon he walked down from his home a few blocks away and found Jack working on an outdoor carpentry project. Witold watched in silence for a few minutes—"with a look of increasing horror on his face," as Jack likes to tell the story—then offered to come back with some power tools and "experience."

"I didn't want our first bookstore in the town to close because the owner killed himself hacking at lumber," Witold said later. "Such technique! I had never seen it before."

A Catholic Zen Buddhist from Poland who'd done his higher education in Spain, Witold suggested speakers for International Nights and, later, Gourmet Nights featuring cuisine from many traditions. He is an incredible cook, and we've enjoyed many evenings on his front porch, sipping good vintage wines and snacking on dark chocolate and strawberries while watching the sun set. He inlayed the porch's beautiful mosaic tiles himself, and did most of the refurbishments inside his elegant home.

Anne, a Spanish professor at the college and a longtime American resident of Spain, often joins us. Anne's house sits just a block farther from the bookstore than Witold's, and they shared— through a series of innocent yet convoluted circumstances—custody of a plump brown dog named Josephine, now of blessed memory. Sweet Josie of the melting-chocolate eyes led many people to make erroneous assumptions about what else her human parents might have shared.

Anne, Jack, Witold, and I were sitting around his dining room table one night in January when Witold dropped our first hint that the shop might be more stable than we could see. (He also delivered just about the best backhanded compliment I've ever gotten.)

"Everyone comes through your store," he said. "It is like a community center without a swimming pool. You are the most talked-about couple in Big Stone. And you analyze the people who live here so very well. What do you say when people ask about me?"

I'd never been called an elegant gossip before, but given that small towns are pretty much fueled by gossip and church suppers, likely someone had at some point called us something worse. And it was a fair cop. I do tend to overthink and underact in most situations; Jack says my solution to any problem is to analyze it into submission.

Besides, Witold was really asking a specific question. As Jane Austen noted, a man in possession of a comfortable home and good fortune must be in want of a wife. The fortysomething market of eligible bachelors tends to run low in Big Stone Gap. Our tall, gray-eyed, college professor friend, fabulous classical guitarist, cook par excellence and adept handyman, excited interest among breasted Americans—and he knew it.

What most people didn't know, although Anne, Jack, and I did, was that Witold had for the last year been trying very hard to marry someone, a lovely woman named Ashia, waiting in Poland behind a tight net of international regulations about bringing her children into a foreign country on a marriage visa.

Privacy is a carefully guarded commodity in modern America, so I knew Witold had subtly asked me how many people knew about his fiancée. Still, I couldn't resist the rare opportunity to get one over on the guy.

"Well, I just tell anyone who asks that your former life partner Anne used to be a guy, but after her successful sex change it didn't work for the two of you as a couple anymore, but you'd parted amiably, as evidenced by the sharing of Josephine, your dog."

Witold let that sift through his English-to-Polish filter as Jack and Anne howled with laughter. Then he rose without a word, took up the plate bearing my slice of mushroom-Gruyère quiche with raspberry chutney garnish, and set it down in front of Josie.

But Witold doesn't hold a grudge. When he and Ashia were finally able to marry a couple of years later, we hosted their wedding shower at the bookstore. Themed "Essentials for Establishing a Comfortable American Home," among its gifts were six rolls of duct tape in assorted colors, a collection of plastic cups from fast-food establishments, a coffee can of rusty nuts and bolts, and a lifetime supply of Tupperware containers with unmatched lids. We toasted the bride and groom with wine drunk from another gift: a dozen mugs advertising tourist traps no one could remember visiting.

But going back to that night at Witold's house, not long after our first successful ceilidh dance and an International Night debut, his casual comment about a "community center" gave us our first indication that the bookstore was making its mark. A throwaway line to him, it reverberated as we walked home.

Jack said, "Community center. There you go. I believe we might just be in with the bricks."

Terribly British, really. At the moment when I most felt like jumping up and down screaming, "We did it! We're in, we're in!" my husband squeezed my hand and said, "Good for us."

Good for us? Indeed. Keep calm and carry on.

So we went back to thinking up crazy stunts— er, special events—to hold at the bookstore. We celebrated Old World holidays as they appeared on the calendar: Burns Night, St. Andrew's Night, Celtic Christmas. I'd always wanted to run a murder mystery, so we started hosting them twice a year, featuring a recurring character: book-slinger John Bach, who with each subsequent murder becomes more nervous as people keep dying in his place of business. My husband dislikes acting despite his innate talent for it, so he really hams it up; I think repressed distaste at having to play the role fuels his growing despair as Bach.

Murders we have held include "Oh Dear oh Deer" featuring Dirk Deerslayer, a ladykiller and deer hunter who finally got his comeuppance surrounded by the beauty queens he'd spurned in years past; "Death Among the Cookbooks," the tale of two offed spinster sister authors and "a list of suspects longer than a lasagna noodle"; and "Books Run Amok," in which Jane Eyre stabbed Hester Prynne in a case of mistaken identity after Anna Karenina and Rhett Butler had a tryst in the mystery room, Long John Silver and Rip Van Winkle proved unreliable witnesses due to intoxication, and Miss Marple ran off with Jay Gatsby. Members of the writing group usually sculpt the plots, although Grace, Jack's guitar student; Jodi, a former local reporter who took a city government job and knows where all the bodies are buried (literally and figuratively); and Elissa, my photographer friend, have each created one as well. Murders involving town officials proved to be especially popular (no comment). All our victims have been great sports about being bludgeoned, poisoned, shot, or otherwise done in. As one recent murderee commented, "Honey, it beats election night."

Surrounded by these and other silly activities, we went whistling forward, advancing confidently in the direction of our dreams. Up to our ears in special events and paperbacks, we were meeting interesting new customers every day, gaining friends, establishing our reputation as a community center where people wanted to be. We thought we were "in." And we were, once again, blissfully ignorant. We had no idea how easily we could lose that goodwill, reputation, and customer base in one fell swoop.

Chapter 7
God Bless You for Trying, Losers

Experience: that most brutal of teachers.
But you learn. My God, do you learn.
— C. S. Lewis, from one of
his popular lecture topics

MURDER TURNED TO CHARACTER ASSAS-sination just a few weeks later, when we fell afoul of a town clique. My day job's boss held a long-standing position in an intricate network of Old Families and locals; when that job fell apart, so did the shop's navigation system through those mazes of interrelations.

Why I'd left one government agency for the same bureaucracy in another state remains a mystery filed under Sudden Flight from Common Sense, but I did. One day my boss helped me understand that my job was on the line unless I changed my thinking on a couple of key issues. For me, those issues represented the very core of what I considered integrity, and I lost it.

A part of me constantly regretted not standing

my ground in the Snake Pit; I'd made a decision not to get embroiled further and fled, but with hindsight, that move felt less like taking the moral high ground, and more like getting the hell out of Dodge. Now here I stood with a second chance at speaking up for truth, justice, and social equity. (Cue the orchestra's string section.)

I said what I thought, got fired, and walked home rejoicing to be a member of the "went down with integrity" club at last. Yes, that's called a martyr complex, and it's neither logical nor clever, but oh, it felt so good when all that bottled-up compliance exploded into one loud (and fairly self-righteous) "NO!"

Those of you who have lived in a small town will know that a firing is almost as good as a car wreck for the topic of lunch conversations. In the immediate aftermath, the local business association's head refused to display our flyers in her shop window; our friend and town councilor Garth asked another councilor if she'd ever visited the bookstore, and she replied, "I hadn't thought about it"; and we got "inadvertently left off" a list of businesses eligible for a community award. *You have offended one of our own; have the good sense to go quietly,* the unspoken message came via not-entirely-subtle channels—even as our customer pool grew.

If we'd had any sense, there wouldn't have been a bookstore in the first place. Sweet irony: looking back, we now realize that at the moment when it would have made the most sense to pack up, the possibility had disappeared from our minds. In choosing not to—actually, not so much choosing as forgetting we had the option—we weren't being thrawn (that's Scottish for stubborn); it's just that we had a dream going, and Jack had promised no more drifting, no living on other people's agendas. Our bookstore, do or die. All for one, and buy one, get one free.

As each day went by, we wanted more and more to stay in Big Stone. Every Thursday, my hubby would pull open the weekly paper and read aloud the news columns from various contributors—about grandchildren coming to visit, families who went out to eat, opinions on the color someone had painted her house: sweet news from genuine people living a quiet life well.

We really, really wanted a piece of that non-action.

Not only were the people genuine *and* fun—albeit since I got fired some no longer held the same opinion of us—but the physical town of Big Stone Gap is truly, madly, amazingly beautiful. A bowl of mountains alternates between surreal morning fogs, snowy slopes, summer flowers, and the splendor of autumn's leaves. The Gap dazzles the eye in every season. Even the downtown buildings, shabby from years of economic downturn, show the most interesting span of twentieth-century architecture one could find in a single location.

In short, Big Stone looked like a great place to spend the rest of our lives. I don't remember a moment when we looked at each other and said, "We're not leaving, are we?" but Jack and I both knew we weren't going anywhere if we could help it. We'd fallen in love, and that meant settling in for the long haul.

So instead of packing up in the face of adversity, we dug into our extra energy reserves, prepared to eat air, and with increased free time and desperation, delivered flyers advertising our special events to a widening circle of banks and clinics and hairdressers, chatting to potential customers all the way. Lots of new people did come to see us as a result of our efforts, while a few of our regulars stopped—not very many, just a couple. A friend from my former job had amassed quite a healthy credit in our blue ledger of trade swaps; the afternoon of my firing, she arrived with her adult daughter in tow, wiped out the balance with four armloads of paperbacks, and disappeared. We never saw her or her children again.

That kind of thing let us know how the back-alley gossip hummed; we figured we could beat it over time, but it's no fun when people are suspicious of you. The "you aren't from here" snake, which everyone who moves into a small community deals with at some point, became a hydra rearing its ugly "you aren't one of us, you won't ever understand us, you're trying to change us, you're the outsiders who will never be accepted" heads—and in an extra ironic twist, that suspicion appeared because of losing my job, an act I believed had returned my integrity. *Won't be a snake in the pit? Okay, how about a shut-out failure instead?*

Most of us have figured out by now that those aren't the only two choices life offers. It bothered me that people thought ill of us, but it didn't define me. Or Jack. Or the bookstore. We were more concerned about the effect it might have on our customer pool, which slumped in the weeks after I got sent home in disgrace.

Soon after I got fired, Garth popped in for coffee and asked how we were doing. I spent the next ten minutes ranting and raving in full-blown Pity Party mode. How we had people we didn't even know calling us "uppity incomers," and—even worse—people we barely knew running in to gleefully tell us that we were getting called that. How the other chamber-of-commerce types wouldn't come near the shop.

When I finally exhausted myself and sat down at my antique kitchen table—sacrificed to hosting the store's coffee service where we offered *free coffee,* so why weren't people taking us up on it?!—my wise friend said, "Honey, this ain't got as much to do with you gettin' fired as people wonderin' if you're gonna stay. I know you and Jack are good people, but you look like every other City Sophisticate Discovering Rural Paradise. They set up a business, it makes money or doesn't, they fold up and get a tax write-off, or they take off with the loot back to the city. Ain't nobody thinks you're really gonna stay very long. You've got no ties to the community, so why should they bother to make friends? It's like fosterin' a puppy; sure, it's sweet, but don't get attached 'cause you'll just get your heart broke when it goes."

"Ties to the community?" I shot back. "You mean like having a *real* job in town, not just a bookstore we didn't ask anyone's permission to start but that just might make it despite the in-club not shopping here, because a bunch of other really nice people are?"

Garth rocked back in his chair and lifted the brim of his cap—and beamed at me. "Well, sweetheart, you *do* have a bit of spark left in you. Good. I was afraid the last little while mighta burned you out."

I hate it when men who are neither my husband nor my uncle call me sweetheart, but it also seemed like a good moment to keep my mouth shut and let him talk. Garth returned the chair's front two legs to the ground with a thud, leaned forward, and crossed his arms on the table,

124

locking eyes with me. "Yeah, honey, that's what they mean. You got no reason to stay now, have you?"

"I've got about 5,200 reasons," I replied, waving my hand at the bookshelves, "and that doesn't count the friends we've made, like Mike and Heather and Teri and . . ." I stopped as Garth smiled again.

"So you think you belong here now, got a good life goin'? Fine. Prove you're someone who belongs here. 'Cause you been sayin' all along, right from the day you opened, that you an' Jack were 'just tryin' out this bookstore thing, gonna see if it could work.' So make it work."

In Scotland, that's called getting hoisted by your own petard, when something you say comes back to haunt you. But I wasn't ready to admit culpability yet.

"At our opening day, they talked about how great it was to see economic development, new entrepreneurs, all that, and now they don't shop here just because one of their friends is mad at me." I all but sniffed, wiping an imaginary spill from the coffee counter.

Garth snorted. "Cut the princess crap, sister. You and I both know small towns are all about who's friends with who. You pissed off somebody's friend; give it time and it'll blow over—assumin' you're comittin' for the long haul. Why should anyone commit to you if you're just playin' around? You got to be around a while, show a little respect and humility for our way of life here in town, before anyone'll take you seriously. Suspicion's always earned, just not necessarily by the people it falls on. Haven't you ever dated somebody on the rebound? This whole town is on the rebound."

"How do we stick around if no one takes us seriously enough to shop here?" I whined, although his rebound analogy made me grin. It's hard to whine and grin at the same time.

He grinned back. "That, baby girl, is the part we ain't figured out yet. Now pull up your bootstraps and prove you can be part of this place. And, honey, don't give anyone more power than they've got. There's plenty of locals can see the good in having a new business run by nice people. People like havin' a bookstore, I know; they tell me. And there's plenty of 'em as like you and Jack; they like all that crazy stuff you two organize. The rest'll come around. Give 'em time."

Exit power-player pal, coffee refill in travel mug. He didn't drop any change in the donation pot for it.

Garth was right; I had openly said we were "just trying out" the idea of a bookstore. We'd refused to go into debt just so we could make a clean getaway if needed; Jack called the little protected lump in our bank account "Wendy's emergency flight fund." Partly that caution stemmed from still feeling unsettled; letting anyone else know how important my bookshop was to me would make me vulnerable again. It had been a casual acquaintance, something we could walk away from easily. Problem was, now we were in love with Big Stone.

That "we might stay, we might not" had also been hedging our bets against straight-out failure. Like the rest of the community, we hadn't been sure a bookstore would work, mentally or physically.

A crazy little three-part syllogism echoes like a drumbeat through the Appalachian Coalfields: people outstanding in their field can go anywhere they want; you are here; therefore, you must not be very good at what you do, because who wants to be here?

The Coalfields are emptying. If you ask someone outside Central Appalachia to name our region's top export, they would say coal, but the more accurate answer is college students. Newly minted, educated adults make up what's called in British Isles history "a bloody Flight of Earls." The best and brightest of the eighteen-to-twenty-five-year-olds flee this scenic wonderland of economic stagnation with their entrepreneurial spirits, energy, ideas, and babies, headed for the cities. The county's population drops by something like 5 percent every year, mostly young'uns crazy to hurl themselves against the walls of what they figure will be a larger life. Mountains may have formed their backbones, but dreams light their eyes.

Living in a shrinking community meant every customer had to be wooed, feted, and treated like a precious commodity. They needed to believe in us, but the very fact that we'd chosen to settle in their town negated trust in our prowess. Four book clubs within half an hour's drive never entered the store in its first year, even though we put out the word that we did bulk orders. Without rancor, and without ever really putting it in words, their members assumed—as one told us later—that we wouldn't be as good as someplace bigger, somewhere else, or just surfing the Net. What could a bookshop in the tiny town of Big Stone Gap offer sufficient to change established buying habits?

A woman came into our shop the day after one of Christopher Paolini's books became available for preorder. When I explained that we didn't have it on hand but I could order it for her, she sniffed. "I figured a place like this wouldn't have it; I'll get it in Kingsport." I tried to explain that no one would have it until the preorders were released, but she walked out midword.

In Scotland, it's known as "too wee, too poor, too stupid" when a small place (like Scotland itself) is considered ineffectual. My M.D. pal

Elizabeth says she and other regional docs often hit against that unspoken assumption when traveling: "Our IQ plummets seconds after they ask where we're from." Yet stereotyping is not a simple art form; both Elizabeth and my photographer friend Elissa have experienced denigration of their skills within their own communities. Neighbors prefer to seek medical care or photographs from a city agency. And that's leaving aside the allure and convenience of online services and retailers.

Elissa took me to lunch one day—I think friends and regular customers kept feeding us because they thought we would starve otherwise—and I told her about Garth's soliloquy. Elissa, four feet eleven inches tall and not a pontificator by nature, blew a gasket.

"Americans en masse have been conditioned to think that bigger is better, box stores and online are the only places worth shopping, buy your stuff from some major brand label and don't accept anything that looks out of the ordinary. Nothing that was made by your neighbor could be any good. Why shop local when local is so small and familiar, and online is so cheap and easy and dazzling?

"Here in our neck of the woods, we've been suckered and snowed until we don't understand the value of supporting ourselves. We could benefit so much as a town from the talents of the people who live here, but instead we die by our own self-strangulation, because if somebody does start a service or a store, they have to run the gauntlet you're running now, Wendy. 'Are you one of us? Are you good enough? Do you think you're too good? Are you trying to change us?' Or they have to put up with that 'Yeah, but it's from here so it must be crap' crap. And that's a real pity, but that's also how it is, and I don't think it will ever change."

I stared at her, and Elissa took a sip of Coke. "That's how I feel," she said. "You gonna eat those fries?"

A limited belief in the prowess of anything considered local, coupled with hefty suspicion of nonnatives, is a tricky hand to play. Amid the innuendoes and nuances, relationships between insiders and outsiders—and who gets called which—can be as subtle as a homemade quilt. You glance at it and see a pattern, but when you look again, you notice alignments and contrasts that change the pattern's intent; a third look reveals tiny stitches rolling over the colored pieces in contours and swirls, holding the whole thing together. All this makes it a little tricky for well-meaning souls from outside to waltz into town and act natural.

We had been, however briefly, insiders, but now some people wanted us to be outsiders again. Time to smile, persevere, and make clear that we weren't playing to anyone's stereotype. What we didn't know, within the misery of those weeks of being talked down, was how much fun getting out of the Slough of Despond and back into the Inside Track would be.

CHAPTER 8

Stephen Saved Our Bacon Day

There must be, not a balance of power, but a community of power; not organized rivalries, but an organized peace.
—Woodrow Wilson,
"Peace Without Victory,"
Address to the U.S. Senate,
January 21, 1917

MY HUSBAND WAS SANGUINE AS the rumor mill continued spitting toads instead of diamonds about our little bookstore, and people we barely knew continued to enjoy telling us about it. "We're doing fine; stop worrying; if some people choose not to shop with us, it doesn't matter; plenty do. And you've got to question the motives of people who want to tell you the nasty things other people are saying."

Still, I continued to cast about for ways of saying, "Can't we all just get along?" in a friendly, nonchallenging way. Eventually I hit upon a cunning plan—political, but not too; clever, but not overly ambitious.

"You should join a local civic club," I urged my homebody husband one night as we sat down to a cold plate of sliced vegetables and cheese.

He shot me the look of a raccoon in headlights, little glittering eyes holding a mute appeal against imminent death. "Why me?"

"You're the male." My logic was infallible. "The rumors will stop once everyone sees we don't want to fight, and that we're doing good things for the area. Plus, you'll be guaranteed a square meal once a week at their meetings." I gnawed a pepper slice. Between money and time, cooking at our house had become more fantasy than nonfiction.

Jack stared at the quartered tomato on his plate. "Hmmm," he said.

A Kiwanis chapter boasted many of the town's movers and shakers. Joining turned out to be expensive, but we figured our gain in goodwill would balance the cost. I asked a local pastor if he'd sponsor Jack. He appeared delighted to do so.

We didn't know my former boss was their current president. We didn't know some members embraced the belief that we needed to leave like good little bad guys. A letter arrived in short order, rejecting Jack's membership and thanking us for our interest in the Kiwanis Club, a group "dedicated to making Big Stone Gap an even better place to live."

My husband, one of the gentlest creatures God ever put on Earth, folded the letter back into its envelope with a wan smile. "Well, I guess we know when we're not wanted."

Truth, justice, and social equity; we're just trying this bookstore thing out; suspicion's earned, honey. The voices ran like rats through my brain, vicious little claws out for blood. *The Coalfields are dying, strangled by our own hands; no one wants to be here, so why do you?*

"And so will everyone else," I snapped back at Jack, snatching up the car keys.

Accustomed to dealing with my overdeveloped sense of fair play (okay, martyr complex) Jack headed me off at the door. "Where are you going?" he sighed.

"To buy the best document frame Walmart sells," I practically snarled. As realization dawned, he threw back his head and laughed, then went with me to pick out a nice oak frame matching the pillars in our front rooms. We spent two days' worth of grocery money on it and hung the Kiwanis rejection letter in the shop—prominently.

It made us feel better, and it sure made customers laugh, but staring at that document one night, I took mental stock. Operating a bookshop at starvation wages, we had taken a direct hit to our ability to improve the customer pool. And even though we were recovering, we couldn't seem to shake the label of aggressive incomers riding the fifth horse of the Apocalypse: Change.

Again and again, my mind returned to the question of why some people talked trash about our store, going round and round like the teddy bear of British finger rhyme fame, circling a garden of dead ends. Jack, passing by the front room table as I sat trapped in my death spiral, noticed and wrapped his arms around me. "Never mind, dear. We have each other, and our health."

But no health insurance! We couldn't afford it once I'd lost the day job.

I wallowed in despairing self-pity for longer than I'd care to admit, praying for deliverance but doing nothing to help myself. That's not a healthy combination. Renting inside one's own skin is soul-destroying.

Enter the paladin on his white horse, lance extended. In this case, the lance strongly resembled a fountain pen (and yes, it is mightier than the sword). Stephen Igo, a reporter who covered Southwest Virginia for the *Kingsport Times-News*, called about doing a feature on the shop. He and Jack spent an afternoon together, Stephen plying Jack with questions, Jack stuffing Stephen full of fresh-baked shortbread. The completed article ran above the fold with a three-column color picture on Sunday's front page.

In short, it could not have been better.

Among the highlights, it said that "Tales of the Lonesome Pine is a not-just-a-used-book-shop (www.scottishsongandstory.co.uk) staffed by Beck's genuine brogue, Wendy, two cats—Beulah and Val-Kyttie—and two dogs, Zora and Bert," and that since opening the shop had "drawn the merely curious, the seriously artistic, and the bonkers over books.

"In their case, 'there goes the neighborhood' means in a wondrously delightful direction. While browsing for books, visitors are invited to sit a spell—in fact, a sign tells them to do just that— and sip a cup of coffee or tea while nibbling on homemade shortbread—Beck got the recipe from his mother—or tablet, a sort of Scottish fudge. Another sign reads, 'if you have change to throw in the pot, great. No worries if not. We welcome browsers and hangers out.'

"Beck and Welch and their furry staff also offer a good book-swapping deal, a free books bin on the porch, arts and crafts on consignment, and a few other sideshows like, well, sideshows. There's the writing group, needlework nights, puppet shows, house concerts, and occasional Celtic folk music and dancing. Toss in some children's events plus a couple of fascinating chats with Beck himself, and you've got just an inkling of what all goes on in a bookstore operated on the principles of imagination and love of life."

I cried the first time I read it.

In our early years, when we opened on Sunday afternoons, the hours frequently passed without customers. Stephen's article came out on Sunday; Gary, Teri's husband, brought us a copy of the paper with many congratulations. I sighed, smiled, and prepared to open the store. Assuming we'd have no customers as usual, I intended to spend the afternoon tidying the free books we'd recently set out there.

I stepped onto the porch, OPEN sign in my hand to hang on the outer door's iron grille—and eight retirees looked up from poking amid the books, and smiled. "The British baking sounds good, but we sure hope you've got iced tea in there!" one said. They'd driven from Kingsport for a nice afternoon outing, spurred by the Igo article.

"It just looked so lovely in the picture." One of the women sighed, tilting her head back to take in the oak columns and decorative scrolling inside the shop. "And now I see it in person, it's even better. Oh! What a pretty cat!" She'd spotted Beulah, mincing about with her tail fluffed for the visitors. Her voice took on celebrity-tinged reverence as she asked, "Is she the one from the photo?!"

A lot of things changed that day. The chair-woman of the local business association appeared, all smiles. We had flyers? Why didn't she take a couple to put in her shop window? We got congratulatory e-mails from two Kiwanians.

Visitors chatted merrily as they perused the shelves:

"Heard you were here. Always meant to come in, saw that photo and said, 'C'mon, kids, today's the day.'"

"I didn't know y'all were here. Wow! You take books in trade?"

"What gorgeous woodwork, and you built the shelves yourself? We're so glad to have a bookstore in town at last. What made you settle in Big Stone?"

"Hey, this letter, did you really get rejected by the Kiwanis club here??!! That's a hoot! We have one in Norton [the next town over]. Wanna join?"

Seventy lovely people flowed through our doors that Sunday summer afternoon. I made four pitchers of iced tea. Our photocopier godparents took me to Little Mexico that night in celebration. (Jack left the day after the interview to lead his annual Scotland and Ireland tour; he got to read the article online from abroad, while yours truly had to cope with the tea. Not that I'm complaining, mind.) Business in the months that followed picked up considerably. Our regulars congratulated us; new friends came to visit, and a few of the old ones we'd lost came back as though nothing had ever happened.

We e-mailed Stephen that we'd name our next cat after him. And some—not all, but most—rifts healed. We weren't going anywhere now, and everyone knew it; equally important, people understood that we didn't want to fight. A bookshop run on imagination and love of life, yes, and thank you; fighting and rivalry, not so much. A lot of people in the region wanted a bookstore, and we wanted to live in Big Stone Gap.

So time worked its magic. Right after Stephen's article, a couple of civic functions asked for some upscale books as door prizes, we donated several boxes to the hospital, and I started helping a church we didn't attend cook lunches for unemployed people. At the request of a mother whose library program had fallen through the night before, Jack read Scottish poems to the local kindergarteners in full kilt and regalia; shortly thereafter we got asked to do a "celebrity reading" for Dr. Seuss's birthday at the local elementary, and then the music department at the high school called about a program of Scottish songs, and a new customer wanted to know if I would make balloon animals for her child's birthday party. . . .

Thus the ill wind blew itself out. The Kiwanis letter still hangs in our shop, but its poison leached out the bottom, dried up, and flaked away long ago. Now it's a reminder not to take ourselves or others so seriously; that this, too, shall pass. Local power players bring in out-of-town friends or family and point it out with a belly laugh: "That's the letter I was telling you about. Isn't that just typical small-town crap?" Browsers relate eye-rolling stories of their own clashes with cliques. Most humans are blessed with the natural ability to laugh at ourselves, and time—coupled with a good sense of humor and refusing to play "an eye for an eye" games—heals most wounds.

CHAPTER 9

Catty Behavior, or How Beulah Taught Us to Stand Tall, Quit Whining, and Have Fun

There were cats, cats, sitting on the mats,
At the (book)store, at the (book)store.
There were cats, cats, sitting on the mats
At the Quartermaster's (book)store.
　　　　　—British children's folk song
　　　　　(the Jack and Wendy version)

T HE PHOTO STEPHEN TOOK FOR the *Times*
article showed my husband leaning on the
back of a waist-high sleepbuilt. Looming large at
shelf front, eyes looking into the souls of her
readers, our younger cat Beulah (Customer
Relations Specialist) reclined on the cushion kept
there for her comfort and convenience.

We are convinced Stephen's lovely article—
charming though it was about our zest for life,
Scottish shortbread giveaways, and beautiful
woodwork—would never have made the Sunday
paper's front page without Beulah's cool stare.

The picture exuded charm, and people inundated the shop for weeks afterward, demanding to meet Miss Beulah. They bought books while waiting their turn for her attentions. She became known as Beuls to her familiars.

Beulah is an unusually pretty cat of distinctive coloring. Soft hues of gray, pink, and peach blend within her fur. Some cat-savvy patrons call her a dilute tortoiseshell; others say she is peaches and cream. With a pale fawn tuxedo bib and Hemingway thumbs, Beulah is what Scots term a *stotar*, or in plain English, a good-looking female.

All of this annoys our older cat, Val-Kyttie, to no end. Val-Kyttie is Scottish, has thick black fur tinged with reddish-brown, and is green-eyed—in both senses of the word. That cat is jealous all over. (She also has one white toe ring and a white bikini on her stomach. A word of warning: if you ever come to visit our shop, do not make the mistake of believing Val-Kyttie is friendly, and try to see the bikini. We can't pay for your stitches.)

Val-Kyttie and Beulah have the relationship of teen sisters forced to share a room: adversarial. Named for the famous Wagnerian ride of the Val-Kytties, the elder of this pair came to us tiny and fearless at four weeks of age, from a home for distressed gentlecats in Edinburgh. In later years she flew the Atlantic to become yet another expatriate Scot. When we adopted the American

144

Beulah at just ten months of age, Val-Kyttie was six. Forever after, she would refer to her little sister only as "that girl the church sent over."

For her part, Beulah tried to act as acolyte to Val-Kyttie's high priesthood. She kept away, rolled over, left food, anything to avoid a fight, but it remained clear that Val-Kyttie had it in for Beuls from the moment we brought her in off the street. The daily tension between them would blossom into overt aggression if the humans went away overnight. On our return Beulah could be found crying in the basement, while Val-Kyttie licked her tail in feigned innocence. Her posture said, "What, down there yowling again? Hmmph, these young cats have no dignity. She should move on."

A funny thing happened in the weeks after Stephen's front-page picture of Beulah. As the waterfall from its publicity slowed to a steady current of regular customers, Beulah took up position on a table under the article, which we laminated and put on the wall. (I'm not sure why the Kiwanis rejection received an oak frame while Stephen got plastic, but there you go.) Jack swore that Beuls pointed her Hemingway thumb at the article when customers arrived, as much as to say, "See that? That's me. I do autographs."

Val-Kyttie was incensed by Stephen's photo and made her opinions clear in that way only household pets can: statement poops. Val-Kyttie does not normally think outside the box, but for three days, she strategically located her excretions where they could do the most damage: at the head of the stairs; next to a bookshelf five minutes after opening. Her crowning sarcastic achievement appeared a foot outside her hooded tray, perfectly centered before its entry door.

Had she spoken aloud, Val-Kyttie's message could not have been clearer: the photo should have been of her, the Senior Ranking Staff Animal. That cute little junior assistant in the tight miniskirt had usurped her matronly authority. After we'd spent a few days picking up statement poops while murmuring soothing endearments about understanding how she felt, Val-Kyttie, clearly fed up with our sensitive-parent routine, reverted to her trademark violence. As she'd done so often before, she stalked in a menacing manner to where Beuls sat washing her tuxedo bib. I prepared to intervene, but this time when Val-Kyttie closed in, gentle, compliant little Beulah reached out, claws extended, and swifter than a striking snake bopped her big sis a good one on the head. Then she ran like hell, but the point had been made. Val-Kyttie sat down, too stunned to pursue.

Jack is convinced that her picture in the paper empowered Beulah to stand up to Val-Kyttie. Not once since its publication have we found her crying for rescue in the basement. We didn't spend any more time crying, either, and we knew just how Beulah felt. To everything there is a season:

a time to hide in the basement, and a time to post things in prominent positions where everyone sees them; a time to get cut down, and a time to watch in astonishment as someone you don't even know tells everyone how beautifully you're blossoming.

Stephen gave us a hefty boost, with a ribbon tied 'round it.

For those of you feeling bad for her, Val-Kyttie did receive revenge for her stolen glory. One spring day, a customer admired Miss Beulah as Val-Kyttie lounged nearby, eavesdropping. Beulah, a skinny, slinky stray when she arrived, had filled out over the winter into a magnificent creature, very much resembling a woman at the opera in a fur coat. She sat, dignified and majestic, accepting compliments as the customer rubbed her head, prattling baby talk. "Aren't you just the prettiest thing?! So regal, so beautiful! And when are your kittens due?"

I swear to you that Val-Kyttie guffawed as Beulah slunk away, tail dragging in humiliation.

In all the years our shop has been open, two customers have been put off by the cats—one allergic, one afraid—while a thousand or more have brought other people to meet them. Boyfriends introduced significant others to demonstrate a sensitive side, patting Beulah while sneaking "is it working" glances at their dates. Usually the girls were caught up in stroking Beuls, murmuring endearments as they fondled her cheeks and tail. The boys looked envious. Couples brought elderly parents. "This is the cat I was telling you about, Mom; isn't she pretty?" Adults brought children. "See the kitty Mommy told you about? Pet gently, now." Beulah, a tolerant cat by nature, rarely used the bolt-holes secreted throughout the shop, while Val-Kyttie, as shop manager, preferred not to fraternize with customers. The whole establishment catered in design and policy to every whim of the two permanent staff cats and the myriad fosters who have found forever homes via the bookstore. (To date we count twenty-nine cats, plus seven dogs.) One shelf beneath a window sports a three-by-five card taped flat, announcing "this space reserved for feline staff." Whoever arrives first basks there on sunny days.

One day I heard giggling and looked up to behold Beulah on one side of a shelf, pushing cookbooks with her paw toward the customer opposite. The lady caught them as they fell, pleased as punch. She even bought one. "If Beuls likes it, that's all the recommendation I need," she assured us as our cat sat on the mat, cleaning her push paw. The customer later brought us molasses cookies from the recipe book. Jack and I found them delicious, although Madam Customer Relations Specialist didn't care for them.

Such is the life of a bookshop staff cat. It's good work if you can get it.

CHAPTER 10

Saved by the Cell
(and the Napkin Dispensers,
and the Corkboards)

*The only thing worse than being talked
about is not being talked about.*

—Oscar Wilde,
The Picture of Dorian Gray

As THE MONTHS ROLLED BY, we understood
that finding ways to advertise had to remain
high on our daily task list—right next to evaluating
trade credit, stocking shelves, and keeping the
place clean. Stephen's article had given us a
rocket-propelled boost, and the customers he'd
made aware of us were bringing customers themselves. Grassroots advertising can't be bought. It
meant we ran the kind of place people wanted
friends to visit—a happy thing to know.

Still, we now understood that we had to make
our own way forward. Special events helped, as
did the unlimited flyer-book swap with Gary and
Teri, but we spent a lot of time cooking up

schemes to publicize both wares and events. Also, we had intended to outlaw cell phones in the store, but never got around to making a sign saying so. This proved fortuitous, because people talking on cell phones came into our shop often. One day a woman walked in, looked around, and pulled out her phone before either of us could say hello.

WOMAN: [Pause] Hey, it's me. Guess what, there's a bookstore in town. [Pause] No, *our* town. [Pause] Yes there is, I'm standing in it. [Pause] Dunno. [To Jack] How long ya been here?

JACK: Not long.

WOMAN [into phone]: Not long. And it's great! There's lotsa Dean Koontzes. They have [reels off several titles]. Say again? [picks up three books]. Okay, got those. [Pause] I dunno. [To Jack] How much are these?

JACK [points to sign: PRICES ARE MARKED IN PENCIL ON FIRST PAGE OF BOOK.]

WOMAN [looks in books, incredulous]: Cheap! [Pause] Yeah, sure. [Pulls more titles from shelf] You oughta come down here. They got lotsa stuff. [Pause] Okay, bye. [Disconnects, smiles at us] I'm gonna get these for her. That was my son's parole officer. She's great. I hope he marries her.

Reader, did she marry him?

Perfectly capable of recognizing a good thing once it fell into our lap, we never did make that sign. Buzz about our shop flew along cordless lines, while the noise level we'd feared never materialized. Shoppers rang friends, family, and coworkers from the bookstore floor to tell them where they were and what great deals we had. Many people bought books for whomever they were talking to. Often, when the person on the other end showed up, they mentioned being referred by a friend.

Resuscitated by all that mouth to mouth, we nosed around for more free advertising opportunities. Our town boasted a popular diner-cum-pharmacy, the Mutual (made famous by Adriana Trigiani's novels). In the real-life diner, eating plays second fiddle to social interaction, but the cast of characters is extensive and eclectic. Most of them don't frequent the bookstore but become stalwart supporters of our being in town, all the same. We ate there once a week for at least a year before being "accepted" as one of the regulars. Other regulars include Bo and Jack, retired mining brothers with wicked senses of humor; Eulis the Korean War veteran, his wife, Annie, and their son, both men long-haul truck drivers; the Gathering of Women Who Lunch, which meets in the corner at the only table large enough to hold six people—and woe betide anyone who stakes a claim before the ladies arrive; plus town councilor Cotton, town maintenance men Donnie and Smokey, about-town handyman and grass mower David; Bill-I-Used-to-Drive-the-School-Bus; and the rest. We meet them there most mornings and gather the day's news, plus a weekly supply of opinions.

Bill-the-Bus uttered my favorite Big Stone Gap quote of all time. The day after the nation elected its first African-American president, as the rest of the men sat and pontificated on the state and future trajectory of the union, Bill gripped the tray guard on the luncheon counter and cleared his throat. Since he was the oldest person in the shop, ninety-three at the time, everyone else stopped to listen to what he had to say.

In a loud voice, he intoned, "Lord, the world is changin' more ever' day. Little Debbies used to be $1.39. Now they're $1.59 [shakes head]. I don't know what's gonna happen to us all."

Jack and I enjoy being Mutual regulars when scheduling permits. Once we reappeared after a two-week hiatus due to busy-life syndrome. Annie, eyeing us as we passed her booth, grinned. "Go away. I'm 'feart of strangers." When I went to an out-of-town conference without Jack, they teased me that he'd been breakfasting in the company of a young blonde. And when he came back from his second trip to Scotland, they informed him I'd been seeing the short-order cook.

There's nothing quite like that special sense of belonging evidenced by your friends teasing the living daylights out of you.

Napkin dispensers sit near the wall at each Mutual booth, and one morning after thinking it over, I hunted down Pat Bean. Miss Bean is a town legend, the octogenarian diner manager, a dear friend, and a bastion of good sense in a world of absurdity. When she broke her arm after tripping on a nearby city's sidewalk, Jack asked if she planned to sue. "Good grief," she snapped. "If I can't walk straight, is that the city's fault?" That's our Miss Bean.

"Would you care if I put a list of upcoming bookshop events behind these?" I showed her the napkin dispenser space. Miss Bean didn't mind so long as we laminated them first, and within a month every tourism stop in town followed this example. For about twenty dollars a year, we put our quarterly events calendar in the paths of some five hundred people a week.

Bookmarks, Stephen-Saved-Our-Bacon-Day, special events galore, napkin dispensers, endorsement from the Mutual crowd and the rest of it all meshed into something that worked just like "real" advertising. Sans money, we still had time, unlimited photocopies, and personal energy. That proved enough to accomplish more than one might have thought. We had a first-anniversary party for the shop and limped more or less confidently in the direction of our dream: a peaceful and fun life full of books in a community that we appreciated, and that appreciated us.

And one April night, some eighteen months after that long-ago Grand Opening, Jack stood up from doing our quarterly taxes, stretched like a cat in the sun, and said, "Let's go to Little Mexico."

Any day without cooking is a good one for me, but we'd been careful about unnecessary spending for so long, it had become second nature. As he folded up the accounts, I asked, "Eating out? What are we celebrating?"

My husband gave a beatific smile and began ticking off fingers. "We have enough money to buy what we need to eat; we have paid-up phone, light, and heat bills." He dropped finger-counting and spread his arms wide as if to embrace the shelf-lined walls. "We are filling this house with the accumulated wisdom of humanity; people are bringing in books; people are buying books; and we have made a bunch of kooky, adorable friends." He wrapped his arms around me and nibbled my ear. "We're celebrating happiness." Then he kissed me.

So we went (a bit later) to Little Mexico, bowed our heads over chips with salsa to thank God for so many blessings, and smiled at each other as we clinked sangria glasses. Solvency is good. Fried salt is great. Ear nibbles are wonderful.

CHAPTER 11

A Book's Value Versus Its Price

Not everything that counts can be counted,
and not everything that can be counted,
counts.
—Albert Einstein, chalked on the
blackboard in his office at the Institute for
Advanced Study at Princeton

SO WE WERE MAKING IT! We had reached the point where the bookstore kept the lights burning and food on the table. Our meager earnings didn't stretch to health insurance and other luxuries, so I eventually accepted a staff position at a nearby college, basically working for benefits. With coverage from this, and the cash flow from the shop, we were solvent. Careful rather than comfortable, but solvent.

People were bringing books to trade by the carton—which scored me significant points with Linda, my college department's secretary. Social sciences was scheduled to move en masse one summer, and Linda bemoaned her hard lot at having to find enough boxes for twelve pro-fessors. I started bringing her carloads from the store. Within a week we had filled a twenty-by-twenty room with cardboard—and now I never have trouble getting photocopies on short notice.

Yet the boxes of books people brought in occasionally had a dark side. Jack and I had been blissfully ignorant about how often bookstores intersected with bereaved humans, but as business accelerated, books from a death or divorce scenario appeared at least once a month.

Families experiencing loss have a lot of mental and physical baggage to deal with. It is humbling to unpack someone else's life history from a box at the best of times, but people moving, or clearing a departed loved one's bookshelf, are rarely having the best of times. And their boxes were so very revealing. Bookshelf anthropology is easy; if you want to know who someone is, investigate their home library. Correlating a person's books to his or her journey from cradle to grave requires little imagination, yet feels almost as invasive as brain surgery. You don't want to know this much about strangers.

One morning two men dropped off eight sacks of books because their mom had moved to the nursing home. "We're not much on reading but didn't wanna sling 'em in the Dumpster," said one. "Thought you could use 'em."

The bags gave evidence of a sweet, full life: a

bunch of books on cooking with herbs and organic gardening. Several bread-making collections. A worn hardback on home decorating on a budget, margins full of handwritten notes. A James Dobson title on raising godly boys. Two erotic novels—not Harlequins; we are talking Fanny Hill here. A whole row of Little Golden Books, and a 1955 set of Childcraft encyclopedias, worn to bits. (However they turned out on reading, Mama raised the boys with good books around!) *Arthritis and Folk Medicine. How to Eat Away Arthritis. Coping with Arthritis.* Funny Christian pocket books about aging. Four books, hardly touched at all, on occupational therapy activities for the elderly to do at home. And a paperback on Alzheimer's, still in shrink wrap.

It wasn't hard to piece together how her life had unfolded, but it was poignant.

Another day, a man with a dolly maneuvered three boxes of books through the shop door, and we got a sharp lesson on the warning signs of a bereaved husband. Most customers didn't come with dollies or avert their eyes when you smiled at them or look as though they hadn't slept for days. I took a stab at what I wasn't yet experienced enough to understand. "Clearing out a house?" He looked so awful; maybe he'd been working too hard?

People handle loss differently. In a mixed marriage (reader married to nonreader) the nonreader quite often will bring the late spouse's entire library to the used book store and just donate them. Sometimes grieving souls want everything finished within sight of the funeral.

Not even glancing up, the man with the dolly shook his head as he stacked boxes in the middle of our front room. A baseball cap shadowed his face. "My wife died. Wanted someone who'd appreciate 'em to have her books."

Jack said, "I'll put the kettle on."

A Scotsman saying he'll put the kettle on sends a coded message. British households consider kettles symbols of friendship, sustenance, and strength. In a crisis, the first thing one does is make tea. But British men aren't so different from others in the species. Announcing their intentions of handling the kettle divides the labor. They bring you and the person in crisis a tea tray loaded with all the needed accoutrements, and set it down gently before you. Then they bugger off as fast as they can go.

Although I didn't know it then, the man with the dolly was the first of many. From him I learned that the archetype of a stoic mountaineer who's a sweetie inside relied upon a fairly accurate description of most Coalfields men.

"She was a big reader. Spent a lot of time in stores like this'un. I musta followed her through half of Georgia, waitin' while she looked at books." He took a gulp from the coffee Jack had

158

made. (Normally Jack makes tea, but husbands are often coffee drinkers; he's learned to ask.)

I wanted to show appreciation, so looked for clues as to her personality in the titles. "Oh, she liked Bennett Cerf! She must have been one fun lady."

He smiled. "Yeah. She was." His eyes grew suspiciously red beneath his hat brim, and he cleared his throat. "Anyway, like I said, wanted somebody who'd appreciate 'em to have 'em."

Sometimes Jack would sit with us as the husband talked, or leave us alone if a bereaved wife or daughter sat at the table instead, clinking her teaspoon against the mug as words poured out of her. The best we could do was listen, show appreciation for the life the book titles revealed, and pretend not to notice when someone was crying. Not all the stories were sweet. Customers shedding a loved one's books sometimes had ugly things to say, and wanted a safe space to tell how their family broke apart when Daddy died.

The bookstore became that safe space not so much through design as by default. Neither Jack nor I have a counseling credential, but how could we ignore the red eyes under those hat brims, the verbal fishhooks people tossed out in comments like "I don't live here anymore, just came back for a funeral." Or "do you have a copy of *Jacob Have I Loved*? I'm a twin—well, was, am, I mean, my sister just died." Or "Figured I'd bring these old books of Mom's to you. Heh. They're about the only thing we didn't fight over."

Some terrible death stories are floating around out there: families coming apart because of small stuff, sisters at blows about Mom's care, brothers fighting over toolboxes. We had a hard time grasping some of the scenarios—and a harder time just listening without comment, keeping the tea flowing and our mouths shut. But that creation of a safe place where people could just talk without judgment or advice coming back at them became part of the bookstore ethos.

My maternal grandmother had a good death. She lived summers in her own little Ohio apartment and spent winters with my parents in Tennessee. Soon after Nanny turned ninety-two and had a couple of unpleasant skirmishes with her stove, Mom, a recently retired geriatric nurse, said to her, "Okay, here's the deal: you can go to a nursing home, or you can come live with us permanently."

Nanny pouted, fussed, pulled out all the stops. When called upon, she could be a real drama queen. (Mom says I take after her, but I don't see it.) But in the end she held a massive garage sale, packed suitcases full of the sentimental stuff she couldn't bear to leave behind, and moved herself, lock, stock, and wheelchair to Mom and Dad's suburban ranch house—where she had her own room but not nearly enough space.

Mom had been looking forward to it. Although a physical train wreck, Nanny could run mental circles around most people, and you didn't want to get on the sharp side of her wit. Her fingers were still nimble, and Mom figured on five or so more good years of quilting, cooking, and catfighting. She and Nanny sparred like schoolteachers from different colleges.

Two weeks after Nanny moved in, she began sliding downhill fast. A veteran nursing-home staffer, Mom knew what she was seeing; her mother had given up. Mom called my sister and me, sputtering, "She couldn't stay in Ohio. She set fire to her sweater sleeve. She can't stand up by herself. She couldn't stay there alone."

Tracy and I knew guilt when we heard it and told Mom what she already knew: that she'd done the right thing. "Nanny always did it her way, and that's what she's doing now." And we came to say good-bye. Everybody knew.

Three weeks to the day that Nanny came to live in Tennessee, Mom was helping her into bed as both of them fussed at each other. Nanny yelped that Mom hurt her. Mom martyr-sighed and replied that Nanny had been startled, not hurt, and couldn't she tell the difference? Nanny snapped, "I ain't talkin' to you no more," and died of a sudden stroke.

Telling the story to Tracy and me, Mom choked back sobs. My sister and I eyed each other sidelong, then burst into laughter. Mom gave a weak, wet grin. "It is [sniff] kinda funny [snuffle], isn't it?"

We still miss Nanny, but what a blessed relief guilt-free mourning brings. We loved her, valued her, and if we didn't always do what she wanted, we did what she needed, especially Mom. Nanny died knowing it. And she certainly did it her way.

The more our customers told us about their family tragedies, the more grateful I became for Nanny's peaceful yet drama-queen passage. We didn't know, back in the starry-eyed days of "we're going to run a bookstore someday," that an unlicensed counseling office would make up part of its operation, but we tried to do the best we could once we figured it out. Even if you don't know the right thing to say, everyone deserves to be listened to.

As an ethnographer, I understood that we had "stranger value" operating, when talking to someone you don't know in a space you don't regularly inhabit feels safer than sharing with friends or relations. Many of the people who told us tales of woe were occasional customers, people whose names we might not even have known when they started talking. That worked—for them and for us. The act of sitting across the table listening, cups of tea in hand, asking a pertinent but not-too-invasive question now and again, seemed to be enough. People wanted to be listened to, valued, validated. The kettle boiled and emptied, boiled and emptied as we measured out our lives with tea and coffee spoons.

In all honesty, the hardest part came not during their stories, but afterward, when those boxes full of artifacts representing the personalities of beloved parents, siblings, even children who had left the family one way or another, became commodities that needed a price tag before they hit our shop floor.

It seemed such a cynical flip—like that moment in *A Christmas Carol* when the domestic staff sold Scrooge's bed curtains and cuff links. Bookshop owners are meant to price and sell books, but it felt creepy, the first time a weeping woman went away and we stared at her dead daughter's library, spread in plastic tubs across our front room floor. *Is this what we've become, literary vultures profiting from the death of others?*

Once a young man in camouflage, sporting a buzz cut, carried in a box of books, mostly Christian and female-oriented. *These have to be his wife or girlfriend's books,* I thought. Did she know he'd brought them? Where was she? Usually people bring in their own stuff, unless . . . she was dead?

Something must have registered on my face as I bent over a box, turning a women's devotional Bible—its pink hardback cover bedecked with flower sprigs—in my hands. Without a word, the guy reached past me and pulled out a book: *Keeping Your Marriage Alive.*

"Didn't work," he said, setting it on the table and reaching down for another: *10 Rules for a Godly Marriage.* "She left me. I was in Iraq, and when I got home, she'd gone off with a guy she met at work."

That lad saw a box full of memory grenades, not books. And he wanted to redeem them. I priced the lot—giving him a little extra for mental anguish—and entered his trade credit in our big blue ledger. He got about twenty-eight dollars, and I hope he also got a clean sweep.

That's the basic difference between price and value: one is calculated in dollars, the other in moments of memory. Bookshop owners contribute order and balance to a crazy, tilting world by dealing from the privileged yet precarious position of knowing the difference between these two things.

Jack likened valuing books from deaths and divorces to cleaning out an old junk drawer, wondering over the history of each object. *"For Sale: Baby shoes, never worn"* Hemingway wrote, simultaneously inventing and perfecting flash fiction as a genre. The untold story is often heartbreaking. One just has to get on with things and learn not to internalize the pain of others— otherwise you'd shut down, like Sue Monk Kidd's character May in *The Secret Life of Bees.* (If you haven't read it, you should!)

Fortunately, family losses were not the bulk of our trade-ins, and most books didn't carry such heavy baggage. Bestsellers, for example, tend to zip in and out of secondhand stores with casual emotional attachments and mercurial price changes. They are the one-night stands of the book-selling world.

Say Stephen King's newest book hits the market at top retail value; six weeks later (give or take) it reaches preloved stores like ours, where customers have left their names on a waiting list. Once the list is satisfied, King's latest goes on our current bestsellers shelf marked at half the cover price, later migrating to the horror shelf at one third the price. A few more sell, but by then the bestseller has been out awhile. The day comes when a second copy arrives, then a third, yet no one wants to buy them. The golden window closes.

Used book stores require vigilance in keeping up to date on popular books, but they also need consistently excellent public relations. This presents ye olde bookstore owners with a problem. From the customer's point of view, she paid close to thirty dollars new but got offered seven dollars credit for the King novel at the height of its secondhand desirability, when we'd sell it for fifteen dollars. It gets worse. Eventually the trade value falls to two dollars, then "Sorry, can't use it," because multiple copies line the shelves. Will that request-denied customer return? How could we avoid emptying the shop of more sellable titles while not refusing a customer's trade-ins, if the trade-ins were has-beens?

On this question, the Internet failed me. I scoured secondhand sales sites to no avail. I asked friends who ran bookshops, and they rolled their eyes. "Hardback fiction? That way lies madness." But they could afford not to stock it; their bookstores sat in metro areas where every customer didn't have to be treated as a limited, precious commodity. We courted ours within a small pond, one flyer, one conversation, at a time. Refusing books on a regular basis wasn't an option.

As Winnie-the-Pooh used to say, "It's hard for a bear of very little brain," but after a bit of trial and error I created Quick Trades (QT). Bestsellers in multiple copies went to the Quick Trades, a practically unusable closet space in the back of the house, next to the garage, with deep shelves. It had probably been intended for storing camping equipment and car parts; it was a lousy place for books, but since these were going to be free, we figured people wouldn't mind so much.

QTs swap one for one; it started as two in for one out, but we had so many in just a few months, it became better to simply recycle them. You can only get a Quick Trade for a Quick Trade. We now have so many that customers who spend more than five dollars get a free book from Quick Trades as well, which makes people practically giddy with glee. There's just something about freebies that appeals to humans.

Meanwhile, people who only read the big names just swap has-been for has-been, and since what is available in Quick Trades depends on the luck of that day, customers often buy from our shelves as well. If someone becomes unhappy for some reason, we use QT to cheer them up: "And we'd like you to have a free book to show our gratitude for bringing that problem to our attention." During Big Stone's annual Customer Appreciation Weekend, everyone who entered Tales got a free book, whether they bought anything or not. That generated an interested load of future customers.

The QT shelf continues to be a self-perpetuating wonder. No matter how many books we offload, we still have a shelf full of Quick Trades. Once again, goodwill proved to be low maintenance.

But, like everything else, a balance needed to be struck. Soon after opening we discovered our town had a small gang of disenfranchised Vietnam vets, guys who never came home in their minds. These men mostly lived in an apartment row within walking distance. They popped in fairly regularly, but never took free books from the porch. Such an act appeared to be beneath their dignity. So we started selling them QT books for a quarter here, fifty cents there—a deal we did not offer other customers. Cut 'em some slack; these men fought the war that keeps on giving. They would plunk down a dollar, have the fun of a good browse, and then head home with comic books, torn-cover classics, and duplicate hardbacks of the latest Michael Connelly or John Connolly. We felt good about that.

One day I took some Bibles from the free bin (they went straight there unless scholarly references) and put them in a box marked BARGAIN BIN, 25 CENTS EACH. I set this next to the Quick Trades so the vets would be sure to see it. That afternoon one of our regular customers, a special needs lad, came by. He observed the bargain bin and fixed me with a reproachful eye.

"T'ain't right to charge for a Bible," he said, scooping up the lot. Cradling them in his arms, he carried his cargo back outside to the free area, spine straight with righteous indignation. Thus ended my career as an interfering do-gooder.

Well, not quite. I began volunteering one day a month at our local library after we "murdered" Chris, the head librarian, at one of our special events. Budget slashed, staff hiring frozen, Chris needed funding. She knew that I understood how to value books, because I'd told her that some of the items on her library's "For Sale" trolley were worth much more than the one dollar per

168

hardback, fifty cents per paperback she charged. Once I even went to Chris with a book in my hand and said, "If I buy this and take it home, it will sell for ten dollars by nightfall." But she didn't have a mechanism in place to value and sell these titles, and she was concerned that the time needed to set it up wouldn't pay enough dividends on the investment.

When her budget eventually fell low enough to require layoffs, Chris took me up on the offer of help and we established an online selling account for the library. We began checking her surplus inventory and between us got about one hundred books online within a day. The first week, our new project made enough money to catch the attention of her library board, which expressed unbounded enthusiasm. What's more, this small branch in a rural system became immediate training leaders because the rest of the district wanted to know how she'd done it. In appreciation, Chris offered to plan our next murder mystery: a helpful library volunteer would get bludgeoned to death with a bookend. I don't know where she gets her creativity.

Our most important rule about pricing books turned out to be "Don't guess; check." One of my favorite quotes is by John Kenneth Galbraith: "If all else fails, immortality can be assured by spectacular error." Nowhere is this truer than in a used book store's pricing madness.

A while back, the college where I now teach held a book sale. Afterward they offered us the remains for a very low sum, and we hauled three pickup truckloads of books into our front rooms. In the rush to clear the shop floor of musty academic tomes in boxes, we priced one non-descript textbook with the nonenticing title of *The Gendered Society* at four dollars and stuck it on the shelf.

A few months later, this book got moved during a cleanup and Jack valued it on Half.com, a useful Web site for checking what others are asking for a title. We usually valued volumes as they came in, but when we got swamped right after that college sale, pricing moved from "I checked" to "I guessed."

In this case, I guessed wrong; the tome was selling for sixty-five dollars. We sold ours online within the week, but it had been in our shop for three months, a bargain for anyone who knew better.

All booksellers have spectacular mistake stories. I'm not even going to tell you about the day I consigned an autographed copy of Jesse Stuart's *The Thread That Runs So True* to the free bin. Every used bookseller can repeat this cautionary tale using a different title. The most expensive one we know about personally belongs to our friends Cuz and Jan, who sold an autographed copy of Douglas Adams's *The Hitchhiker's Guide to the*

Galaxy for six dollars—then spotted it on eBay a few days later, bidding up to six hundred dollars. Anywhere used book aficionados gather, stories about "the one that got away" get wilder and more expensive as post-trade-show drinks flow.

Usually the rise and fall of a book's price is prosaic and allied more with time than emotion. Still, we never forget that books are more than the words on the page. They mark the important moments in our life journeys. One of the boxes from that college book sale held several great titles on British history, all with the same woman's name inked inside their front covers. Her name also appeared on a few cards and letters stashed between their pages. A notecard in a nonfiction work on the correspondence of sixteenth-century British monarchs held the following: "Hey girl, you're gonna beat this! You're strong, smart, and taking good care of yourself. Let's go to Hawaii next year. Do you think someday scholars will write books about our e-mails?"

In a Philippa Gregory novel and dated some six months later, a handwritten letter read, "So sorry to hear about your troubles, and we hope your health continues to hold. God bless you in the coming year and call us if you need anything."

The last note appeared on heavy personalized stationery from a senior college official, tucked inside an Elizabethan romance. "Dear X, as you and I both know, waiting in that chemo room is a royal pain. Here's something I used to pass the time and change the venue a little bit. Regards, Y." The book sale had raised funds for a scholarship in Professor X's memory after she succumbed to cancer.

Yes, they are commodities, but we still handle other people's books with care. There's a whole lot of life in them—and not just in the words.

CHAPTER 12
I Dream About Running a Bookstore Someday . . .

In the room the women come and go
Talking of Michelangelo.

—T. S. Eliot,
"The Love Song of J. Alfred Prufrock"

A LTHOUGH WE TAKE SATISFACTION IN being a safe place for people to tell their stories, please don't get the impression that running a bookshop is all bittersweetness and light. Much of it is dusting and heavy lifting.

About two years passed with us flying by the seat of our pants before we finally felt like we had a clue as to what we should be doing. Finally, we more or less understood what the regular tasks of advertising, shelving, valuing, and cleaning entailed—and how bad we were at that last one. Left to his own devices, Jack would use the same drinking glass until it dissolved. He considers taking a bath in the tub tantamount to cleaning it. I'm cleaner but not tidier; clutter follows me like an errant puppy. My shoes and socks tend to rest in little piles wherever my feet grow tired of them. Customers trip over these markers all the time, regulars sidestepping them with a wry smile and the comment "Wendy's in today, I see." Jack swears he could track the day's weather and my path through the shop by which items of clothing have been left where.

Bad housekeeping skills provide scope for creativity, however. Wearing fuzzy socks, I can just skim my toes along the edges of the bottom shelves to pick up the accumulated dog and cat hair. We concocted a get-rich scheme to sell pillows stuffed with the furry staff's offcuts, but it came to naught.

The day came when we found to our delight that we could afford to hire a cleaning lady. Becky cleaned for two glorious lemon-scented years before health concerns necessitated her turning us over to our current Wonder Woman, Heather. Hiring a cleaner cost almost as much as the shop averages in a day, but Jack and I are both domestically impaired to the point of being a danger to self and society. Besides, Becky and Heather were and are not so much cleaners as bookstore staff good at cleaning; they offered great ideas and advice, treated the place like their own homes, looked after our animals and the shop if we had to run out to do an errand, and generally deserved triple what we could afford to pay them.

Turning the sanitation department over to professionals left Jack and me free to handle the increasing flow of acquisitions. From our first year of terror that we'd never drum up enough stock to fill the shelves, we had flourished to—as Jack puts it—"the point of regret." We should have been more careful of what we wished for, we realized as each day we sifted through boxes of books, bags of books, miles and stacks and piles of books! And every last one of those little darlings had to be priced and shelved. Just keeping the shop floor clear of trade-ins became a stress factor, because if the boxes and bags got ahead of us, the place resembled less a used book store than a junkyard.

Jack once commented, "It is the sole thing about running this shop that I have come to dislike, pricing the same old genres of romances and thrillers every day." While sorting boxes can be poignant, or even fun if they have surprises in them—say, a beautiful hardback of Asian love poetry, a collection of essays on the Harlem Renaissance, even the occasional cult classic novel—battered lots of old thrillers are by far the most common trade-in.

The trade books arrive in unpredictable clumps, some days none, other days literally hundreds. Sometimes Jack and I wake to a front porch brimming with books left as donations, no name or number on a slip of paper anywhere, just boxes and bags stacked along the railing. We joke, when yet another set of 1970s World Book Encyclopedias blocks our front door, that a desperate mother could no longer feed them. "Please look after these books; thank you." (If you didn't read *Paddington Bear* growing up, that's not going to mean anything to you, but it's not too late; the beloved little guy's antics are still in print.)

A sign to the left of our porch door indicates anything on that side is free for the taking. That's where we put those in bad shape, dated in their appeal, or otherwise past prime. One rain-spattered dull morning, Jack opened the door, used his toes to nudge around inside a plastic sack someone had slung there in the night, discerned it full of Danielle Steel and Mary Higgins Clark hardbacks, and pushed the whole bag across to the free side with his foot before shutting the door again.

In bookselling, as in life, some days are better than others.

The Luv Shack, as we call the outbuilding that houses romances, provided some fun days, although it came to us under difficult circumstances. About three years after we opened, a friend who shall remain nameless got the left foot of fellowship from her church. (Sometimes personality just overrides community in a tiny congregation.) Complicating the situation was that our friend ran a part-time business in the church hall, complete with a large and sturdy storage shack—wooden beams six inches thick—at the back of the property.

"Move it or lose it," ordered a letter, which hinted that the church might retain the building should it still be there after a certain period of time. Dander was up, anger flying, and righteous indignation flamed as only small-town churches can provoke. Our friend offered us the shed if we would haul it off.

Free shed, assembly required, sounded good to me, but Jack had to do the work of disassembling and rebuilding it. Plus, we weren't sure how the church members—many of whom we knew as shop regulars—felt about the whole thing. Jack looked at me. I looked at the overflowing romance shelves, paperbacks dribbling in piles across the shop floor. Jack sighed, and prepared his toolkit.

A pickup truck, two guy pals, three days, and four large pizzas later, we christened The Luv Shack. Three thousand romance novels graced its interior the next day. We put up a sign, LUV SHACK: ROMANCE(S) LIES WITHIN, 3 FOR $1, and toasted this shrine to the failings and foibles of earthly love. As soon as I find a good one, I'm going to put a lifesize cardboard cutout of Elvis Presley in there and hang paper doves from the ceiling.

Bad beginnings can turn redeemable. The Luv Shack soon reinforced our faith in the innate well-meaning-ness of humanity. The shed doesn't lock. Sometimes we came home from a Monday ramble (the shop's closed day) to find a dollar bill clipped to our mailbox. Checking the phone messages after an evening out, I heard a female voice say, "Look under the little mouse statue on your front porch. Y'all weren't open, but I shopped in your shed." Three dollars nestled 'neath the mouse's bum. That sort of thing happens all the time. We told the friend who donated the Luv Shack, and she laughed, then struck a pose, one finger in the air. "The Lord worketh in mysterious ways, belief in humanity to re-establish-eth," she intoned.

We're just glad she's feeling better about the whole thing. Like most small-town dustups, the squabble blew over, and the Luv Shack still graces our front yard, enticing romantics from every walk of life, testimony to the power of redemption.

Most people are polite, honest, and kind. Raised right, they're just happy to have a place to trade in books they've read for ones they haven't. Unfortunately, even the simplest precepts of human decency can get a little muddled after a garage sale. Not often, just once or twice per summer, a savvy sale-holder brings in his or her unsold stuff—still bearing homemade price tags in the fifty-cent range—and turns into a guerrilla bargainer before our eyes, demanding three dollars in trade credit per dog-eared paperback.

Every secondhand shop encounters its odd handful of price warriors, but the poster child for the book clan has to be the Nancy Drew Lady. On a summer afternoon, a woman in her mid-fifties, sporting bottle-red hair in a short curly perm, pink framed glasses, and a pleasant smile, brought in her yard sale leftovers. One glance, and my heart sank. By this time I knew enough about the book business to understand where we were headed.

She had a whole box of Nancy Drews with paper dust jackets, and unfortunately for her, she had put masking tape stickers on them specifying a quarter each. Usually we get the yellow spines of the seventies book clubs, or even the sturdy pink ex-library copies that generations of girls recognize and love from school. Those jacketed volumes with the masking tape that couldn't be removed safely were early—if not first—editions, but the tape would tear that lovely soft old paper the instant we tried to remove it.

The woman also had the Dana Girls in lavender dust jackets, which suggested they could be first editions as well. Both Dana and Drew were Stratemeyer Syndicate productions. The Syndicate created the pseudonym Carolyn Keene in 1930 and used ghostwriters until the Nancy Drew Mystery Stories series closed in 2004. Dana Girls started in 1934, penned by Leslie McFarlane, a man who wrote the first four Danas before stating—as the publishing world's legend has it—

that he preferred starvation to writing another. He then moved on to authoring several Hardy Boys and a film-writing career in Canada.

The Nancy Drew Lady didn't know what she had, evidenced by the price stickers adorning those pretty—and valuable—covers. Alas, almost nothing in the book world is valuable with masking tape on it.

I tried to break it to her gently. "Sell many of these today?"

"About a dozen," she responded, plunking the box on the table. "Little girls filling out their collections, mostly."

"Mmm." That seemed sweet and innocent as an observation on her part. She was a nice lady. I had a good idea of what was about to happen—for some reason, the nicer they are, the harder they fall—so I double-checked the price online before taking the plunge. "Well, these Nancy Drews could be worth a bit."

Her eyes came alight. *Uh-oh.* "Really? How much?"

"Not that this is what they would sell for around here, but one Web site has them at twenty-two dollars per title. But the masking tape—"

I stopped under the force of her stare. Her mouth flew open as her gaze shifted to the box. I'd seen this Jekyll-Hyde flip many times. My lips formed the words alongside her as she said them aloud. "I sold them for twenty-five cents each."

Jack emerged from the mystery room at that moment, and frowned at me. My husband, a gentle soul from the Old World, considers mimicking customers bad form. He is much, much nicer than I am.

"Well"—I lined the oft-delivered words up on the runway—"you couldn't guarantee that they'd sell at that price anyway. In fact"—I segued smoothly into the second half of the bad news—"antique books don't do well in this area. We'd sell these at three dollars each, the going price for Nancy Drews around here. Our clientele would be a lot like yours: little girls and their grand-mothers, filling out their collections." I wouldn't bother explaining again about the masking tape undermining antique status.

The lady swiveled to face me. "You mean you wouldn't give me full value?"

Sure, twenty-five cents. Aloud I said, "If you mean eleven dollars trade credit, no. That's what an urban collector would have paid." *Before the masking tape.*

Her look sharpened. "I meant twenty-two dollars."

My husband, making tea in the kitchen, chuckled. So much for heart-of-gold Old World gentility.

"We don't deal in antique books. You might try taking them to an antique shop or book dealer." I continued smiling, polite and subservient. The antiques guy could talk to her about masking tape.

"How much commission would they charge me?" Her voice cracked like a whip.

"I'm not really up on antique selling. I'd recommend you call someone in the business and ask." *How should I know, lady? Besides, they've got masking tape on them!!!* My patience ebbed. I made a conscious effort to deepen my smile, but it probably looked like growling.

She didn't notice. "Hmm. This doesn't seem fair. If they're worth twenty-two dollars each, and I leave them with you, I'd only get eleven dollars in trade credit." *No you wouldn't,* I opened my mouth to say, exasperated beyond diplomacy, but she was in full-throttle steam-propulsion mode. "That's not realistic. What about a ten percent commission?"

"Ma'am, there is no market for antique books in this area. We don't sell them." *What part of no didn't you understand?*

Her face clouded darker than a thunderstorm. "Why not?"

Oy vey. But I gave her the reasons—well, most of them. "We have a limited amount of space. People interested in old books are usually from out of town, not our regular clientele, and we can't predict their interest with any regularity. We can't afford to take chances on selling antiques in a store that doesn't have long-term climate control for them. They're a specialty market, like on eBay." *MASKING TAPE!!!*

Oops. I spilled the e-word. As her face brightened, I knew what she would ask. Sure enough, behind a bookshelf where she couldn't see him, my husband lip-synched along with her. "Could you sell them for me on eBay?" He cracked up silently at the perfection of his foreknowledge as she continued, "You can keep"—her eyelids and fingers fluttered as she did rapid math—"three dollars per book." She gave me a triumphant yet calculating look. "That's what you would have charged anyway."

Oh, she *was* listening. My husband sipped a mug of tea and raised his eyebrows at me. I stared hard at the mug and sent brain waves for him to pour me one and add a little brandy.

"Unfortunately, eBay doesn't always yield prices sellers might expect. We've done that in the past and not gotten what people anticipated. Just because AbeBooks—that's a Web site for antique books *[don't go there, my mind shouted]*—says twenty-two dollars doesn't mean they'd sell for that, and whether they sell or not, there's still a cost to list them, so we've stopped doing commissions. But of course you can list them yourself." I tried to keep a rising note of hope from my voice. Maybe she'd leave now.

She turned a face deep in calculation toward me. "I can't do eBay; my husband won't let me."

No fool, he.

"Tell me how I could best realize the full value

of these books," she commanded, placing a proprietary hand on her box of masking-taped golden opportunity. A small cloud of dust rose. She snatched the hand away.

From the kitchen, my spouse muttered, "Open your own bookshop." I sneezed as the dust reached my nose, so she didn't hear him. Nobody in town would have believed it anyway. My husband is a saint. I'm the one who loses my cool. Weakly, I repeated that she should visit an antique dealer. Exit the lady, Nancy Drews under one arm. She left a crate of Harlequins for trade credit.

So it isn't all sweetness and sympathy. You really have to like people to run a used book shop, or you'll wind up smacking somebody.

CHAPTER 13

Running an Unlicensed Intellectual Pub

Ignorance and bungling with love are better than wisdom and skill without.
—Henry David Thoreau, *A Week on the Concord and Merrimack River*

GUERRILLA BARGAINERS WERE SIMPLY annoying, while we'd come to a compassionate understanding of bereavement and book clearance. But we hadn't yet seen how bookstores connected to house fires and prisons, or understood how often people would want to tell us about family feuds and other personal matters. Had we known about these elements before setting up shop, I might have dashed out to beg my way into a psychology course first. For most things in life, there's common sense; for everything else, there's a graduate program. . . .

One of our favorite bookshops back in Scotland sat above an Indian restaurant. In addition to the lovely Madras and Vindaloo smells wafting up,

Betsy, the proprietor, could have been ordered from a catalog of stock-and-trade colorful local characters. A small round woman with white hair and a posh Edinburgh accent, Betsy often told us, years before we opened our own shop, that browsing was a special pleasure customers looked forward to in a bookstore. She said that "a used book store operator is many things: counselor, literary critic, research guru, manager, shelf stocker, cleaner, coffeemaker, child protective services agent, custodian, and, oh yes, salesperson. So wait until the customer tells you what's needed; maybe all they want is a browse. If they want something else, they'll make it clear to you."

We found Betsy's advice invaluable in later years. One day a new customer entered the store, looked around a few minutes, then walked up to Jack and launched the following conversation:

PERSON: Wow, cool, a bookstore! How long y'all been here?

JACK: About two years—

PERSON: Wow, what kind of accent is that?

JACK: Scottish. I'm from—

PERSON: Wow, cool! My family's from Ireland. I'm gonna visit there someday. Tell me about Ireland.

JACK: Well, I'm not—

PERSON: I hear it's beautiful.

JACK [giving up]: Yes, lovely. Green hills, rolling landscapes, the coastline is—

PERSON: Wow, cool! Got any books on turtles?

JACK [to Wendy]: Do we have books on turtles?

WENDY: We have books on everything! [a blatant lie; at the time we had about sixteen thousand books] Do you mean fiction, facts on them in the wild, or the Christian children's book Janette Oke wrote about turtles?

PERSON [eyes glazing]: Uh, my daughter got a turtle for her birthday. It lives in a tank in her bedroom.

WENDY [pointing to nonfiction]: We have a couple of books on aquatic animal care. Let me show you.

PERSON: Wow, great. We got her the turtle after her mom took off. We thought it would help her cope, you know, give her something to look after.

This kind of information leakage happens all the time. Sometimes it's funny; sometimes it's not. Customers tell us about fights with cancer, nasty exes, beautiful grandchildren, despicable bosses, coping with life's big moments, stupid relatives, stupid relatives, stupid relatives, and how they intend to marry or kill so and so. People need to talk. We're the bartenders to whom everyone tells their troubles in this intellectual pub. Let them talk. Perhaps it makes the world a better place. At worst, it gets things out of their systems.

As it stands, when people reveal any form of neediness in the shop, they're stuck with our more or less benevolent ineptitude. Jack and I have different gifts regarding customers. I've got a great memory for faces, so I greet people by name. Jack is crap at remembering names, let alone faces, so he just smiles at everyone and asks, "Been in before?" in that gorgeous Scots burr. Guess which one they like better? Sigh. We ask customers if they want coffee or tea, point out the shortbread, and leave them alone until they start asking questions.

About four months after we opened, a woman we'd never seen before came in searching for a handful of fairly eclectic titles: *Communion* by Whitley Strieber, an out-of-print book called *Small Holdings*, an Ann Rule true crime paperback, and several classics. I stacked these on the table and left her to peruse. By turns quiet and garrulous, she talked over me as I started to answer her questions, ignoring my answers. Truth be told, she seemed . . . odd.

The woman sat down to assess her gathered armful, ignoring our offers of tea and queries as to whether she had enough light.

"Do you have *The Tao of Pooh*?" she snapped.

Miffed at her tone, I fetched it. As I handed it over, tears pooled in her eyes.

Jack looked at me. "I'll put the kettle on."

"Um, everything okay?" I asked, offering a tissue.

She scrubbed her eyes. "I lost these books. I'm replacing them."

"Sure, lost," I said, clueless.

She looked up at me; it was almost a glare. "Do I want to tell you this?" she asked, as if no one else were in the room. "Okay, but you asked for it. My house burned down. I lost everything. My dogs, three of them, burned. Everything burned. I'm replacing the books I lost." She looked back down at her stack.

Eeep. I sat down at the table and toyed with the sugar-bowl lid. "Well," I said, "that sucks."

The woman gave a half smile. "Yeah. It does."

When she'd made her final selections, we gave her *The Tao of Pooh* free of charge. "Everyone needs a little help rebuilding."

"I didn't tell you the story so you'd give me a discount," she barked. Jack rolled his eyes and disappeared into his man-cave. Beulah's not the only one with boltholes.

"No, we know that," I said, dropping the books into a bag. "Everybody deserves a break now and then. Look after yourself."

She didn't leave. Instead I made some more tea and we sat in the shop for two hours while she told the story—a horrific story, so you don't need to know it. Suffice it to say, she lanced the wound that day, letting out pent-up poison.

And that was that, we thought. We'd given a woman coping with serious trauma a book. But she became the first of many. Due to the rural nature of the mountain bowl surrounding us, fires are a regular hazard. Even though we have a county—nay, region—full of the best volunteer firefighters in the world, if something up on the mountain starts burning, it's going to finish before anybody can get up one of those narrow switch-backed roads to save it. At least once a quarter, someone comes into our shop seeking replacements for titles lost in a fire.

Did you know that one of the first things a fire victim replaces is their favorite book from childhood? We didn't until a man asked for Syd Hoff's *Danny and the Dinosaur*, and Jack said something about children loving that classic.

"For me," the man said, without a trace of emotion. "Lost it when my house burned. Had it since I was a boy. Want another one."

A man told us about his teacher reading the class *Beautiful Joe*. A woman described climbing her grandparents' apple tree to devour *Heidi*; another had grown up pretending to be Sara Crewe in *A Little Princess*, waiting for her father to find her. Then they described the fires in which they lost each book—and a whole lot more.

We give fire victims one of their chosen books for free. There isn't much else anyone can do. And I've found the outer edges of my inner strength. Ye gods and little fishhooks, fire stories have horrors that humans shouldn't hear, let alone live. But they keep coming, so we keep putting the kettle on. Another lesson for bookshop owners: "Learn how to listen yet let it pass through you." Thanks to some therapist friends, I have finally acquired that tough skill. But it wasn't part of our anticipated job description.

The fire victims' sad recountings were hard to listen to, although loss and pain should be respected. But with the professional shoppers, we reached the limits of our patience. Professional shoppers are akin to guerrilla bargainers, but rather than the people who hold the garage sales (like the Nancy Drew Lady) they are the hagglers and bargain hunters who frequent them—like Fiona and me.

As word got out about our trade-in policy, professional shoppers who frequented yard sales started bringing in books, intending to sell them for a profit. Since I had bought quite a lot of our opening inventory at such events, I knew by now what worked and what didn't. Plus I could recognize the signs of items bought on the cheap, including masking-tape damage. Usually people understood if we said a book didn't suit our shop, and we rarely refused books unless they were just too old or too damaged. But as the years passed and we gathered quite the collection of Cornwalls, Grishams, and Silhouette or Harlequin romances, we stopped taking some of the most common titles and authors. That's when we found out the word "no" didn't appear in everyone's vocabulary.

A young man we'll call "Jim" fell in love with an out-of-print book culled from our personal collection, brought over from Britain. He asked us to set it aside for him. Back in the early days of the shop we had no restrictions on our trade policy; you brought us books, a dollar amount got written into the ledger under your name, and you could spend it cross-genre on whatever you wanted. This was a mistake we corrected after Jim.

Jim began bringing us romances bought for ten cents at sales, price stickers still on them. At that time we stuck to our policy and accepted them in trade at twenty-five cents credit value, then later wound up selling them for three for a dollar. Not good math. (Have I mentioned before that we didn't know what we were doing when we started?)

The book Jim wanted cost fifty dollars. You guessed it; he brought us two hundred romances over two weeks. We gave him the out-of-print, British-publisher-only antique volume and he walked out happy while we crammed two hundred Harlequins from the 1980s and 1990s onto a shelf.

Not only had we given away a valuable book,

we'd created a monster. He kept bringing books scavenged in yard sales, picked up in thrift stores, even—as he bragged to someone else who told us later—found in the trash. Some of those little paperbacks were in dire condition, and we began to refuse a few of the worst. The pile of paperbacks we told him he couldn't receive credit for grew with each successive visit. Finally we gave up on the "this is the last time" speech and just point-blank explained that we could not accept the stuff he'd brought.

To our surprise Jim politely but firmly told us these latest trades were just like what he'd been bringing for weeks, that he expected the same treatment he'd been receiving to date, and that we'd better not mess with him because he knew people.

Book mobsters? In the Gap? Who knew?

To be fair to Jim, there was a lot going on in his life. To be fair to ourselves, we didn't want to be part of it. He continued his slow smolder and we continued stonewalling until he finally stopped bringing in trades. I can't say that we were sorry.

It's not that professional garage salers are a bad lot on the whole—we like Fiona just fine and she never annoyed anyone, weaving her magic on various lawns. But some people will consider a used book store tantamount to their personal cash cow. A small handful of customers have proven resolute about not spending money with us, and likely wouldn't see this as detrimental to the fact that they enjoy having the store in town in the first place. It's like people who cruise new book stores for titles, then go home and buy them off Amazon. They want the cheapest price they can get, and don't see the effects their buying habits have on local stores—or why that should matter to them.

The No Cash Crew, as Jack calls them, haul in copious amounts of books for trade credit, but when the credit runs out won't pay cash for anything. We keep an eye on what they bring, and once explained to a customer that we knew her books had come from the library's castoffs trolley for fifty cents, so couldn't credit them at half the retail price of twelve dollars as she was asking, although we still liked her and found her a worthwhile person. Losing a few pro bargainers over the years has not hurt us. We try to be nice, but some people define nice only as your doing what they want.

Again, exceptions abound. Barbara, one of our earliest customers, was a professional garage saler, but asked us straight-out what we wanted, then brought us Westerns, older science fiction, and certain children's authors based on a list of "can't keep 'em in stock" titles we gave her. Barbara proved a pleasure to work with. We called her "our outsource buyer." And about four years into the relationship, she gave us a sweet smile and announced her plan to open a used book store forty miles away. We wished her well and offered her some overstock. When we're down that way, we pop in on our "godchild," and Barbara still comes to see us when she's in the area.

Barbara works a day job as a prison guard, and remains one of the few people we met who already knew the role that bookshops play in the lives of families with incarcerated members. The first time a woman appeared in Tales of the Lonesome Pine clutching titles she'd purchased elsewhere, asking if we would mail them to her inmate son, we were so perplexed that she had to explain what she wanted twice, slowly. Until that moment, we had no idea that prisons don't allow inmates paperbacks unless they're mailed from a bookstore. (And they can't have hardbacks.)

We do now. Once a package came from a prison with a form letter stating the books we had sent couldn't be given to the requested inmate, having been deemed inappropriate by the warden. Inside lay two titles we'd never seen before, both new, both on U.S. army intelligence interrogation techniques. To this day, we have no idea who mailed them.

A jolly man of about six foot five comes in quarterly, bearing sudoku puzzle books. He gives us postage money plus "a little extra," as he puts it, to mail them to his incarcerated brother. After a few visits we told him we didn't need the tip if he would just cover the postage.

He smiled. "That's nice of you, but I don't want you to get sick of me askin'."

Jack waved his hand in a "pshaw, neighbor" kind of way. "It's okay, really. How long does your brother have left on his sentence?"

"Forty years." The man grinned and put a fiver on the counter. "See y'all next time."

Perhaps most proprietors opened with a more fulsome awareness of what hidden tasks lurk behind a bookshop's doors. Jack and I didn't have a clue—just desire, which with the naive sincerity of high school sweethearts we figured would cover everything. Doesn't love conquer all?

I'll be honest with you; it helps, but working sunup to sundown factors in as well. That "follow your bliss" saying actually has an undercurrent; if you follow your bliss, you'll work hard to get it right. When the occasional customer tells us his or her dream of running a bookstore someday, we recognize our own naïveté in that enthusiasm. They may have some inkling about long hours and low pay, but rarely do they know about the fires, the guerrilla bargainers, the bereavements, or the prisons. Neither did we—then. But we sure do now. In all honesty, the scariest, hardest, saddest, most important stories found in a bookshop aren't in the books; they're in the customers.

CHAPTER 14
Yarn Goddesses

Methinks it is a token of healthy and gentle characteristics, when women of high thoughts and accomplishments love to sew; especially as they are never more at home with their own hearts than while so occupied.

—Nathaniel Hawthorne,
The Marble Faun

BARBARA AND FIONA WEREN'T THE only regulars who helped shape the bookstore's stock and personality. A few months after we opened, Isabel (she of the curling toes) ended her long reign as director of a preschool and donated all her children's books and shelving to us. We still sometimes call the children's area "Isabel's Den."

Although Isabel is a charming and fun person in and of herself, many people keep on her good side because of her years directing the preschool. Sometimes at a Tuesday night needlework session, as seven or eight women sit about the table knitting or crocheting, the *Post* will be lying open to a photo of—for instance—a former Big Stone Gapper, now a famous cardiovascular surgeon living in New York City, winning some national research award at the American Medical Association's annual meeting. Isabel will glance at the photo and say, "Oh, I remember little Jimmy! He used to pick his nose and eat it. A doctor now? My goodness."

Singer Nanci Griffith is right: everybody does die famous in a small town.

Isabel had the idea for a Needlework Night at our bookstore. "It will offer women with like interests the chance to get together and talk, relax, enjoy each other's company," she suggested. We were all for it, and Needlework Nights started monthly, but proved so popular they went weekly in their second year, Isabel at the helm sending newsletters chock-full of patterns, yarn management tips, and related activities. (She also ensures a steady supply of dark chocolate at the gatherings.)

Needlework Nights are akin to having car tires aligned, sans testosterone; they keep us running right as we check attitudes and adjust balances amid the quasi-spiritual atmosphere of feminine companionship. Regulars ebb and flow, but in addition to our fearless leader, Isabel, the group includes: Fiona, who has mastered every step in

198

crafting a sweater from birthing the lamb to casting off the cuffs (and she once copped to knowing how to artificially inseminate ewes); Elizabeth, forbidden to tell any more stories about women in the ER with needles through their sternums because they knitted in a moving car; and Becky, our first barrel-full-of-laughs professional cleaning lady and world's sweetest soul. After we hired her and raved about her phenomenal cleaning, several other Needle-workers and townswomen vied for her services— and she became so overworked, she recruited Heather to clean for us.

Along with these stalwarts of the bookstore's inception, Needlework Night attracted Lynne, a lifelong Big Stone Gap resident who now winters in Florida and summers at the old homestead. Lynne, in her eighties and a cancer survivor, showed up at one of our Dulcimer Sundays (a jam session for mountain dulcimer players) and inspired us all; she became such a regular at the shop that she sometimes staffs it when Jack and I go on short holidays.

Needlework Night enjoys a cast of sporadic attenders, too—women like Sarah, the doctoral student in medical anthropology who spent a year in town doing fieldwork and pleased us all immensely by giving birth to a girl so we could make tiny pink hats and booties with pom-poms; Marnie, self-appointed rescuer of every stray dog for forty miles; Mary Ann, jewelry maker extraordinaire; Erin, able to recite the plot of every play published since 1630; Kathy, the loud and amiable town socialite married to Garth; Joan, just at the cusp of launching two teenage children into the wide world; Witold's wife Ashia; and scattered others.

Part of the fun is never knowing what dynamic will be operating on any given night. For instance, if Joan and Ashia attend, we all try to behave ourselves because they are such dignified ladies, but the problem is that Isabel and I together really don't retain dignity; it slides right through our "not in public" filters and runs out our sensible low-heeled pumps. Once we get started, well, it is an all-female group, so an hour rarely passes without someone uttering the word "penis." Or calling down curses not normally heard from the mouths of steel magnolias of the mountain variety—at least, not in public.

And while we never outright told men they couldn't be part of Needlework Nights, when a husband pulled his chair up to the table one evening, the girls, without a word or look passing between us, began telling childbearing stories. As Elizabeth launched into a detailed and vivid description of her daughter's breech birth, Garth grew so pale that Jack appeared with a bottle of Scotch and hauled him upstairs. At the end of the night Kathy yelled, "Okay, y'all can come down now." The boys returned with a rosy glow over their earlier pallor. Garth often came back to "keep Jack company" after that, but he never bellied up to the yarn bar again.

Some of the yarn goddesses ply their trades in our shop: Fiona's pottery, Isabel's quirky dishcloths (her specialty remains one with the state of Virginia outlined in raised stitches, but she also knits a mean pine tree), and my crocheted novelties grace the shelf set aside for local handicrafts. Our shop's welcome mat and kitchen privacy curtain are crocheted from "plarn," aka plastic bags cut into strips; people think these two items are cute, so we never say we were trying, in our early years, to save the thirty dollars a curtain and mat would have cost us. Once, when Fiona exchanged a lovely oval mat she'd woven for another friend's quilted placements, Isabel joked that they had traded their ply.

I joined Round the Mountain, an artisan co-op, as a chair caner. It's a hobby that takes me into the Zen of physical crafting; when I'm done being nowhere thinking about nothing, the chair has a nice patterned seat. Photographers, potters, painters, and fiber wizards brought their wares to sell at the store. We organized a percentage split, and regional crafts became part of our tourism draw. Our selection criteria remains pretty basic: is it handmade and do we like it? Later we added: have we sold enough within a year to justify the space? Keeping it simple works well for everyone involved.

The Yarn Goddesses have had many adventures. We used to belly dance together—but only after swearing undying secrecy about what happened in the class, so I can't tell you any of those funny stories. When the belly-dancing instructor also became pregnant and gave birth to a girl, we were so happy to have another reason for making cute little pink layette sets that we forgave her for not starting up the class again.

Instead, we took up water aerobics en masse and that produced a fair few funny stories as well, also verboten. (Once your friends know you're writing a book, they can get quite persnickety about spending time with you.) But the Night Mr. Dickens Got Out trumped every other silly thing we've done as a group.

Isabel has a rescued border collie. She picked up the dog while on a trip with me to Pittsburgh, helping our friend Jerry price and clear the library of his late wife after Stefni lost a dignified battle to cancer. The dog needed a home and Isabel, as she explained to her husband William on our return, needed a dog. He came with the name Charley, but was so full of himself—plus had a foster brother named Marley, already in residence—that his nickname became Mr. Dickens.

One night as the Yarn Goddesses settled in, a frantic phone call came from William. Charley had gotten out of the yard and run—barking joyously rather than gently—into that good night. Evening traffic had started picking up and, to put it plainly, this dog's intelligence was on a par with your average turnip truck.

Dread seized the room. Isabel went out the door, brown hair flying, as the rest of us mobilized: Garth and Jack were shouted down from upstairs to do search-and-rescue duty in Garth's red pickup, and Fiona and Becky stayed to work the phones while Kathy and I set out on foot to cut Charley-the-Idiot off from the main road.

We searched and whistled and called and barked, but saw neither hide nor hair of Mr. Dickens. Twenty weary minutes later, a vehicle pulled up in front of Kathy and me, blinding us with its headlights. From inside the cab a man said, "Hey, you girls are cute. Wanna go for a ride?"

I like to think Kathy recognized her husband's voice, but who knows? We rounded the side of the truck and Charley stuck his needle nose out the window to give Kathy a big wet ear kiss. The boys were heroes.

"How'd you find him so fast?" Kathy asked.

Garth puffed out his chest. "Charley's a guy. We thought like guys. Where does a guy go when he runs off? We found 'im across the creek, serenading a little girl Doberman."

Kathy fixed Charley with a stern gaze. He

blinked and licked himself. Kathy swiveled her steel blue eyes to Garth, who blinked and scratched his armpit.

We dumped Charley back inside the yard, gate firmly latched, and waved good-bye to William, who bubbled with gratitude. Back at the bookstore, Isabel had returned to pace the floor in tears. When we burst in with the good news, a bottle of wine appeared. It wasn't ours; we don't have a liquor license and would never serve alcohol at a bookshop function. We herded everyone upstairs to drink unencumbered in our second-floor home instead.

As we toasted dogs we had known, a sharp "crack" sounded outside. Whatever. We opened a second bottle of wine. A few minutes later, somebody said, "What are those flashing lights?"

Eight college-educated adults pressed their noses against the windowpane, wineglasses in hand, to behold the bookstore cordoned off by police. After one look, Garth—a volunteer fire-fighter and long-standing member of the local council—set his whiskey glass carefully atop a dresser and moved to the other side of the room.

Isabel, from one of the Gap's oldest families, marched down the stairs. A minute later she returned. "If we leave quietly, they won't press charges." She was kidding, but Garth still looked pale.

It turned out that the ancient guide wire on a

nearby streetlight, growing tauter as the pole settled over the years, had reached breaking point and snapped without warning. The fallen pole's top end lay just a couple of feet from the store's front walk. Since the pole had an electrical wire attached, streetlights and traffic signals were out in the neighborhood; the police had arrived to reroute vehicles and to keep people away from the downed wire.

We traipsed downstairs and sat on the porch, toasting the Uniformed Ones with wine and whiskey glasses—except Garth, who "forgot" his upstairs. He chatted with the officers as one by one the girls sobered enough to drive home. Fiona drove over the now-dead wire when she zigzagged off in her SUV, but not because of drink. She drives like that all the time.

CHAPTER 15

What Happens in the Bookstore, Stays in the Bookstore

If A equals success in life, then A equals XYZ. X is work, Y is play, and Z is keeping your mouth shut.
—Albert Einstein, *Observer*,
January 15, 1950

A NICE YOUNG LAD CAME shopping for James Pattersons one spring day. Knowing "Tucker" from church, I'd assessed him as more of a classical guy. He belonged to a local book club whose members wouldn't have been caught reading Patterson in their own bathtubs, let alone publicly. Tucker didn't even know the title he wanted (out of the seventy-two-plus the Patterson industry has published). He just knew it was "the first one."

"*Along Came a Spider*?"

"That sounds right," he responded.

"How did you get interested in this author?" I asked, suspecting his answer as I led him to the mystery-and-thrillers room.

A sheepish expression crossed his face. "I met this girl."

Trying not to laugh, I handed over the paperback. Sure, I could have told him then that the relationship wouldn't work out, but it was none of my business.

Tucker returned for two more Pattersons before the breakup. He later married a nice woman with a taste for Lee Smith. As a wedding present, we gave them a dozen cozies with titles like *Marriage Is Murder* and *To Love and to Perish*. (In case the term is unfamiliar, the best description ever for "cozies" is "murder mysteries where no one cares who got killed because they're all distracted by cooking new recipes or following intricate handicraft instructions.")

Tucker and his new wife "Vicki" shopped with us regularly until they moved away. Once I suggested Vicki try a Patterson.

She scanned a back blurb. "Maybe. I've read a couple, but Tucker never has."

I didn't think fast enough. "No, he bought some when . . ." My voice trailed off.

Tucker's wife looked at me, an expression that could only be described as a smiling frown on her face. Then, with an indecipherable wink, she strode briskly into the front room where Tucker browsed classics. Ignoring the other customers, she waved the Patterson in the air and shrieked, "You liar! You said you never dated that slut!!"

We put a sign over our computer: WHITB, SITB. (What happens in the bookstore stays in the bookstore.) The sign reminds us that shopkeeping in a small town requires a particular kind of etiquette, and a lot of keeping silent. Sure, word of mouth at the speed of cell phone helped us become a profitable business, but all that nice buzz had a sugar-crazed little sister who kicked us pretty hard in the shins: gossip.

It's no secret that the delights of gossip present a double-edged sword; people like to discuss events while they are half formed, each storyteller interpreting in his or her own image what might have happened and why. This makes operating any small-town business—and particularly one in which people talk as openly as a bookstore—a constant study in tact and reserve. Ask any hairdresser. Small-town business operators know too much about people, and if any of it slips out, trouble will plague our houses like a pack of tigers.

Sending news faster than truth or accuracy, gossip is as much a staple of small-town life as the Fourth of July civic fireworks. We'd been on the receiving end of enough negative buzz to resolve that our shop would become what one customer termed "a little Switzerland," a safe place where anyone could say anything without fear of its being repeated. (At least, not until this book came out. . . .) We would become a third place.

Third places are those needed spaces, neither home nor work, where we are known by our names and valued for being whatever we decide to be—the clown, the intellectual, the quiet person. Being part of a family is a wonderful thing, and I'm all for team-building at work, but having a place where you don't have to be anything to anyone makes a pleasant breather.

Small stores have traditionally filled this role throughout history—tearooms, bakeries, yarn stores, greenhouses, and bookshops owned by families who treat their establishments as sacred trusts and customers with friendly dignity. You probably have such an icon in your life, because even in the face of online retailers and box stores, we little guys tend to adapt and stick with splendid, flexible resilience. We're needed. Think what your life would look like without your own third space. (And if the spirit moves you, tell them so next time you're buying something there!)

Although we tried hard to protect this sacred trust, occasionally things went haywire—like the time a local pastor and his missus attended one of the shop's semiannual murder mysteries. Five short years into the ministry as a second profession, he'd retired from thirty long ones in the merchant marines. He was a real human being, for which we loved him and his sweet, wise wife. During the course of the Friday evening mystery, the reverend's assigned character, a rough kind of bloke, needed to behave rudely. He did a good job. Neither Jack nor I thought twice about it.

It's Friday, but Sunday's coming. . . .

By the time people sat down to Sunday dinner the poor guy was defending his entire ministry as the rumor mill caught, chewed, reformed, added significant pulp fiction to and spit back the single salty word he'd said in character.

First we found it funny, but when we realized just how deep judgment currents were running, we felt like character assassins. We called him to apologize, offer to help, whatever he needed, but he sounded sanguine.

"Better not do any murders for a while, but I want you to know, we had a great time. Believe me, this is small stuff compared to what some pastors put up with."

Guilt still haunts us over "Pastorgate." WHITB, SITB is our policy, but no one can control what others say or do—or what others decide to say about what someone does. And yes, life would get pretty awful if we expected everyone to behave according to the same rules. But that safe third space, the little neutral Switzerland we thought we'd created, wasn't immune to the flash fires of gossip, which was disappointing.

Sometimes you really do want to go where everybody knows your name. And sometimes you want to be where people know you only as "that short, pleasant woman who reads J. A. Jance." Either way you slice it, a used book store should be able to serve it up, the place where people got to define themselves for themselves.

CHAPTER 16

Growing into Ourselves

It does not matter how slowly you go as long as you do not stop.

—Confucius

EVEN AS WE WORKED TOWARD becoming the place where everyone could find safe harbor, physical space was rapidly becoming a precious commodity in the bookstore. Tales of the Lonesome Pine opened in our long front parlor and sucked up the side bedroom (which became the mysteries and thrillers room) a few months later. Personal space compressed as the shop grew. When the downstairs kitchen succumbed to cookbooks, crafts, "-ologies" and gender studies soon after Stephen-Saved-Our-Bacon Sunday, a countertop laden with cookery gadgets sustained us. Our teakettle boiled up perfect four-minute eggs, while the rice cooker turned out beautiful potatoes. A (metal) sieve atop the boiling potatoes would steam broccoli to perfection. Crock-Pots didn't just make good stew, they wafted homey smells; we sold more cookbooks with the slow cooker on. The Asian fusion meals Jack produced in our electric skillet were pure delights.

Gadget Corner lasted about a year, until we scraped together enough money to renovate the upstairs kitchen. It sat in the back outside corner of the house, painted white since tiny windows in slanting alcoves let in so little natural light. I liked the sea-green tiled floor, so reminiscent of my paternal grandmother's odd taste in kitchen colors, but its best feature was the 1950s vintage stove. Previous occupants had for some reason left this brand-new antique unused, its plastic-wrapped instruction book and meat probe waiting patiently on the pristine oven shelf. The manual sported the usual house babe with a flared skirt belted waspishly around the waist, high heels, bobbed wavy hair, and a gleaming smile. Valued online, the manual turned out to be collectible and sold for an obscene amount of money (which helped buy the new fridge). We learned by trial and error how to work the oven.

The second year, the enclosed side porch became the envisioned children's area of our early dreams, and Jack built a shelf for humor in the bathroom. (It sat within easy reach of the toilet. Sales rose. Did this make us flush with success?) Year three, the downstairs closets became "book nooks" for young adult literature and Jack lost his back-room man-cave to

Westerns and war novels. A year later he enclosed the carport, ostensibly for my chair-caning sideline, but the books for sale online wound up segregated out there.

Four years and ten months after we opened, we reached a carrying capacity of thirty-eight thousand volumes when Jack refused to put a bookshelf in the downstairs bathtub. I pointed out that two tubs remained in the upstairs bathrooms, one an ancient claw-foot big enough to scald a cow, but he only responded, "Some things are beyond the pale." Of course, he said it in that cute Scottish accent, so it didn't sound like saying no.

Learning to maintain private and public space upstairs and downstairs didn't come easy. Once we arrived home from an elegant evening of music feeling frisky, which led to a most satisfying romp 'round the paranormal romances. The next morning a guy came in looking for vampire novels. Draped across the Christine Feehans lay my bra.

We instituted a walk through the store just before opening each morning, doing a quick check for things that might frighten or confuse customers. I remain notorious for doing laundry of an evening, then forgetting the next morning that certain intimate items, which in Britain are called "smalls," hang drying in our downstairs—public—bathroom.

As Jack and I settled into the roles of colorful

local bookstore owners, we continued trying to give customers the space they needed while staying in business. As an example, a young woman telling me about her mother's death mentioned feeling isolated, unable to talk to friends about the trauma of her mother dying so young. She made a half-sniffling, half-giggling reference to the movie *Ghost* and said she almost wished she believed in psychics just so she could talk to her mom one more time.

It's that ever-present balancing act: on the one hand, people who visit independent bookshops tend to like hearing recommendations; on the other, hawking books to crying customers could not only offend, but seem cynical and caustic. Add in that Jack and I need enough money to eat, and you see the problem. Where's the line?

I didn't want to play the pushy salesperson with that young woman, so just mentioned that in *A Grief Observed*, C. S. Lewis said something similar. She asked who he was, and what else the book said. Fine, that meant I should show her the book. If she hadn't asked, I wouldn't have said anything else about it.

Selling used books is not like selling most other things. Food must be palatable; clothes should fit; paint has to be the right color. But books? On the one hand they are all things to all people, on the other a different thing to every person who buys one: entertainment, information source, inspiration and motivation, a talisman of wisdom, even a mile marker on one's journey. The reason someone wants a book can vary widely, from household decor to seeking enlightenment.

For instance, it's a documented phenomenon that people who survive extended periods in graduate school find they can't read for pleasure anymore—at least for a while. Finishing my Ph.D., I realized with horror that a pastime that had sustained and encouraged me since the age of three had been crushed by the weight of so many pages read purely for informational gain. Too many books addle the brain, indeed.

Trying to get through even the lightest of fiction, that winter of my post-doctoral discontent, I found myself repeatedly skimming for basic plot and meaning, using the same techniques I'd mastered for academic survival. No longer possible the slow savoring of book, wine, fireplace, cat and couch; now it was grasp the gist and move on. Many post-docs have similar tales of woe.

And of being cured. My magic reconnection came in *Beach Music* by Pat Conroy. It held sentences so beautiful, so interesting and twisty in their wording, I had to stop flying past and think about what he meant. One has to inhale Conroy's constructions slowly or they don't make landfall on the brain. Soon I was reading as God intended, sentence by beautiful sentence, savoring the descriptions and the drama. And when the book ended, I'd enjoyed it. Not getting information from it, but reading it.

Thanks, Mr. Conroy.

We observe a lot of "book reunions" among browsers, when people reconnect to books that mark an epoch or turning point from their past (as Conroy did me). Sometimes they find something that's been lost so long, they've forgotten they were looking for it.

One drizzly day a woman in her fifties picked up a copy of Jessamyn West's *Except for Me and Thee*, lying atop a pile waiting to be priced. (Although bad weather usually lessens customer traffic, on this hectic morning the front table sagged beneath trade-ins.) Frowning at the illustrated cover, she said to herself, "Is this—?" She opened the book and read a few lines. A slow smile crept across her face. "It is," she said with quiet conviction, folded the book shut, and handed it to me.

"Special book?" I asked, writing up the sale.

"My mother read it to me when I was sick in the seventh grade and missed a month of school," she said. "I don't think I ever knew the name of it. I'd really forgotten all about it until I saw that picture." She pointed to the cover, a colored line drawing of a barn in winter, some animals in the foreground, a human figure walking between them. Her finger lingered on the jacket, tracing the man's footprints through the snow; I don't know if she knew that a smile lingered in her eyes as well.

It's that kind of thing that makes it—well, there's no better word for it—happy-ifying, to run a bookstore. (Yes, okay, it isn't a "real" word, but don't you think it should be?) Still, take such moments as part of the whole, because book reunions, while sweet, are not the bulk of our transactions. Neither, for that matter, is intellectual discourse.

People who visit our shop sometimes drop hints that they'd like to open a bookstore "someday." They say how delightful it sounds to be surrounded by books and ideas all day long, to spend languid afternoons on literature's great themes; to find a good debate partner about whether Doyle's Sherlock Holmes has become the thinking man's Elvis (what with Laurie King marrying him to a girl half his age in her books, the Dr. Who lads creating a charismatic thirty-something sociopath for British telly, and Jeremy Brett's ghost chasing action hero Jude Law's Watson across the big screen); to compare Cormac McCarthy's mired-in-despair novel *The Road* to the stiff-upper-lip despair of Nevil Shute's *On the Beach*, then both of these to Dean Ing's shoot-your-way-back-from-the-apocalypse paperbacks; to hand literature professors cups of tea as they rail against the trend of twice-told classics—Mr. Darcy a vampire? Louisa May Alcott solving Special Victims Unit crimes?

Becky Thatcher raising Tom Sawyer's love child? Tiny Tim operating a brothel in London??!! (All these fractured-looking-glass tales have been published and rest between covers on our shop shelves.)

Trouble is, there's rarely time to have those great conversations, because we're too busy looking up orders and hunting down mildew. Anyone getting starry-eyed about owning a bookstore should ask herself a few questions: Can you lift a box weighing fifty pounds? Do you know what cat pee on paper smells like—and can you get it out? Will you exude patience while solving puzzles that start, "I'm looking for a book . . ." and peter out somewhere between "it has 'The' in the title" and "It has a red cover and the author was a soldier whose last name started with S. Or was it Z?" I've already told you about the life stories you're going to hear, many of them unpleasant.

The essential criterion for running a bookstore is less "Do you like books?" than "Do you like people?" Ironically, we find that having unlimited access to more reading material than we ever could have imagined means we read less. Chuck and Dee Robinson own Village Books, a new-and-used location in Bellingham, Washington, a shop I visit regularly because my friend Cami lives there and we are both bibliophiles. He once said in an interview with business writer Robert Spector, "If you're opening a bookstore because you love reading books, then become a night watchman because you'll be able to read more books that way." He was right. It's amazing how just the sight of so much intellectual fodder quells the appetite, let alone how little time remains to read once the shelves have been straightened, the day's swap credits assessed and put away, and the sales taxes tallied.

And yet, in one of life's great paradoxes, we admit that in the midst of having very little time to do as we like, we very much like what we are doing. In the novel *A Ring of Endless Light*, Madeleine L'Engle's teen protagonist realizes she is most contentedly herself when concentrating wholeheartedly on something else. Mihaly Csikszentmihalyi wrote in *Flow* that we get into a zone, absorbed in doing something needful that we know how to do, unaware that we're enjoying ourselves until we stop. *The Happiness Project*'s Gretchen Rubin described a happiness fog, enveloping you wholly but turning ethereal the moment you become aware of it.

Jack and I spend our days sorting crimes from cookbooks; helping customers find a particular self-help tome while listening to the havoc the problem they need help with is wreaking in their lives; explaining why we won't buy 1940s encyclopedias; nodding in encouragement as someone outlines plans for a novel he'll write someday. It's all about the customers, 24/7. Yet in those moments of concentrating on what other people need, want, long for, we catch glimpses of own contentment, fluttering like that elusive bluebird just at the edge of our sight line.

Chapter 17

Reading Rekindled

*Many people, other than the authors,
contribute to the making of a book, from
the first person who had the bright idea of
alphabetic writing through the inventor of
movable type to the lumberjacks who
felled the trees that were pulped for its
printing. It is not customary to acknowl-
edge the trees themselves, though their
commitment is total.*
        —Richard Forsyth and Roy Rada,
                Machine Learning

S O ONE MUST ASK: IF running a bookstore is
such a happy thing, why are there fewer and
fewer of them?

When we started Tales of the Lonesome Pine, we
were light worriers and big dreamers. Fortunately,
we had friends to do the heavy worrying for us;
they called us weekly from places across the States
and Scotland, just to outline their fears and explain
in simple terms why we were doomed to failure.

223

First, they wondered if a used book store could hold its own against those giant (one could say Amazonian) Internet book retailers.

Yes, we answered—firmly—and secondhanders will stand strong for years to come, because physically entering a used bookshop is charming. Fantasy authors Terry Pratchett and Neil Gaiman created L-space to explain libraries. These magical buildings house more than the sum of their parts while time warps, bends, and refracts heedless of nature's laws. Bookstores have that and more. In B-space, book-lined walls buffer against the world's bustling while browsing calms the soul and satisfies the mind.

People pop into our store daily, saying, "A few minutes to kill, so thought I'd look around." They're not going to buy anything; they just want to pull some peaceful, book-scented air through their lungs. We're glad people think of us that way. Human beings breathe slower in a bookstore. Secondhand book stores are full of enticing displays, polished brass, and fresh-brewed coffee smells. Bookshops assault the senses in a happy way.

Big chain booksellers often do cute and clever things like set tiny overstuffed wing chairs in the children's area, or outline bodies in the mystery section. Small shops don't always have room for such displays, although I have seen many a Halloween jack-o'-lantern reading on a mom-and-pop's front step. In our shop, we put a wine bottle on top of the theology shelf—ha-ha—and my aunt's silver tea service over literature. And at Christmas, a lighted reindeer with his head down graces the front lawn, a pair of large cardboard glasses perched on his snout, his nose literally buried in a giant picture book. People look for him every year, pointing Rudolphus (as he is known in the neighborhood) out to relatives and visitors.

Reindeer continuity aside, used book stores have the distinct advantage of being unknown quantities. Consumers eat at McDonald's because, in Istanbul or Iowa, they know what they're going to get. People investigate preloved book shops because they *don't* know. How often do we have the chance to go treasure hunting in today's world? I like to think of B-space as the slow-food movement for bibliophiles. We like lives replete with ideas and time to think about them. Don't serve us fast-food, bread-padded, watered-down versions of reading material. We want the good stuff and we will take our time to get it.

Bill Peace visits us like clockwork every two weeks, as he has done since our opening day. Bill is the inventor of the "military shuffle." He enters the store and starts at shop right, working his way title by title up and down the shelves around to the next room's door, until the entire perimeter is secured. Then he examines the middle shelves from right to left. Finishing one room, he crosses to the next and repeats the pattern, eventually covering the whole store with his slow, deliberate steps. In his time, Monsieur Peace has bought Christian fiction, books on educational theories, World War II history, a seafood cookbook, several Westerns and war thrillers, a paranormal romance, and some science fiction. He's the kind of guy who would drive Amazon crazy, because their software can't pinpoint his profile well enough to suggest things he might buy. The cookies crumble when trying to pigeonhole a reader like Bill.

One day while ringing up his books, Jack said something about Bill's eclectic tastes. Bill shrugged. "I like what I like, and what I like is to like what I read," he said.

Jack laughed, and Bill clapped him on the shoulder. "'Sides, at my age, I don't really care what other people think. I ain't reachin' for no big brass ring in the middle. I've done my time, I've done my duty, and now I'm gonna sit in my house with my wife and read what I want, when I want." Exit Bill Peace, carrying his bag of miscellaneous supplies for a retirement well lived.

Truth be told, Bill is the kind of reader we dreamed about, back when we started. He is a reader's reader and a delight to watch, going 'round the corners at precise angles with that bearlike gait, bending and straightening as he runs his eyes up and down the shelves, spine by spine. He's so thorough that he takes hours. One winter's night we actually closed the shop at 6 P.M. as usual, thinking everyone was gone—only to have him appear as I was setting the table for supper.

"I'll take these," he said, materializing suddenly from our mystery and thrillers room, holding out a couple of medieval whodunnits. I choked on a little "whoop" of surprise and nearly dropped the plates, but Bill didn't even notice. Jack rang up his purchases, opened the door for him, and turned on the porch light. To this day, I'm not certain he knows we locked him in.

Bill is not the only customer whose tastes vary, or whose enjoyment of the shop has as much to do with ritual and relaxation as with finding a book. My friend Jenny, from the bookstore's writing group, comes in now and then for a cuppa, and after we've talked a while, she goes into "the routine."

Casting her eyes over the shelves in a slow arc, she asks, "Got anything I might like?" in her movie-star languid voice, and I'll haul down a couple of novels or memoirs. Completely unlike Bill in her approach to book shopping, Jenny also has fairly eclectic tastes; she loves not only most of Joan Didion's books, but also Tom Perrotta's *Little Children*—which I hurled across the room around the third chapter. In fact, we joke that if I hate it, Jenny will like it—unless it's a memoir. We both adored *The Prize Winner of Defiance, Ohio* and *The Geography of Love*, and laughed our way through *Mennonite in a Little Black Dress*. But we stay off each other's fiction lists. We want to remain friends.

From Jenny's casual eye sweep to Bill's deliberate steps, people cruise our shop expecting the unexpected. They know that bookshops are magic, and books are the road maps by which misfits find each other.

As former residents of Edinburgh, we once took friends from Spain on an all-day ramble through every used book store in the city (nine at the time), returning exhausted but happy with four bags to lug on the train. Not even speaking the same language, we trundled up Edinburgh's medieval closes and down its back alleys, handling volumes musty and fresh, our Spanish friends communicating by gesture with the shopkeepers who guarded these treasure troves. Years later, looking back on that trip, I know we couldn't have had any deeply meaningful conversations because we shared no common language. Yet I remember vividly what we talked about: literary themes from European folktales common to Spain and the British Isles. We compared heroes and villains and motifs, discussed why witches show themselves in daytime England but nighttime Spain, pitted the Irish giant Cuchulain against the Spanish Caravinaigre.

Bookshops are magic.

Big-name box bookstores have installed cafés

and armchairs precisely because people like to hang out around books. Next time you're in one of those cavernous megasellers, see for yourself how they've worked to create ambiance. Look at the shelf placement, how they've been arranged to mark off cozy little reading nooks. Somebody's tried very hard to make you forget you're in a warehouse.

Fine, said our killjoy friends who stop in from time to time to explain why we're doomed. So a bricks-and-mortar store still works. Now what about iPads and Kindles and Nooks?

Shut up, we responded. And pass the wine.

Actually, that's not how we feel about e-books. What's so horrible about e-readers, anyway—either the devices or the humans who use them? I'm a big fan of literacy in any form, digital pulse or printed pulp. Why should e-books spark an either-or division among readers? Couldn't there be room in our futures for both paper pulp and electronic pulse?

I first had an e-reader in my hand about eight years before they hit the American market, when I lived in Britain and worked with recovering addicts. About a third of the guys in the "rehab-instead-of-jail" program were dyslexic. (Did you know that dyslexia affects one out of ten people in the United States and Europe, but that one in four convicts is dyslexic? Think about it a sec.)

E-readers offered a "cool" way to engage these

lads on the topic of reading in the first place; while Dick and Jane were neither hip nor happening, having one's hands on any electronic device was. Add to that the promise of a laptop loaner if they read an entire e-book, and those boys had big incentives to write some of the most interesting reviews I ever read. My favorite remains a young man who compared Captain Ahab to his former drug supplier: "They both just concentrated on what they wanted and didn't care who got hurt."

So, e-readers, eye readers, what's the difference? Reading is good for us, and if gleaning words from a computer screen is a little harder on the eyes and softer on the brain (as studies are beginning to suggest—something about screens not stimulating the correct eye muscles to make us think, so instead we remain passively observant; the same disconnect happens when watching television), at least it's still words, not pictures.

Here's the thing Jack and I have observed from our perch above the electronic fray: books aren't just words. They're objects with specific, physical, desirable properties. I asked a friend with two daughters what books meant to her family, and she waxed eloquent for a full two minutes on their properties: "literal sponges for our tears and muffles for our guffaws; conveyors of knowledge; the hard evidence of our studies; sharing in an adventure or an illness; and companionship with as many other people as there are copies sold."

We let that rest for a moment, sipping our coffee, then Tonia laughed. "And I don't know if you want to hear this, but my daughters built a castle out of books for their dolls. They made the walls and the roof and the steps up to it, all from books. And they made a book garage at the back for the princess to park her pony and her sports car."

Try that with a Kindle. The pony would do unspeakable things to the interface circuitry.

When we started our shop, we couldn't bear to think a single physical volume should ever be thrown away; that reticence birthed the free book section on our front porch. Surrounded by a bunch of old Reader's Digest Condensed Books and *The Guinness Book of World Records* from the 1980s, we stuck them out there hoping someone would want them. Yet as time went on, and we saw just how many geriatric tomes lumbered into Tales of the Lonesome Pine, their information, ideologies, or inspirational power corroded by time, we pitched a box here or there into a Dumpster—never without a wee twinge. They deserved respect for their contribution, after all; we would never treat people or pets that way in their old age.

But they kept coming, the books no one wanted. Even though we flat-out told people we didn't deal in rare or old books, our shop still attracted a lot of older volumes in poor shape, scribbled in with ink or otherwise too damaged to be considered true antiques. We never have figured out what to do with these "old dears," as Jack calls them. We displayed a couple of 1900s textbooks on raising children just because people found them so charming. One depicted (complete with illustrations) how to build a "baby cager," a device like a playpen that hung from a window so Baby could safely get fresh air. (The book highly recommended these cages for those in walk-up tenements: "economical and efficient for the busy mother who must do her own housework.") Another tallied the cost of raising a boy against raising a girl. Believe it not, gentle readers, boys were more expensive, because parents had to factor in college. The beautifully embossed, leather-covered *Light at Eventide: A Book of Poetic Comfort for the Aged* went to Isabel for a birthday ending in a zero. The poems ran heavily to sunsets and angels folding their snow-white wings. (Isabel didn't speak to me for three days, but I think she secretly liked it. It was a very pretty book . . .)

Although it may be borderline apostasy to treat these linen-and-leather tomes with less dignity so late in their great and far-reaching lives, I must admit that they make great gag gifts. When our photocopier godmother Teri gave birth to a boy after three girls, we sent her *The Boy and His*

Daily Living, published in 1908 (the one with the "boys go to college, girls do not" costs list). Olivia, our writing group coordinator's daughter, received a copy of *Light on Dark Corners - A Complete Sexual Science and a Guide to Purity and Physical Manhood - Advice to Maiden, Wife, and Mother, Love, Courtship, and Marriage* on the occasion of her seventeenth birthday. (Her parents were not so very amused, and you really don't want to know what this 1897 book suggested about the morals of girls who went to co-ed colleges.)

But by the time we'd been running a few years, books that had seen their fifteen minutes of fame rise and fade were turning into craft projects: angels for Christmas trees, flying mobiles of birds, crudely fashioned twisted-paper statues of literary scenes, even experiments with making our own pop-up books. I made a couple dozen purses, and still carry mine, crafted from a 1935 book called *Earning and Spending the Family Income* (a helpful tome that explained what I should do with my husband's paycheck when he brought it home and turned it over to me). Support columns for end tables. Shelves. Planters. Jewelry boxes. It's amazing how superglue and nails can transform a useless object (and there it is, folks, spelled out in black and white) into a piece of art.

Bibliophiles recognize that books are not just ideas trapped between covers, but artifacts, mile markers on our life journey. "I think of my bookshelf as a trophy of accomplishment," said an academic friend of mine. "I look at their spines and remember where I was when I read them, and what I got out of them. And I have a side of the room for books I'm going to read, and a side for books I've read. So I can revisit old friends, or try something new."

My friend John shared a house, a dog, and a cat with me when we lived in Newfoundland during our graduate studies. He laughed at the idea that "the book is dead and only the information is important. So say people who like digital media. I still organize my life according to a micro-geographic model wherein I know what I know based upon what the piles I've made contain. Plus my cats like to sleep on certain books, which is how I know they're important. Cats have historically been hoarders of useful information."

Books are physical objects that cause responses to their tactile dimensions. Sara Nelson, in her memoir *So Many Books, So Little Time*, talked about remembering where she was when she read a book, being transported back to that time and place when she held it in her hands. Even a book's smell will evoke memories. "A book reads the better which is our own, and has been so long known to us, that we know the topography of its blots, and dog's ears, and can trace the dirt in it to having read it at tea with buttered muffins," said Charles Lamb (yes, that guy who redid the Shakespeare stories for kids back in the 1800s).

And books can become, when their shelf life truly has ended, objects of art. Perhaps you read about the mysterious and exquisite little sculptures, most crafted from Ian Rankin novels, which graced several book festivals and shops in Britain in 2011? These creations spawned a fashion for similar objects around the world, and one now finds altered books in many artistic poses. I like to think those sculptures gave their host books dignity at the end of their lives, a kind of final promise: when you can no longer be read as an objet d'art a scalpel and some glue will turn you physically into one, and people will continue to admire, appreciate, and enjoy you, oh lovely little book. It seems right and proper. God grant us all such a dignified end.

Books, be they physical objects or electronic pulses, are way cool. They are idea houses. So let those who want to read from machines. Those who love the feel, the smell, the gilt edging and the pretty covers and the soft paper, and the kinetic memories will enjoy the physical objects. Either form can be an artifact. So long as we're all reading, and gaining joy from it, does it really matter so much?

And yet . . . it might. E-readers have taken down the big bricks-and-mortar booksellers. Think about it; although this can't be laid solely at the feet of e-readers, Borders is gone. Waldenbooks is past history, along with Crown and B. Dalton. That pretty much leaves us Barnes & Noble (now the only place where one can buy Nook e-books), Powell's if you're lucky enough to live near one, and a few big independent stores, including, in our part of the world, Joseph-Beth in Lexington and Malaprop's in Asheville.

The demise of larger retails lets a whole bunch of mom-and-pop bookshops stand out in bas-relief against the starker landscape. The more things fall apart when the center cannot hold, the more small-business owners are picking up the pieces and planting them in their own home soil. Amazing though it may seem, the broken bits tend to take ready root and grow.

Estimates from the book industry suggest that one in four U.S. bookstores is secondhand, and that there are more preloved book shops now than ten years ago, perhaps by as much as 10 percent. Some futurists believe that only secondhand book shops will still exist in the next century, the new retailers made redundant by e-readers. That may be true if we turn to reading e-books so totally that print runs stop, and while I hate to see the new-only team so threatened, I'm willing to accept that future bookselling establishments may focus on used, or be amalgams of used and new. Can you imagine a world without bookstores? These aren't just places where shoppers buy books; they are community hubs, people's third places. Who will listen to the fire stories, the novel plots, if not booksellers? Will the computer make you a cup of tea?

Jack and I sat down one night and made a list of all the functions our shop served in our region, and realized that, while books anchor our purpose, some of the things we do have only a tenuous connection to them. Four years earlier, Witold had been the first to name us a community center, and he was right. People meet at our place to share activities they like, such as needlework, art films, international infotainments, gourmet meals, lectures on everything from science to politics, game nights, and house concerts.

We're one of just a couple of places where you can buy a green salad or vegetarian soup in our whole county. And we're the only place where you can have honest-to-goodness Scottish tea and shortbread. We can afford to serve food that other, bigger restaurants can't because we don't rely on food sales for money; it's supplemental.

Newcomers come by and say, "We just moved here and saw your sign" or, more often, "and so-and-so told me to come down and meet you." They ask questions, tell us how they're feeling, talk about what they're looking for in their new home or job, describe where they came from, and get a cup of tea. We're an unofficial welcome wagon cum support group for bookish people.

We're where people can talk. You don't have to

know us, or be known by us, to sit down at the table and tell the story of your mom's going to the nursing home, recite the poem you're writing, or disgorge any other story lying heavy within you. We tend to call this being an intellectual pub, but Jack's pastor friend Tony has another name for it.

Tony drops by at least twice a week for a cuppa and a quiet chat with Jack, but one day he ambled in when the place was a madhouse. We have a customer who has fixated on Jack's guitar playing; Chuck was following him around like a puppy asking about chords as Jack briskly sorted books that a rather impatient woman we'd never seen before had brought in to trade. One of the Vietnam vets idled his way through a pile of value paperbacks while keeping up a running mono-logue to which Jack occasionally answered, "Mhmm." Meanwhile, "Nikki," a regular customer whose dying sister was married to a schmuck who wouldn't let anyone visit her, cried softly into her cup of tea as I handed over Kleenex and shortbread, calling the creep husband names all the while. (Nikki and I knew each other well by this point, so she didn't mind my comments.)

Instead of leaving, Tony poured himself a mug of tea and ambled over to the vet, engaging him in conversation. When the last of this crew had gone and we sat down to the now-stone-cold teapot with Tony, he started laughing. "Y'all are the luckiest people on Earth," he said. "And this place is a church. No, think about it." His waving hands negated our exhausted murmurs of dissent. "Churches are where people get fed. That guy [the vet] didn't have any money and you gave him five books for a dollar. Churches are where people talk about their sadness. That woman cried and you gave her Kleenex and a hug. Churches are places where we connect with God. You're his hands and feet on Earth. Jack, you let that kid follow you and talk nonstop, and never once lost patience. Y'all are running a church!"

Sure, Tony, whatever. It doesn't feel like a church, more like a dusty, dog-hairy, 38K-strong collection of objects that have to stay more or less within certain spaces, including a children's room that gets hit by cyclones at least twice a day. If anyone wants to call it by a nicer name, go for it; we're just dancing as fast as we can while smiling.

But Tony was right about one thing: even on days when it all seems to be going pear-shaped (that's Scottish for everything going wrong) we still know we're blessed beyond reason to be doing what we're doing.

And, despite the moments of madness like the one above, we are a quiet place to change pace for a few moments. I can't tell you the number of customers who come in and say they're waiting for their wife/husband to pick up something at the pharmacy, their daughter/son to get a haircut down the block, their friend who is exercising at the gym next door. Waiting, they stroll around our shelves. They're not going to buy anything; they just want to be in a cool (or warm) place with quiet music and friendly people. They know they're welcome. Sometimes people sit at the tea table, not checking e-mails, not using their cell phone, just sitting, legs stretched out in front of them, letting their eyes flick over the shelves, little half smiles on their faces. They'll point to a book and say, "I read that in college/the army/the year I got married. It changed my life/was the stupidest thing I'd ever read." And I swear to you—Jack and I have watched this often enough to document it—their breathing changes. It slows down. Their shoulders relax. Their eyes get soft.

E-readers will mess up that intellectual pub/ church, soft-eyed slow breathing phenomenon as they reduce the bookstore population. Where are folks going to get the same space in which to relax? Where will those who need to talk be heard in cyberspace? People need their third spaces, and if e-readers get too uppity, they could reduce the number of such safe houses available.

I doubt that e-readers could eliminate the whole herd, though, to mix and mutilate a metaphor. Consider that a predator usually takes down some of the weaker creatures around the edges, not the strong ones in the middle. E-readers, in contrast, seem more likely to kill the strong than the weak. Borders went, but not the little independent shop across town. If the strength of a store rests primarily in its ability to get the best deals by buying bulk and passing those savings on to customers, then it has a problem when the online market opens up cheap and easy acquisition without the middleman or -woman. But if the strength of a store rests in the proprietor's ability to spend time with each customer, to help them find what they want and match disposable income to adequate pricing, or to just listen to them, well, these are enduring qualities. And except for price matching, they are human qualities.

Store owners—at least until they can be replicated online—are why I think small bookstores will be around even when the last leviathan disappears, harpooned by an e-reader. Physical brick-and-mortar bookshops are watering holes for human intellects and spirits. E-readers and books bought online don't let you tell the story of why you wanted to buy them. Amazon neither knows nor cares that you want a red-hot romance to distract your friend during chemo; that the book of wedding cake designs you seek is because you're going to make one for your daughter-in-law-to-be since her parents can't afford to put on the wedding, but you've never made such a thing before and you're scared to death. Small and independent shop owners care. We're good listeners. That's probably because we're humans, just like the people who shop with us. Perhaps someday computers will be good listeners, too. Hmm; will that make the world more like heaven or hell?

When customers start conversations, be it about their last relationship, their jerk boss, or their aspirations as artists, they are like the people in *Farenheit 451*, living books who must tell you their stories or die. And the book they want to discuss is one that's written on them, inside them, hidden from the rest of humanity. They don't want to pontificate on the great themes of literature, but to tell you the great themes of their lives. The personalities of Meg, Jo, Beth, and Amy are not their target; they want you to understand why their family is a mess. It's not the process of writing but of being human they explore, explain, question. We're all of us running the gauntlet from articulate to desperate, Quixotes tilting at our particular windmills, Psyches searching for our one and only Cupid. Perhaps the nicest thing bookstore owners do for the world is not sell people stories, but listen to people's stories.

When we listen to each other, we validate each other. As near as I can tell, everyone in the world wants and needs validation. Mom-and-pop book-sellers are different from the box stores and the computers; because we're not just selling to be selling; we're selling to keep the connections between storytellers, storied lives, and story readers active.

And that connection is why we will be—why we must be—standing small and proud in your children's future. Do you know the Aesop's fable about the oak and the reed? The oak offered to protect the reed from a coming storm, but the wind cracked the oak at its roots and blew it over. As it floated past, the oak called out how surprising it was that its mightiness had not withstood the storm, yet that wimpy little reed still stood by the side of the river. The reed called back that being small and flexible sometimes proved wiser than being the biggest.

Customers love being treated like individuals almost as much as they love good prices—although if you've been to a big-box store lately, you may join me in a growing concern that we as a nation have sacrificed the first for the second. Independent bookstores—be their stock preloved or new—may become thinner on the ground, start selling e-books and sandwiches to make ends meet, have to consider carefully what we ask people to pay . . . but we're not dying. We're not even coughing, just doing what mom-and-pops have done for generations: tracking market trends on the big screen and listening to customer needs in the neighborhood, then flexing to meet them while being polite and human and good listeners.

CHAPTER 18

Last Cowboy

When I was young, I admired clever people. Now that I am old, I admire kind people.

—Abraham Joshua Heschel

A PLEASANT BUT RUGGED MAN whose name we didn't know came in every week or two and browsed the Westerns and war section (what we call Guys with Big Guns). One day he emerged with three torrid romance novels that had been misplaced. Set in the Wild West though they were, their author was one of the great bodice-rippers (buckskin-rippers?) of all time. Yet because they'd been stuck in Westerns, this rather manly man bought them happily—something I feel certain he wouldn't have done had he seen them in romances.

Those particular copies were hardbacks missing their dust covers, so the usual picture of an improbably proportioned redhead bent backward over the supporting limb of (pick one) a tall mustached man wearing a leather vest and chaps/a tall, dark, and bronze bare-chested man wearing feathers and fringed buckskin/a horse wasn't in evidence. That's probably why Jack put them in the wrong place. (You didn't think I was going to cop to that, did you?)

After the customer had gone, we moved more of that author's books to Westerns, but just those that didn't have overt romance covers. He bought them all next visit.

The dude was happy; he liked her writing. We were happy; we'd sold several titles from a fairly prolific older author to someone who genuinely liked them without embarrassing our customer. The rush of happy endorphins from matching the right books with the right people fuels bookshop owners; it provides our natural high.

Despite temptation, I learned not to make too much fun of Westerns after a customer and his daughter showed me what they could mean to another person's spirit.

A diffident, slight man with the improbable nickname of "Wee Willie" shopped regularly with us. His nickname alone should have been enough to arouse sympathy, but Wee Willie could talk the hind leg off a donkey, a pair of horses, and an entire herd of antelope. The guy never stopped. From the moment he entered the shop with his customary "Hey, y'all! How's life?" until he backed out the door with a week's supply of reading material, Willie talked.

"I got me a new computer, gotta figure out how to start it up and then I'm in business! Not business, I mean, not like y'all, but I mean my own business, not a home business, but the stuff I gotta take care of at home, you know, paperwork and all that, gotta get that done. My daughter's helping me get it set up, the computer. She's got her own business, she's a veterinarian. When she was little I'd allus say, 'Now you be gentle with animals, honey. Never trust anyone's not good to an animal.' Boy, I like dogs. Why I'd as soon kick my own mother as kick a dog. Had me a little dog, last year, she died from cancer. I didn't know dogs got cancer 'til my daughter said. Boy, I was tore up. Not like I cried or nothing but it sure did hurt me. Not hurt like physical, I mean, I was in the war, I got shot and that hurt, but you know what I mean."

I'd learned some time ago to let him flow while giving polite, smiling, monosyllabic answers that didn't offer any foothold into a new subject. The thing that kept his listeners from pushing Wee Willie off a cliff was his good-natured soul. Willie's innate kindness radiated to everything and everyone around him. Willie always patted our two dogs over the fence before coming into the shop, stroked Beulah and called her a beautiful girl, thanked us for opening the first bookstore ever in his hometown. He just couldn't talk about one subject for more than a minute, or stop talking longer than ten seconds.

"I like books, boy, I like books, and I can afford to buy 'em, you know what I mean, I ain't bragging or nothing but I had me a good job and now I'm retired and I can buy the books I want, you know. I got the money, not like you, ma'am, with your good education an' all, but I done all right. Worked forty-two years as a maintenance man and I done all right."

Always clean and happy, Wee Willie sported in summer a sleeveless undershirt and a baseball cap with Bermuda shorts. In winter his long gray overcoat never revealed its secrets. An infectious smile remained his biggest accessory. He could grin to rival the moon's rays.

If only he would grin without talking, I thought, absolving myself with the Southern get-out-of-jail-free card for uncharitable speech by adding, *Bless his heart.*

We planned a party to celebrate the shop's five-year anniversary, and began inviting favorite customers. Wee Willie never signed up for our e-mail list, so Jack gave him the flyer reserved for those we felt should be honored with attending this special occasion.

Willie looked at the birthday cake on the invitation. "Whose birthday?" he asked. "Oh gee, never mind, I'll just read it, silly me, it'll be great, I'll see you on the day. I love parties, I'll make sure to bring the doggies some treats and thanks again for inviting me. I been to lots of parties, of course, but they're allus fun. It's so fun to come here. Y'all are some of my favorite people and I ain't just saying that, I mean it, y'all are so nice and I just love coming here. Well now, I better get on down the road. See you then!" He waved the flyer and backed out the door, talking.

About a month later, in the season between Thanksgiving and Christmas, a tall woman with black hair to her waist walked into the shop and asked if we took books as donations. I said of course, but we would give book credit if she preferred.

She shook her head. "The books aren't mine and I live in Charlottesville," she said. "My dad didn't have many books, but there's maybe two boxes. I don't know if you can use them or not. They're old, but hardly touched at all."

I recognized a death-in-the-family scenario as I helped her bring in the small stash.

"There's not much to Dad's collection, nothing sentimental or that I'd care to read myself, but I hated to just throw them away, and the VA already got the rest."

"Your dad was a veteran," I remarked, setting down a box and digging inside: a pristine set of Shakespeare's works, hardbound in cheap red covers. We saw a lot of these; somebody must have been door-to-door selling in the seventies. A

King James Bible, a copy of *War and Peace*, Owen Wister's *The Virginian*. An encyclopedia set circa 1960.

I explained our free book policy and suggested that was the place for the encyclopedias. "A lot of local women like to make book angels for Christmas, so they'll be glad to pick up hardbacks now." I smiled with an apologetic little bookseller's shrug, as if to say, *What else can one do with old encyclopedias?*

The woman smiled back with sad eyes. "Dad used them for shelf decoration, too."

"Computers have changed a lot of things," I responded, checking the Shakespeare set for silverfish.

She shook her head. "He had one, but never really learned to use it. I was always going to come up one day and help him get started." She shrugged. "Busy time. Too late." Her voice cracked under suppressed pain.

I'll never know if that would have been enough to make me realize who she was, because just then I flipped open the cover of the King James. Spidery script spelled out "Presented to William—."

It hit like a Taser jolt.

My head flew up. "You're not . . . is Wee Willie . . . ?"

She smiled, regaining control. "My daddy. You remember him! He loved this place. Came down almost every week, but I guess you know that.

He'd always call and tell me about how nice you two were, how pretty the cat was, Bella, is that her name? He loved visiting. Had a heart attack. Guess you didn't hear."

"We loved having him," I replied, begging God to understand as I embraced Willie's bereaved daughter. "I'm so sorry."

She nodded, swallowing as professional women do when they don't want to lose it, so I turned the conversation back to business. "Are there any more books to bring in? Wee—your dad bought a lot of Westerns from us over the years, and those are really popular."

Something—pallor, shadow, a cloud of confusion—cast itself over the room. She squinted at me, eyes wrinkled in a way so similar to Willie's that a lump rose in my throat, catching me off guard. *I should have been nicer to the little guy. What else did he have besides reading?*

I babbled on. "Assuming you don't want to keep his Westerns. Perhaps they're sentimental. He loved them so. As I'm sure you know. Knew. Know. Sorry."

"Daddy loved Westerns," she said in a measured tone, as if trying to determine whether the words were true.

"Yes," I said in assurance, but she shook her head, exasperated.

"I know he did." Asperity tinged her voice. "He loved to watch them on TV. But I didn't realize you didn't know. He never would have told you. He was so proud of having friends like you. Educated. He was big on education. Look at me. He put me through college."

Was that noise she made a laugh or a sob? "Daddy couldn't read. He'd come here to buy books for the VA. He must have given them a couple hundred."

My mouth opened, but my jaw worked without sound. When the power of speech returned, I heard myself say, "Bless his heart. Um, if there's anything we can do." The words fell, lame and pathetic, against the wall of her grief.

She reached out and squeezed my shoulder. "You did it already. You and your husband gave Daddy dignity these last years. He loved coming here. Bless *your* hearts. Bye now."

And that was that. Wee Willie never came talking through the door again. But that Christmas we asked another customer with connections to the VA to take a box of donations there in Wee Willie's honor. We picked out covers Wee Willie would have liked: men holding guns and snarling, yet looking nobler and gentler than one might expect, and I cried the whole time.

Maybe the best we can do for each other in our small ways is still better than the big guns ever will. Could a computer have seen in those covers what Wee Willie did? Would a box store have given him dignity?

CHAPTER 19
Living Large in a Small-Town Bookstore

Books are delightful society. If you go into a room and find it full of books—even without taking them from the shelves they seem to speak to you, to bid you welcome.
—William Ewart Gladstone

PEOPLE WHO LIKE TO READ love being in massed assemblages of books: bookstores, libraries, homes where the walls are lined with shelves and spines. Such places are magical. For me, I suppose this knowledge stems back to trips to the library as a kid, which were always celebrated events. Whether I took books home or not, I just loved the smell, the touch, the sight of all those stacks towering to the sky. (I was short.)

The library I frequented was attached to an old house used as storage and administrative space, connected to the more prosaic cinder-block-and-fluorescent-lights building via a ramp and a rather forbidding industrial door with one small window much too high for a child. From my first visit as a preschooler to my last before moving away as a college student, I wanted to make a mad dash for that ramp, ducking under grasping librarians, rushing up, away into that house where—I just knew—the Mad Hatter held his everlasting tea party, Bilbo Baggins sat in front of a glowing hearth ready to talk of adventure, and Pickles the Fire Cat waited for me to scratch his ears. I just had to get past the librarian guards—something I never managed. On some days, I still fantasize about going back to that library, explaining it all, and asking to pass through the forbidden door.

But I'm old enough to know that the delicate porcelain figurines of imagination should not be hurled against the walls of reality. Better to keep one's dreams intact and be happy with the memories of that long-ago real library. I still remember with a little ripple of pleasure how fascinating it was to play games in the stacks. Pick a shelf. How many books with red covers? Divide by the number of books written by women, count that number of spines over from the top left, or middle bottom, and check that book out—unless it looked horrible, in which case I would cheat and take one next to it. (What's the point of inventing a game if you can't break the rules?)

Such a little bookworm was I that searching for a particular book, or the place where certain subjects were corralled, felt almost as rewarding as actually checking one out. The hunt became its own thrill, regardless of whether prey actually got speared. I could read the fairy tales of every land at 398.2, and just up from there were books about exotic festivals I'd never heard of, let alone celebrated. (How did one pronounce "Eid"? my six-year-old self wondered.) Travel writers lurked around 912, but could pop up in other places as well. And in 780, I could even take out sheet music and play it on my piano at home. Plus there were the wild-card turn racks, display cases, and general fiction alphabetized by author. You could look up a favorite novelist, then investigate the people on either side just to see if they were interesting. I don't think I have ever left a library without feeling a twinge of regret, a vague sense of panic that I'd missed something important, that stories, people, and ideas were still in there waiting for me to find them so they could tell me secrets.

I remember as a very young child being warned that libraries and bookstores were quiet places where noise wasn't allowed. Here was yet another thing the adults had gotten wrong, for these book houses pulsed with sounds; they just weren't noisy. The books hummed. The collective noise they made was like riding on a large boat where the motor's steady thrum and tickle vibrated below one's sneakers, ignorable until you listened, then omnipresent and relentless, the sound that carried you forward. Each book brimmed with noises it wanted to make inside your head the moment you opened it; only the shut covers prevented it from shouting ideas, impulses, proverbs, and plots into that sterile silence. What an enigma (a word my young self wouldn't know for years) that such a false sense of quietude should be imposed on this obviously noisy place. It felt the same as the subversive, subliminal hush of a lunchroom where kids were plotting—just a temporary absence of noise until adult backs were turned.

Childish . . . and yet, have you ever stood outside on very still nights and let your ears adjust until you could hear the soft hum of overhead power lines? When I head downstairs in the morning to brew coffee, I hear that sound again— the low throbbing of the books in our shop, pulsing with energy, waiting. And the childhood sensation that they stopped talking to each other only because I came into the room returns. Perhaps that's what makes people breathe slower in the bookstore; without knowing it, they adjust their rhythm to the gentle pulsing of the books.

Of course, if this childhood fancy were true, then some of the books in our shop would be swearing at us. Idyllic libraries with straight shelves and neat rows may have well-behaved volumes; ours look more as though they've been in a drunken brawl. They await us in the morning sloughed across the table, stacked alongside overflowing shelves, stuck in windowsills, hanging off the turn rack I found in a thrift store and brought home in my little Honda's backseat. (I had to keep the windows open so the rack could stick straight out either side. Lots of honks on the highway from that escapade, but the state policeman just grinned as he passed.) Our bookshop is the Lonesome Gulch Saloon to a library's Eastern Boarding School for Young Ladies.

At night I sometimes browse the peaceful chaos of our shelves with no intention of actually choosing something, just wanting to see what's there, playing the old library games. I look at covers—that you can't judge books by them is just one more lie we teach our children—and weigh pros and cons. Then I might choose a volume or, feeling luxurious, two or three. With potential gems in hand, I flip off the light and head to our wooden staircase, groping my way up by feel. The bookstore is wired so that you have to extinguish the downstairs chandelier (just four bulbs in iron hooks, but it looks very distinguished). Then you must cross in darkness to the stairs and climb them before hitting the switch for the second-story landing's dome light.

Here's yet another dichotomy about running a bookstore: on the one hand, it's a sacred trust, a third place where people can find a listening ear and the wisdom of the ages; on the other, it's a building that has to be kept clean and lit. And as much trouble as Jack and I had trouble keeping the place clean, keeping the lights on proved worse.

It's our own fault that we're slobs, but when we started running out of space sometime during year three, we had to cover the first-floor staircase's light switch with a bookshelf that ended up resting right against the toggle. To use the light would require moving a whole stack of hardbacks, then feeling around with a stick between wood and wall. It became far simpler to just leave it off and creep up the stairs, hands outstretched. This lazy attitude led to a nightly ritual I have come to adore.

Zora the black Lab likes to sit as silent sentinel halfway up the staircase; bumping into her tempts a heart attack each time. In the evening, it's fairly common that one of us will be working on domestic chores upstairs while the other is in the shop taking care of business. From her point of view, Zora is only fulfilling the duty of watching over us both, but hunting a black dog on the inky staircase each night is no great treat, especially as she sometimes stretches out lengthwise—a fuzzy, benevolent speed bump. Or, as A. A. Milne put it in what we think of as Zora's theme song:

Halfway down the stairs is a stair where I sit:
There isn't any other stair quite like it.

As Jack is usually the last one to come to bed, I will lie in our room reading, one ear tuned to hear the moment when dog and human connect: the thud of his outstretched hands hitting the wall, followed by his muffled oath and the *tap-tap-tap* of Zora's wagging tail against the wood. It never fails to reduce me to giggles. Ah, bliss.

Jack talks about installing a motion detector, perhaps a clapper or some voice-activated thing, but we haven't to date. Blame for this procrastination rests squarely and solely on my father. How can I put this? I am the daughter of a card-carrying gadget geek. My dad never met a machine he didn't like. As children my sister and I had LEGO out the wazoo, plus a Thingmaker (remember "Goop"?!) and Tinkertoys and Lite-Brite. If it made something, said something, turned something on and off, or involved new and improved electronic circuitry, my dad had to have it. (But it might interest you to know, my father has yet to purchase a Kindle.)

After Jack and I married, we lived in Scotland for several years, so visited the old home place annually. On arrival—by which I mean, in the car from the airport—Dad would fill us in on all the new gadgets he'd acquired during the interval, and speak with disgust and a dismissive hand wave of those he'd discarded.

My mother, a patient soul by nature, has used the same drip coffeepot since 1990, despite Dad's best efforts. She usually sat with a book, smiling, as Dad showed us how to work the National Weather Alert monitor, the talking bathroom scale (*Why?!*) and, one memorable year, the Light Commander.

Jack and I slept on the fold-out living room couch, flanked by two lamps with separate wall switches. One required either advanced yoga positions or getting out of bed to reach its off button. Father, recognizing a chance to own another gadget, decided this logistical problem could be solved with a voice-activated mechanism. He spent an hour that first night drilling us on its special features and passwords: "Light Commander, Light Off," and the equally unforgettable "Light Commander, Light On."

Mom rolled her eyes and headed for bed as Jack and I repeated these modern abracadabras to Dad's satisfaction. Only then would he go away.

More than an hour later, Jack put down his book and yawned. I had long since fallen into a doze with a paperback on my face. Jack removed it, tucked the covers over my inert shoulders, and placed my glasses on the bedside table. Then he turned to the lamp.

"Light Commander, Light Off."

There was no response.

He repeated the command, a little louder. Nope. He tried softer. Nada.

Jack thought a moment, then realized his accent

would be flummoxing the gadget's settings. He adjusted his Scots clip to a Tennessee drawl.

"Laaahhhht CahmAINder, Laaaaaaght AAAAA-hhhhhfffff."

The lamp ignored him.

Perhaps he had the wording wrong. "Light Commander, Turn Off."

The bulb burned merrily—or, as Jack said later, brighter.

Lying with my back to him, I listened to my normally unflappable husband lose patience with each successive attempt. Truth be told, I was enjoying the performance very much, and trying not to end it by laughing out loud.

"Light Commander, Eff Off!" he snarled, and I couldn't suppress a honking giggly snort. Reaching behind Jack to where the couch bed left an opening to the wall, I yanked the plug from its socket and handed it to him, biting my pillow to stifle the giggles.

So it is understandable that Jack hasn't followed through with his intentions regarding the upstairs light—or, for that matter, the other weird places where illumination sources grace our shop. I have to tell you that lights are a sore point among those brave souls who pinch-hit for us when we make brief forays back into performance, or just run away for a weekend.

I think many people must hear the books humming, recognize that fun energy that thrums through our shop gathering a community around itself, because two years ago, a tax attorney came up to me at the town's annual Christmas parade, put her hand on my shoulder, and said without preamble, "Isabel tells me she loves watching your store, that it's peaceful and fun and pleasant, that it clears the mind. How much would you charge to let me do it for a weekend?"

Tom Sawyer is alive and well and stocking bookshelves in Big Stone Gap. (If you don't remember the famous fence scene Samuel Clemens wrote, wherein Tom suckers a bunch of boys into paying him to whitewash a fence, you should revisit that passage soon.)

Peggy isn't the only person to approach us on the street and offer to work the shop "not for pay, just for fun, if y'all go away for a weekend. It just sounded like a good time, something I'd enjoy." Once we'd been around long enough, that classic pendulum swing of small-town life sputtered into motion, and word went out that Jack and Wendy's place was good fun not just to visit, but to be part of. Jack often says, "Nothing breeds success like success. And people want to own a piece of what they like."

Needless to say, we love that our shop is that easy to get a sitter for, but we do recognize the unfortunate light switch quirks in our baby. In order to understand this idiosyncrasy, you're going to need a floor plan.

Tales of the Lonesome Pine Used Books has seven rooms, plus the outdoor Luv Shack. As bookshops go, we are small "but pack a wallop," as Garth once commented. Three rooms run across the front with only sliding pocket doors to separate them. If you were standing just inside the door with your back to the Free Books Porch, you would be in Local Lit, where we feature new and used titles by area artists, a Trigiani table, and CDs from many regional musicians. Southern and historical fiction also have shelves in this room, as do memoirs and other nonfiction narratives. To your left would be general fiction; literature, poetry, and writing; art and photography books; science fiction, fantasy, and paranormal romances (werewolves, vampires, and demons, oh my; or, as Jack calls them, "Fur and Fang Flings").

On the opposite side of the store is what we casually term the "nonfiction room," something of a misnomer since its central shelves hold Christian novels. Along the edges run science, education, comparative religion, history, travel, entertainment (mostly music and television), biography, and economics. Directly opposite this shelf, customers find the shop sign they like best: "Humor is in the bathroom—seriously." (Hey, we just flat ran out of room. Danielle Steel, Barbara Taylor Bradford, and Barbara Delinsky are in there, too. It's not an editorial comment.)

To the right of the bathroom is the staircase

leading to our living quarters, where the dogs hang out on plush pillows during the day, whining at customers until they reach their hands over the baby gate blocking the lower landing and pet them. Opposite the staircase is a single shelf sporting another favorite sign: PATTERSON, CORNWALL, GRISHAM, THE CLARKS: AND THANK YOU BUT, NO, WE DON'T WANT TO BUY ANY. It is this overloaded bestseller shelf that incapacitates the downstairs switch for the upstairs light. I know (1) it's not James Patterson's fault and (2) he probably wouldn't care, but we feel a twinge of resentment every time we restock his section. If we could just sell down his pile of books, we could get the use of this switch back . . .

Straight on from here lies the Mysteries and Thrillers Room, with a small porch jutting off it holding the Children's section. A former coat closet became the Teen Nook. Back to the bathroom and going left, you enter the half of our kitchen given over to the shop, where we keep—what else?—cookbooks. Also crafts, gardening, and horror. (The paranormals pushed horror out of the fiction room. Jack swore he could hear Robert McCammon's werewolves snarling at the John Saul and Peter Straub novels.)

The door at the back of the former kitchen leads to what was Jack's man-cave, now shared with the rest of the species as the Guys with Big Guns section. To the left of the man-cave a door leads to the carport Jack enclosed for my chair caning business, which slowly got taken over by books advertised for sale online. Just before the garage door, a small but deep closet houses the infamous Quick Trades section. Although people often cite QT as their favorite section, they tend not to linger because Beulah and Val-Kyttie's side-by-side litter boxes rest just below the bottom shelf. (The girls won't share a bathroom.)

It stinks that we can't afford to overlook the space above the litter boxes, but that's not the worst place we've squeezed out a few more feet. Straining to use every nook and corner efficiently, Jack has modified shelves to fit against windows, across counters, into the kitchen crannies reserved for a stove and refrigerator. I once threatened to crochet a hammock and drape it from the ceiling to hold tiny gift books—the fleas of the second-hand selling world. The silly wee things fall into crevices everywhere until Heather's broom liberates them.

Now, with that floor plan in mind, what could bring more pleasure than to be the guest manager presiding over such an exotic flock of humming, throbbing, tightly packed books for a day? Friends do indeed clamor to be on the substitute book-slinger list. Paige, a student from the college, lived in the guest room one summer in return for watching the shop while Jack and I traveled; we got the idea from the famous Shakespeare and

Company bookstore in Paris. When he counted up one night, Jack named more than thirty people who have helped out at what friends nicknamed "The Beckwelch Bookselling Cooperative."

But none of them can find the light switches.

As every inch of our establishment's wall space from the floor to six feet up is covered with shelving, the switches are hidden by books. We always tell the store-sitter what titles they lurk behind, but at the end of the day we come home to a dark bookstore operated by flashlight and candles—or worse. Once we arrived to find all the volumes from the third shelf of histories—the next section over from where the switch actually nestled—on the floor and that day's guest seller sitting in the gathered gloom, draining a bottle of wine.

Our favorite seller-and-switch story is the time we pulled up at midnight to every light still blazing. A moment later, the phone rang, and Peggy's voice said without preamble, "I remembered how hard it was to find them last time, so as soon as you showed me where they were and left, I went around and turned them all on. They stayed on all day."

Good friend, bad electric bill. But one has to admire Peggy's problem-solving prowess—not to mention her ability to recognize the sound of our motor driving past her house. (Actually, that's not an unusual skill in a small town.)

My friend Jenny, from the writing group, says, "If it weren't for the damn light switches, this would be a great gig. There's a whole different kind of energy to this place: busy, yet calm at the same time. I don't know any other work environments like that."

When my friends say such things, I remember the hum of the libraries that graced my childhood—and smile.

CHAPTER 20
The Network

It is not so much our friends' help that helps us as the confident knowledge that they will help us.

—Epicurus

JACK AND I MISSED THE exact moment when we changed from "those new people who own that place" to "Jack and Wendy, who run our town's bookstore." Too busy running "that place" to notice the gentle slip from suspicion to trust, we just looked up one day and found ourselves surrounded by a network of customers, friends, and fellow citizens.

However, we can pinpoint the day our new status came home to roost. (In retrospect, people begging to take a turn at the helm should have been a clue, but most of those people had become friends as well as customers, so we didn't take it too seriously.)

One summer Saturday, some five years into our sojourn as bookstore owners, a man shuffled in and stood at the door of the fiction room, looking around in a vague sort of way. Typing on my laptop at the table, I glanced up and smiled as Jack headed toward him with his customary "Good morning! Help you find something?"

The man said, "Well, do you have any books about reading?"

I suppressed a snort of laughter.

"What type of reading?" Jack said, ever polite.

"Well," the man drawled, eyes moving from Jack, to me, back to Jack, "about learning to read."

A couple of things were starting to sink in: the way he stood, slumped and still; the fact that his eyes didn't roam the shelves, which is what most people's do even while they're speaking to one of us. They can't wait to get started, but this man stood, bearlike, eyes darting back and forth.

Jack shot me a look that said *out of my league here,* so I smiled at this potential customer. "Who is learning to read, a child or an adult?"

"Me," he answered. "I need to learn to read."

Ah. Got it. Hey, good for you! I thought. Aloud, I said, "Okay. We have some literacy—um, some books about learning to read here, but do you have someone who can help you, because most of them are designed to be used by someone who can read, and they go over them with the person who can't. You would have a hard time using them yourself."

"Oh. Well, no. I live alone."

"You're going to want someone to help you, because it's really hard to learn to read by yourself. I'm pretty sure there are classes here in town. Let me check." I pulled my laptop lid open again and thought fast. I didn't have a clue where such classes might be held, but could think of three people who would: Isabel, who was on every do-gooder board of directors for forty miles; Jessica, a counselor at the local college; and Paul, the director of a youth agency.

As the man expounded on his story, I e-mailed all three: *Help! Man in bookstore needs instant answers on literacy classes; he can recognize his own name, no numeracy or literacy beyond that. Please call!*

Within two minutes, the phone rang. Jessica asked for some details, then told me where to send "Steve." No sooner had I hung up with her than the phone rang again.

"Tell me to call, then be on the phone?" Isabel scolded. "Lemme talk at 'im."

Jack walked Steve over to the location where classes were held, which turned out to be just a few blocks from his home. (We were afraid he'd get nervous about finding it based on street signs and landmarks.) While he was gone, the phone rang again—someone from the youth agency had phoned the person who ran the classes, and she was returning my call.

When he got back, Jack sat at the table fingering

a cool drink—it had to have been at least ninety degrees out there—and said, "That was amazing."

"I'm feeling a bit dazed myself," I said. "Fifty-four years old, and only able to read his name?"

Jack's hand waved in negation. "I meant how fast we activated the network. He got hooked up within—what, ten minutes?"

I hadn't thought about the undercurrents of what had happened, but its import suddenly flooded me. First, a man who probably felt that he had every reason to be suspicious of judgment or ridicule from those incomer owners had walked into our store and asked for help. Next, I had known who to call. And last, all three of the people contacted returned my call almost instantly—on a Saturday.

Jack leaned back in his chair and stretched his arms over his head. "I don't know which feels better: helping him, or getting help to help him."

Four years earlier, at Witold's house, the moment when he'd called us a community center had passed quietly; we'd thought we were settled in then, but later discovered a bit more work to be done. This moment also passed without a great deal of hoopla, and it stuck; one day we were outsiders, the next an integral part of the duct tape and black jelly beans and baling wire that holds society together. And while we can tell you the day we knew our status had changed, the exact point when it did slipped past in a blur of just getting on with what was in front of us to do.

Helping to keep a community cohesive is part of what a bricks-and-mortar bookstore does; what computer could handle the day-to-day doings of a bookshop with half as much dignity, grace, or humor? Of course, a computer probably would be too logical to get into such precarious positions in the first place.

Running a bookstore is one big bundle of paradoxes. It is joyfully absurd, yet about the time you think you'll die laughing, someone comes along with a story that breaks your heart. It is poignant and painful, but when you get depressed by the human needs and grievances, balm from twenty generations of collected wisdom waits on the shelves. Not to mention the collected wisdom of friends.

If I had to pinpoint the biggest gift this place has given us, it would be creating a sense of belonging, of community. Take the time our friend Becky's sister died, after a long, tense illness that ripped at the fabric of the family. While Becky and her husband attended the funeral, Isabel and Jack split cat-sitting duties for Chunky Monkey, Patches, and Minnie. (I was traveling a fair bit so couldn't participate.)

Becky's three cats took little notice of the new sitters one way or another, and no one worried about a thing until Becky and Tony returned.

Tony called that afternoon. "Where's Chunky?"
Uh-ohhhh.

Turns out Chunks had taken advantage of the new arrangements to fulfill his lifelong dream of seeing the outside world firsthand. He'd slipped through the front door during either Isabel's or Jack's visit. The fact that it could not be ascertained on whose watch he escaped meant both Isabel and Jack felt like miserable heaps of failure.

"She didn't need this, the day after a funeral," was all Tony said, driving the knife in deeper with that one gentle statement. Jack, Isabel, and I swung into overdrive.

Flyers sporting Chunky Monkey's picture went up on telephone poles, store windows, anything that held still long enough. No one called. Becky, Isabel, and I patrolled the streets, calling "Chuuuuuunkeeeeeee." No cat answered.

The second week, we took out an ad in the local paper. Two days later, a woman called Becky. "I think I have your tomcat. I found him in the grocery store parking lot. I opened my car door and asked if he wanted to come home with me, and the big guy jumped right in."

The woman couldn't get to Becky's house before seven that evening, so Becky was on tenterhooks. "Chunky's not that friendly. Would he do that, just hop in somebody's car? But maybe he was hungry, poor baby."

All day long it went on like that, until the woman arrived. None of us was there except Tony, who told us later that when the lady carried the cat up to the door, Becky reached out and grabbed him in exuberance. *"Chunks!"* she shrieked as the cat cuddled against her bosom, purring and rubbing and smiling.

The woman had become attached to her foundling, so she'd rather hoped it wasn't Becky's cat. Becky, being Becky, had been feeding two tuxedo-colored kittens in her garage, cuddly creatures who longed for a life of soft laps and caresses. She moved swiftly, introducing the kittens—who were at their most winsome point of fuzzy irresistibility—to her cat's benefactor. The lady went home with the twins, and Chunks moved back onto Becky's lap.

Except . . .

The Tuesday after the reunion, when the usual gang of women met for Needlework Night, Becky stayed home to bond with Chunky, and talk turned to the happy ending.

"Have you seen the new Chunky?" Isabel asked me as we stitched.

"What do you mean, 'new Chunky'?" I replied.

"He's older. And oranger, and has more stripes. And he's really friendly. I don't remember too well what Chunky looked like, but I always thought he was more . . . yellow. Not to mention standoffish."

Lynne chimed in. "Yeah, he seems . . . different."

I opened my mouth, but Sarah beat me to it. "Still, if Becky's happy, what does it matter?"

We all nodded assent. "Difficult funeral, hard times, what's a little denial if it makes her happy" mutters went 'round the table, and we counted our stitches, content to let it go.

All except Mark, husband to Needlework regular Elizabeth, and a plain dealer. Becky cleans house for Mark and Elizabeth, and Mark and Becky are the best of buddies. Sweeping their kitchen floor that Friday, she prattled on about the change in Chunky's personality (and fur) brought on by "his ordeal."

Mark emitted a skeptical noise. "You know that's not—"

Words died in his throat as gentle Becky suddenly pinned him against a cabinet with her dust mop. "It's Chunky," she growled, shaking the weapon at his abdomen.

"Of course it is, absolutely, right, yeah," Mark babbled, and then slipped away to his man-cave, presumably to get a shot of nerve-calming bourbon. Having Becky yell at you is rather like being attacked by a golden retriever.

Another week passed. The next Needlework Night, Becky mentioned that Minnie Mae, Chunky's sister, showed "reattachment issues. She just doesn't seem to like him anymore." Eyebrows shot up around the table, and someone began talking, fast and high-pitched, about a movie they'd seen the night before.

When the girls left that evening, Isabel hung back and confided to me, "You know, this Chunky thing has got me rattled. I see yellow cats everywhere these days. I've been feeding a stray one under the empty house across the street for almost a week now. Well, good night."

In the middle of the night, I bolted upright. Jack stirred next to me, aided by my hand gripping his shoulder and shaking hard.

"It's Chunky," I said.

Jack sighed the sigh of a husband in peril. "We've been over this before. If Becky thinks it's Chunks, then . . . wait a minute, it *is* Chunky?"

"No, not Chunky, the other Chunky. That Chunky's not him, but the real Chunky, he's Chunky," I said in triumph.

Turning on the bedside table lamp, Jack held his head in his hands. At the foot of the mattress, Bert the terrier jumped down and ambled, stiff-legged and resentful, into the living room to get some sleep.

I clarified. "See, the Chunky that Becky says is Chunky, we all know it's not Chunky, but since she really wants it to be, we're not saying anything. But the Chunky that really is Chunky, that's the stray cat Isabel is feeding under the porch."

Jack stared in disbelief. "Do you mean to tell me that the whole time everyone, including Isabel herself, has been scouring the town for Chunky, Isabel has been feeding him back at her house? And never made the connection? Do you really believe that's possible? Oh, never mind. All right, we'll call first thing in the morning."

By the time we awoke, the story had ended. Isabel had gone home that night and rung Becky. "I know you have Chunky Monkey back and all, but there's a yellow stray across the street from us, and—"

"I'll be over first thing in the morning," Becky said. At dawn, Isabel's doorbell rang. Isabel, yawning, led Becky across the yard to the abandoned house, where she started to rattle a food container. But Becky let out a high, keening "Chuuuuuuuuuuuuunks," and the cat shot from under the house into her arms.

"Oh, poor stray thing," Becky said, her face buried in the cat's fur as he nuzzled and purred, glommed to her chest. "I'll take him to the vet and get him—er, it—checked out." Exit Becky, wearing an extra fur bosom.

Isabel received a phone call later that day. "Don't be mad at me," Becky begged.

Bewildered, Isabel said, "Of course I'm not mad. But why did you keep sayin' that other cat was Chunky if he was still missin'? I might have connected the dots sooner."

"Well, I didn't lie about the other cat, it's just that . . . well, you and Jack were so miserable, and it was just nicer, easier, if I told everyone the other cat was Chunky, and then when you said about this cat, I just couldn't help it, I had to find out. So now we've got our baby boy back plus we've got Dudley."

"Dudley?" Isabel stammered.

"Tony named him that. He's Dudley-Do-Right, because he helped us do right by our friends."

It has to be a sign of love when your friends will deny reality on your behalf. Dudley and Chunky continue to live side by side, brothers in all but biology. And the sisterhood of friends who would go deep into denial for each other continue to live side by side, too, and gather every Tuesday night at the bookstore.

It is easy to love one's friends. Yet even the customers we sometimes wanted to throttle showed us care and concern, made us feel part of a community. Lulu—she of the Scott stamp— came by when I was under the weather, tucked up in bed and croaking. Jack probably didn't look much better, since he'd had to manage the shop, cater to my every whim, and give the hated quiz to my cultural anthropology class the night before. (I had started adjuncting.)

Enter Lulu, slamming open the shop door with her customary "Hey-ho there!"

Jack gave her a halfhearted wave.

LULU: Where's Wendy?

JACK: Sick in bed, I'm afraid.

LULU: Huh.

JACK: [fingers crossed to prevent the wrath of God because he's lying] She'll be sorry to have missed you. After anything special?

LULU: Huh. What're you gonna do for supper?

JACK: Pardon?

LULU: If your wife's sick, what're you gonna eat?

[Stage director's notes: Jack is a better cook than I am. He is a dab hand at curries and omelets and paellas, plus many other fine foods. The idea that he would eat poorly because I was poorly flummoxed him into speechlessness—no easy task.]

LULU: Never mind. Go across to the store and get me a pound of cheddar cheese. You got macaroni noodles? [moving toward kitchen; we still had one downstairs then; Lulu steps over the privacy gate and opens our fridge] Hmm, get me some milk, too.

JACK: Er, I can't leave the shop just now.

LULU: [straightening] Tell you what, this will be easier at my house. Back in a little while.

[Two hours later, Lulu appears just as the bookshop is closing and thrusts a rectangular object wrapped in a towel into Jack's arms.]
LULU: Heat that at 350 until it's warm through. Can't stay. 'Bye.

Jack said it was the best macaroni and cheese he'd eaten since his mother's.

CHAPTER 21

Ceridwen

*It often requires more courage to read
some books than it does to fight a battle.*
—Sutton Elbert Griggs

PERHAPS LIBRARIES AND BOOKSHOPS seemed
noisy in part because they contain such
competing ideas within their walls, varied values
and beliefs that have a hard time living side by
side in people. Certainly Jack and I learned, as we
settled into being a part of the town and the
region, that what a bookshop sells, and to whom,
can be a powerful political (or personal) act open
to many interpretations. But one of the things we
love most about the community that has formed
around the bookstore is its encompassing nature—
and we work hard, consciously, to protect that.

As Quakers, Jack and I believe in Jesus as God's
resurrected sin offering. Beyond that, we're not
big on theology. Yet negotiating even such limited
boundaries in the shop proved tricky. Our part of
Appalachian America has a reputation for . . . shall

we say, seeing things one way only, and we wanted neither to offend those with narrow views nor become part of their team.

The 1800s German poet and journalist Heinrich Heine correctly predicted that "Where one burns books, one will eventually burn people." I'm not going there with my life or my shop, so in addition to Bibles, we sell the Koran, assorted Jewish texts, the Book of Mormon, and tarot cards. The shop opened with two shelves for Christian titles, later joined by a comparative religion shelf. (We thought "comparative religion" sounded encompassing yet noncombative in a predominantly Christian region.) At some point a really nice set of scholarly books on Jewish holy days and rituals came in: Pesach, Seder, Yom Kippur. We shelved these expensive and esoteric volumes in comparative religion, where a browsing woman spotted the handsome blue and brown volumes one day. Her nose wrinkled as she came to me, holding at arm's length an open book showing side-by-side Hebrew and English.

"Why are you selling occult books?" she demanded.

I was speechless. Jack came to my rescue, explaining in his beautiful, get-away-with-murder Scottish accent that the pages taught about rituals found in the Old Testament. The woman, clearly having a hard time understanding Jack's accent, sniffed. He repeated himself, more slowly, until she appeared mollified. Closing the book, she laid it on a shelf.

"Well, I thought that writing was something else. I believe in the New Testament." She had the grace to sound embarrassed. It turned out she thought the writing was Arabic. (Don't ask me about the mental processes that took her from "Arabic" to "occult.")

Quick confession: raised in a religious tradition that perhaps emphasized fear over love, I have worked very hard to kick the apple as far as possible from the tree without undermining the bare essentials. Keith, a college pal who is also a lay pastor, once summed up my theological standpoint as "Jesus is Lord; now let's have tea and cookies." He wasn't being flip, just descriptive.

Quakers tend to be pretty relaxed about theology, believing people who disagree shouldn't be considered evil on that basis alone. Just try talking first, get to know each other, and if you still want to declare the other person Satan incarnate after supper, that option remains open to you. Jack and I keep this as our baseline when dealing with people and books, although I do pray over tarot cards before setting them out. (It seems like a gentle way of quashing any negative influence they might have without pawing the ground, snorting and angling for a chance to lock horns.)

Back when I was a full-time storyteller, the tourism officer from Wigtown—Scotland's town made up of bookshops, like the famous Hay-on-Wye in Wales—hired me to tell stories at a festival. My hubby planned to travel along so we could enjoy some serious browse time prior to the performance, but two weeks before the festival, Jack's ninety-one-year-old mum began failing fast. Jack said not to cancel, but he clearly wouldn't be going with me. The night I left for the gig, Mum went into the hospital, not expected to come out again. I took the scenic route to Wigtown, through a secluded nature preserve, driving along the windy forest road trying to de-stress and not feel guilty. Jack really wanted me to go, but it felt wrong. Suddenly, knowledge hit. She was gone. I glanced at the clock: 7:20 P.M.

On the call home after arriving at the bed and breakfast, Jack told me his mum had died at 7:20 and he didn't want me to come back tonight. The funeral would be as soon as I returned two days hence, the arrangements made long before by Mum herself. Everything should stay as normal as possible. He needed that. We said good night and I hung up the phone, pushed through the fog of unreality to my room, and cried myself to sleep.

Next morning I wandered the village, lost and alone. Each bookstore has a theme in Wigtown, but I wove in and out of the shops indiscriminately. I wound up in Ceridwen's Cauldron, a store carrying Wiccan and alternative healing items. Ceridwen is the Celtic Lady of Inspiration, patron of poets and those seeking wisdom. Willingness to listen to other viewpoints or not, I never would have walked randomly into a Wiccan store had it been a normal day.

It wasn't a normal day, not by a far cry. My mother-in-law, a lovely woman with considerable strength of character, who had held my hand two days before in her hospital room and said, "I'm glad he's got you," was dead. And Jack sat home alone. Nope, not a normal day, not normal at all.

The shop owner chatted to me, asking where I came from, was my trip business or holiday. *Whoosh,* out came the story as guilt and confusion drilled a hole through self-control. Only pride kept me from bursting into tears. At one point I actually heard myself saying, "And I shouldn't even have come in here because I know it's a shop that sells bad things but I wasn't paying attention."

You can only kick that apple so far. . . .

The owner, a round-faced woman with curly black hair, acted as though she dealt with hysterical, grieving bigots every day. She rose, said "Just a minute," and went through a low door in the back wall. She returned a few moments later with a laden tea tray. "Come into the garden." She led me through and indicated a small wooden table in her courtyard. "Sit down and take your time," she said, laying out cup, saucer, milk jug, sugar bowl, and biscuits. "No one comes back here. There are books in the shed if you want something to look at." Exit the owner of Ceridwen's Cauldron, closing the courtyard door behind her.

I waited until the door closed to start sobbing. That's when the extent of her kindness became clear: a box of tissues waited beside the teapot.

That day in Ceridwen's Cauldron reminds me again and again that a little kindness travels a long, long way, while meanness never taught anyone much of anything except how to reciprocate with more meanness. Quakers believe people should be allowed to walk the path toward truth without others setting themselves up as traffic police. If, as the book of Ecclesiastes says, eternity has been placed in the hearts of humans by God, maybe we have to find it for ourselves for it to mean something.

Jack and I have seen firsthand the gracious goodness that comes from people of dissimilar views remembering that we love and are loved by God. Tony who pastors the Presbyterian church just a block down the street came to us with a plan; he wanted to host a monthly gathering called Let's Talk, and thought Tales would be an ideal location. "The bookstore, with so many viewpoints side by side on the shelf, is the perfect venue for bringing people with different ideas together," he said.

The group that formed has few ground rules, the two most important being mutual respect and one-word topics; discussions have covered suffering, happiness, citizenship, and evil. I thought of the Wigtown shop owner—who never told me her name; in my mind she is Ceridwen—often during Let's Talk, but particularly on the night when a grinning man asserted that the Holocaust was God's judgment on the Jewish nation for rejecting Jesus as the Messiah. In the moment that followed, our friend Witold, Polish by birth and tolerant by nature, blinked once. A man whose father was a concentration camp survivor half rose from his seat. The silence lasted only a split second, but tension crackled and the very air seemed to be pushing on us—until Tony asked, in a mild tone, "That viewpoint is difficult for me to understand. Why do you think this?"

The man lost his grin and dissembled a moment before mumbling that he didn't really think that, he'd just wondered if we'd heard the idea before. It turned out that he'd thrown his verbal grenade not as a discussion point, but in hopes of getting a rise out of the assembly. What he got instead was a gentle voice making just enough space for him to set things right. Which he did.

Why do people like to fight about the worst

possible angles of theological reasoning and argue minutiae into the ground? Isn't it better to give each other what Ceridwen gave me—a little space and a lot of kindness?

A couple of years ago, Jack and I started attending that nearby Presbyterian church. I'd been helping with their food bank and lunch delivery program, and liked the women I met there: Virginia Meador and Norma Siemens, matriarchs who kept half the town's social programs functioning with their volunteer hours, and Grace of the perfect trouser pleats and bad mummy jokes. They often invited us to attend, and eventually we did. The nearest Society of Friends (as Quakers are officially known) was a two-hour drive, so our second year in Big Stone, we began hosting a monthly Meeting in the bookstore. Of course, this being a small town, "They've even started their own church!" came rippling back via grass roots anonymity, but we didn't mind. It was kind of cute—and a Quaker group isn't called a church.

The people at our Quaker gathering bring food to share together after each meeting. The meeting before Christmas, Tony suggested we walk down to the fellowship hall with our lunch and share the holiday repast prepared by their congregation. So the Presbyterians, in sweater sets and suit-and-tie, dished up couscous next to the baked ham and declared it good. The Quakers, in denim overalls and swooshy skirts, ate most of the banana pudding, and thanked its makers. The two groups talked pacifism, social justice, and favorite fishing holes. And there was Peace on Earth, Goodwill to People.

CHAPTER 22

The Way We Buy Now (with Apologies to Trollope)

Tough choices face the biblioholic at every step of the way—like choosing between reading and eating, between buying new clothes and buying books, between a reasonable lifestyle and one of penurious but masochistic happiness lived out in the wallow of excess.

—Tom Raabe,
Biblioholism: The Literary Addiction

THE FACT THAT MY HUSBAND is a Scotsman often causes people to joke about frugality. The truth is, Jack is not an avid penny-pincher; I am the queen of thrift stores and garage sales. My husband enjoys a good flea-market ramble as much as I do, but he will buy an item new if needed, or sometimes just because he desires it. Me, my hands shake when I try to pay retail.

Fortunately, what used to be considered parsimony has now become known as the Green Movement.

Previously unthinkable as it may have been to recycle envelopes in professional offices, one can observe them in the twenty-first century issuing from New York high-rises, bearing stickers that proudly proclaim their green credentials. The same goes for biking, walking, or busing to work; what used to be weird is now in vogue.

Jack and I don't shop thrift stores because we want to save money—although that's never been something we scorned. It's more that we figure since the item is already made, the resources for it extracted and expended, then if the bowl/purse/belt/record player/silly little decorative statue is still in good nick, why not use it up instead of starting over? We'd never get a puppy from a pet store or a breeder when so many strays need good homes; why buy a new Crock-Pot if we spot one in a secondhand store? About the only manufactured items Jack and I insist on getting new are big appliances and handmade items.

I recently picked up a hot-air popper at a thrift store for a dollar, after discovering that microwave popcorn—that delicacy so touted and prized back in the 1980s—is pretty bad for you, while your basic corn kernel blown up by heated air scores high in nutrition, low in calories and additives. (It pays to have friends in public health who can interpret nutrition labels.) Most of my clothing comes from garage sales and thrift stores, as does much of Jack's. It's not hard to find things that still look new, have no stains, fit well, and are flattering. Tested those last two criteria in a department store lately?

And of course we bought reading material secondhand long before we started our own shop. Back in Scotland, a little tearoom lined with shelves in the tiny town of Milnathort served as a treat on rainy Saturdays. We'd browse the used books, donate some of our own, have a cuppa, and meander home to sit at the dining room table, reading the afternoon away until it was time to make evening tea.

I can't tell you the number of earrings Jack has bought me at festivals where we were performing, or about the photography, objets d'art, and sometimes even clothing we've purchased at these venues, for ourselves or as gifts. Ambling along the booths between sets, we'd do our yearly birthday and Christmas shopping, confident yuppies seeking out unusual things our family and friends wouldn't have seen (and thus had the chance to buy for themselves) in the box stores and franchised boutiques of America.

We also went in with neighbors and bought a cow (slaughtered and divvied up into one- or two-pound plastic bags, thank you), which soon filled the garage deep-freeze. A friend and I purchased milk goats and pasteurized our own dairy products. I get eggs from a place at the edge of town, where I can see the producers clucking in the yard when I drive by. And during the summer, we load up on veggies at the farmers' markets, one just a block from our house on Saturdays, one Tuesday evenings near the college where I teach. Five fruit trees in our back garden—pear, heirloom apple, and peach—round out the diet nicely. (Those trees give for the nation; the summer we moved in, time that could have been spent getting the bookstore ready to open disappeared into jars of fruit butter and stuffing the freezer with apple bites. We even gave about twenty-five pounds of fresh fruit to the food bank.)

Between the cow, the goat, the chickens, the farmers' market, and our own fruit trees, we source a lot of local food in the summer; visits to the grocery store drop to filling in staples like sugar and whiskey. One day our friend Marcia joined us for dinner, and as we sat down to vegetarian pizza with goat cheese, we realized that we knew the names of those who had produced everything on the table, except the flour in the crust. Even the bottle of wine Marcia brought came from Mountain Rose, the local winery.

Recounting this story at yet another dinner party about a month later, when my husband had made his infamous tandoori beef curry for our friends Mark and Elizabeth, Jack laughed suddenly and stood from his chair. Holding it up, he patted its seat.

"It gets better," he said. "Wendy caned the chair seats we're sitting on, and we bought the frames at garage sales." The four of us started giggling, looking around the room, pointing out the harp Jack built for me (from a kit) for Christmas; the casserole dish holding the curry, crafted by Fiona; the drawing on the wall of wine pouring into a glass, done by an appreciative customer. The big oak table where we sat—which Jack sometimes called the heart of the bookstore because of its position in the center of the fiction room, where so many special events swirled around it—came from an antique store, bought years ago in far-off Snakeland. I recounted with pride how most of our Christmas presents lay wrapped upstairs, handmade items purchased directly from their makers.

Then Mark pointed to the bookshelves Jack had built and said, "Okay, a lot of the things in this house, bookstore, whatever, come straight from the hand of the person who made them, right? What about the books?" As our hilarity and jokes about cheapo Scotsmen turned to blank stares, Mark persisted in his point. "Think about it. We'll each pay more money to have food we trust on the table. But we want to pay less money to have things that are mass produced. Jack bought a harp kit because it was cheaper than buying a ready-made harp."

"Aye, but also because it made the harp more

special," Jack interjected, and I nodded vigorously.

"It means so much more to me to have a harp Jack made than to have an expensive model. And the sound is just lovely. He did a great job on it. Who's to say one bought from someone else would have been so well crafted?" My voice may have held a hint of smug self-righteousness.

"That proves my point," Mark said, smirking. "Some things we get off the highway to shop for—I mean the mainstream marketing highway, you know, buying from Walmart or a big chain store like that. We get off the beaten path because we want them to be special. It may cost more—the food, the materials for these chair seats we're sitting on (and by the way, Wendy, they're really comfortable)—but it's special. And some things we buy because they're cheaper. The harp's more of a fluke; it was cheaper, but it was only nicer to build one yourself because you knew what you were doing, Jack."

I jumped in. "I just read a book about this: *The $64 Tomato*. It's the memoir of a guy who reckons up what it costs to grow his garden—which he does every year because his family's used to the better food from it—and he realizes that it's way, way more expensive than buying the same things at the grocery store."

Mark took the interruption well. "That's what I'm saying. How much of how we shop is about making our lives better, and how much is about convenience, or just not thinking too hard about what we're doing? Which things did you pay more for so you could be happier with them, and which did you pay *less* for so you'd be happier with them? And"—his long finger jabbed again at the bookshelves lining the room—"I'm not letting you off on this point. What about buying books new, as opposed to buying them secondhand?"

I blinked at the shelves. So did Jack and Mark's wife Elizabeth. "I'm not understanding about the books," I finally said.

"Authors make things. They make the words that go in the books. We all like handmade things. You're proud of your handmade presents. You feel like you're supporting artists. But you're selling other people's art in here, and they're not getting any of the money. How do you justify that?" Mark folded his arms across his chest, then unfolded them to fill his glass with locally produced wine.

Gobsmacked is the word in Britain for when someone startles you so totally that you can't speak. Jack and I were gobsmacked.

At the time of this discussion, I think I summed up with something brilliant like "Uhhhhh." Don't be envious; years of storytelling and college teaching converged to make me so articulate on the fly.

Okay, so let's unpack this idea. New book stores—by which I mean stores that deal in new books rather than secondhand—encounter a recurrent sore point in the way people buy now. In this era of online shopping, a few bricks-and-mortar establishments I've seen even have signs up in the window: FIND IT HERE, BUY IT HERE, KEEP US HERE. They're referring to that famous practice some shoppers call e-bargain hunting, when a person identifies a book he or she might like from the shelf of a new book store, jots down the title, then hauls out a smartphone to check if the price on Amazon is cheaper.

Although Jack and I mostly shop used book stores, when we get a rare day out in Asheville, North Carolina, we make sure to stop at Malaprop's, one of the last large independent (as in, not part of a chain) booksellers in the United States. Careful with money as we are, we see it as a point of honor to buy books there, because we believe in the store, the people, and the concept of local buy, local supply. And it's the closest independent bookstore to us—a two-hour drive. That's kind of a warning shot across the bow, don't you think? When you were a kid, how many independent bookshops beckoned within twenty minutes' drive of the house? Where I live now, besides our store there is only a Books-A-Million and one more secondhand bookseller within a forty-five minute drive.

At Malaprop's one August morning, Jack and I cruised the shelves, picking up and putting down various tomes on travel, anthropology, music, even fiction. On this particular summer day, languid and lethargic, I found nothing that suited me—although I did pause briefly over a memoir about small-town life and work that looked interesting. In the end, I didn't deem it enticing enough to buy. Jack got a musical biography while I, out of duty more than desire, bought a book of amigurumi patterns. (Cute baby animals to crochet. Old habits die hard.)

A few weeks later, I happened to be cruising the famous McKay Used Books in Knoxville, Tennessee. McKay is actually a local chain store for secondhand books and music, started by a husband and wife who were so successful they expanded to four locations. Stopping by my favorite section, narrative nonfiction, I spotted the book I'd eschewed at Malaprop's, priced at seventy-five cents. Well heck, I hadn't been willing to take a chance on it for fourteen dollars, but this fraction of a dollar was a no-brainer. I tossed it into my filling cart with nary a second thought.

It turns out I didn't much care for the book and set it aside after a few chapters. This little anecdote can be read (no pun intended) two ways. Perhaps I dodged a $13.25 bullet, because the title wouldn't have pleased jaded-reader me no matter what; this interpretation makes me a wise shopper taking no chances. Or perhaps, if I had paid more for it, I would have tried harder to like the book.

Did expectation diminish with price? No one, me included, will ever know.

What I do know is that not everybody can afford those choices; people on minimum wage, welfare, fixed incomes, and so on have to be careful with their money. No one faults necessary frugality. Jack and I can afford (four years on from the terror of debt and humiliation) to pay more in support of smaller retailers, so we usually do, test-case memoir notwithstanding. We recognize that independent shops depend on local customers; had I been more drawn to that particular memoir, I would have bought it in Malaprop's because I liked being in Malaprop's. It's akin to sitting in a restaurant; the price you're paying isn't for the food—the least cost of being there—but for the service, the seating, the ambiance. That's why you get to complain about stuff; you paid for it.

New book stores are brain food stores. (So are secondhanders, but our retail concerns about sticking around are the wee bit different.) Thus, if you're lucky enough to have a cool little bookshop near you, I'm sure you do your part to keep it there, even if it means a thirteen-dollar gamble now and again.

Back to Mark's point, though. He brought an itchy rubbing awareness of how our bookstore fit into the wider world of reading, echoed a couple of years later when I'd actually written a book and my agent sold it. Suddenly I was an author, someone who would make money (or not) by the number of times the book retailed as a new object.

Elizabeth came over one day soon after I learned the book you are currently reading would be published. She kept me company as I did a long overdue deep clean of the upstairs rooms. When I told her about the more-than-expected advance headed my way, she teased, "Well, you can stop shopping at thrift stores now."

Still in a daze, I blurted the first thing that came to mind. "I didn't write it for money." Which was true.

She responded instantly, looking me in the eye. "I know you didn't. You wrote it because . . ." Her voice trailed into a question.

We stared at each other for a moment; then Elizabeth crossed her arms and raised her eyebrows. "You wrote it, because . . ." One hand untucked to roll in a "here's where you talk" gesture.

Do you know, I hadn't thought about why I'd written it? It just had to be done. Like that old cliché about climbing mountains: because it was there.

Why do writers write? After all, it's dangerous. As Patricia Hampl, an author whose wordcraft I admire, said, "You can't put much on paper before you betray your secret self, try as you will to keep things civil." Carolyn Jourdan, author of the sweet and funny memoir *Heart in the Right*

Place, cautioned me at a luncheon, "Get a psychiatrist to read your book before you publish. You have no idea what you'll be telling people about yourself until you see it in print, and then it's too late."

So why take the chance on putting my whiny, neo-bitchy, self-centered prose about living the bibliophilic dream out there? I think writers write because it's a device to make sense of what's happening around us, to order and calm and clarify our thoughts. We scribble down flashes of insight, observations, ideas because we believe other people will identify with us, understand what we think, feel the same way about something, or even—oh great arrogance—benefit from what we have to relate.

Because it's fun.

I wrote about the bookstore for all those reasons. In the beginning my pages didn't feel important to anyone else, just to Jack and me, but that was enough. I needed something to turn in at the monthly writer's group meetings, after all.

Then my friend Margie got saddled with the early draft.

Margie and I have almost nothing in common, except a wicked dry sense of humor and the belief that students are the ultimate reason for everything professors should do. She heads the natural sciences department at the college where I am on the teaching staff, and is a scientist's scientist. I hate math almost as much as chemistry, but we wound up having coffee once a month because we started a CABs club together. (Cynical Altruist Bitches. So now you know.) Membership is limited to people who do the right thing with martyred sighs and eye rolls, easily identified by their dashing about making stuff happen while complaining loudly that "it won't make a blind bit of difference." You know the type.

Quick but necessary sideline: I have Margie to thank for introducing me to those microscopic "water bears" that live in moss. She picked up a *National Geographic* on the library's coffee table and showed me an article on Tardigrades, complete with colored pictures. Tardigrades, aka water bears, are adorable cuddly looking creatures, complete with little claws and ears and everything.

Writers shouldn't be friends with scientists; it leads to fistfights. Margie rolled her eyes as I waxed eloquent about tardigrades, inventing on the spot a marital structure and kinship system. To her they were organisms; to me, a wee forest society waiting to be written about. We practically got thrown out of the library when Margie shouted me down as I began to verbally imagine how working tardigrade mothers might organize child care on snow days, "when their schools would be closed, of course. It snows inside moss, right? Heck, one flake could wipe out an entire village."

See, writers create because we have to. We'd explode otherwise.

Anyway, one day over coffee I told poor Margie one of the stories I'd jotted down about something that happened in the store, and she howled with laughter (earning us yet another dirty look from the library staff).

"That is really funny; you should write a book." She sighed, wiping her eyes.

"Funny you should say that," I said with a grin.

Margie read the whole draft, then encouraged me to send it off "to someone, you know, out there in publishing." So did my friend Cami, author of a running memoir called *Second Wind*. We'd been friends since high school, and she knew just who "out there" I needed to talk to. A supersonic flash of e-mail exchanges later, this nice New York woman I'd never met wanted to give other people the opportunity to read about what we did in the bookshop. Gratifying, yes. Most gratifying, and I'm grateful. And of course, turning out text is a full-time job for some. For most of us, though, writing is like singing in the shower; we don't do it believing someone will hear us.

So we write because we write. Fine. But how do we get paid for it? Well, most of us don't. And then there's the reality that neither Picasso nor his family received any of the massive fortunes now following his paintings, not to mention the legend of his beach drawings.

One day a man crested a seaside cliff and looked down on another man drawing with a stick in the sand—incredible swirls and lines he recognized as the work of Picasso. Without a camera, before cell phones, he simply sat and watched as the artist drew and drew until the tide came in and washed it all away. Then Pablo went whistling away with his stick over one shoulder.

Do you sing in the shower? Draw in the sand because it's there?

Elizabeth and I were deep in this discussion as we headed downstairs for a glass of something. Mike Ward, a friend of Jack's visiting from Scotland, was cooking evening tea—we love it when Mike visits—and added his thoughts.

"Lots of sales don't benefit the person who made the product, it's not just artistes," Mike said after hearing the gist of our conversation. His voice tinged "artistes" with an edge of something disrespectable. "Handcrafted furniture gets sold and resold, or even passed down in families as priceless. Houses, if they're actually built by one person, don't give the builder anything after the first sale. Speaking of, I think it's unusual in America nowadays—and for that matter in Britain as well—that any given object is made by a single person. Houses are kits, furniture is factory-produced, we buy computers and cars and household appliances that we can't fix ourselves and replace them when they break because there's no one person who created and hooked together all those fiddly bits inside them. No one can fix them, or at least the company tells you that.

"So it's two things that make up this idea. One, we're hard pressed to buy something that just one person made. That being the case, how can we give a living wage to a company and be sure any of it gets to those assembly-line people? Two, when you do get a handcrafted item, be it a house or a harp, it's only the first sale that benefits the creator. And one more thing, so three: books aren't handcrafted. They're a hybrid of original thought and production values. Isn't that the whole e-book question you were wrestling with last week? E-books eliminate production costs, thereby sharing new literature with the masses.

"There's no shame in a secondhand book sale not benefitting the author—although I think if you dig deeper, you'll find it does in the same way checking it out of a library does. It puts the word out—literally! People discover new authors in libraries. So even a bookstore run by an author, Wendy, is doing no harm by selling secondhand. The world has worked like that since the beginning of human trade; you make it, you sell it, and it's not yours anymore. Why should artists get hung up on that when everyone else lets go? It's that first bit that bothers me more, that we don't have much contact with the makers anymore, or the makers with their own items. That's only changed these last fifty years or so, the way I see it."

I always did like Mike.

Matthew Crawford, author of *Shop Class as Soulcraft*, wrote something very similar.

> Both as workers and as consumers, we feel we move in channels that have been projected from afar by vast impersonal forces. . . . Some people respond by learning to grow their own vegetables. . . . These agrarians say they get a deep satisfaction from recovering a more direct relationship to the food they eat. Others take up knitting, and find pride in wearing clothes they have made themselves. The home economics of our grandmothers is suddenly cutting-edge chic—why should this be?
>
> Frugality may be only a thin economic rationalization for a movement that really answers to a deeper need: We want to feel that our world is intelligible, so we can be responsible for it. . . . Many people are trying to recover a field of vision that is basically human in scale, and extricate themselves from dependence on the obscure forces of a global economy.

When Elizabeth and I bought goats, people joked that we were turning into conspiracy theorists, survivalists, weirdos. Goat cheese at the supermarket could be had cheaper and more simply than looking after its source all year, feeding, midwifing, housing, caring. Yes, but the cheese tastes better, and I have fondled the ears and looked into the eyes of the goat responsible. Her milk has been in my hands start to finish. It brings satisfaction, even relaxation, to come home from a hard day's intellectualizing at the college, or to head upstairs from time with the customers and curdle milk. Crawford is on to something with his comment that frugality is just a thin veil for the denied satisfaction of something else we crave.

Being an ethnographer, I have to point out the caveat that Jack and I live well as midrange middle-classers. We may not have a lot of ready cash, but we own a house outright, are dangerously overeducated, have confidence that the police and ambulance will come to our neighborhood if called, and know that family and friends could toss us a credit line if for some reason the bank would not.

Not everybody has these luxuries. In my poststudent years, I lived much closer to the lines of poverty and fear, yet even then the fear was of being "poor," not homeless. Some of my friends couch-surfed their way through graduate school, while others had to drop out of college for lack of that omnipresent-yet-never-enough green stuff we run our society on. Other people aren't in the same lifeboat as I am. Some are even in the water.

Would people in the water pay more to produce their own stuff—clothes, food, furniture, or houses—or are such activities the privilege (responsibility?) of those with enough money and time and leftover energy to do them? People working minimum-wage jobs at box stores may want to own a goat and make their own cheese, but where will the goat live, and when will they have time to milk? Not to mention, does eight hours plus overtime of keeping your retail zone clean and organized, zipping from rack to rack on your feet all day, leave you with enough energy to herd goats?

Jack sings a song by the famous Scottish poet Mary Brooksbank, a mill worker who became a union organizer: "Oh dear me, the world's ill-divided. Them that work the hardest are aye the least provided." That line, said the late Norman Buchan, a ballad singer who represented Glasgow in the United Kingdom parliament, is why he went into politics.

It's also the line that makes me think the way we sell books is honorable and right, and that when my book becomes a commodity traded on the secondhand market, that will be a happy and good thing to point to as an accomplishment in life. Then I can rest on the laurels of my own caned-chair bottoms.

CHAPTER 23

Booking Down the Road Trip

Suck every drop of living out of this life . . .
Sieve out every grain of happiness, grief,
excitement, stillness, or anger that a fully
lived life [can] offer.
                    —Cami Ostman, *Second Wind*

IT WAS PARTLY THE CONVERSATION on "the way we buy now," partly the selling of the book you are reading, that made Jack and me decide to visit other secondhand book stores in a whirlwind tour, heading across Tennessee to Mississippi and Alabama, then back up to Arkansas, Oklahoma, Kansas, Missouri, across to Indiana and Illinois, and down through Kentucky to home sweet home again.

I think we wondered how many like-minded souls were out there being independent booksellers in the face of big-box stores and e-readers. We wanted to hear their stories and tell them ours. So we set off in our 52 mpg electric hybrid to look for America. And in the interest of being as local-friendly as possible, we agreed to eat only at non-chain restaurants for the duration of the trip, and to not allow ourselves to shop in any box stores.

Twelve days, forty-two bookstores, and ten states later, we returned wiser and—given that only eighteen of the forty downtowns we visited were healthy—oddly cheered. In a radio interview after the trip, I said that we went to look for America and found it closed. Of the forty-nine booksellers we'd found via Internet sites or recommendations among friends and other bookshop owners, seven had packed it in.

In fact, the inaugural bookstore we visited in Athens, Tennessee, sported a giant GOING OUT OF BUSINESS banner. We benefited from their half-price closing sale and shared commiserations. As we drove away, I said to Jack, "First bookstore out of the gate, and it's going out of business? Do you believe in omens?"

Jack settled back in the passenger's seat and pulled his flat cap's brim down over his eyes. "No."

About half the bookstores on this excursion were located in strip malls, named things like Book Rack/Nook/Corner/Palace/Exchange, and offered something between ten thousand and twenty-five thousand paperbacks tucked onto homemade shelving. They were usually staffed by the owner. It's part of a bookshop's charm that owners tend to be colorful local characters, or sweethearts who just missed getting a social-work degree. We never met two alike, from Joe in Tupelo, Mississippi, to Joyce in Franklin, Tennessee. Greatest Hits Music & Books is a bookstore-cum-outlet for used movies, CDs, and games. Joe opened the place three and a half years before our visit, and his store is upbeat and messy, like himself. Frankly, if Joe doesn't drive a VW bus, he should. Joe also pulled off one of the best "getting started" capers since our own Walmart bookmark escapade. The third month he was in business, he sneaked out to the Barnes & Noble on the highway bypass and put a flyer for his shop on the windshield of each car in their parking lot. (Go, Joe!)

By contrast, the Book Den, owned by Joyce, is as neatly executed as a cross-stitch pattern. It took only a few minutes of chatting to see how proud Joyce is of her shop, and rightly so. She radiated confidence and vitality as she explained how she'd bought it in 1995 from its previous owner, hired one of her best friends to help her, and settled in for a second career.

Joyce was the first shop owner to mention e-readers; she feared them. "I used to have people come in every two weeks, now they come in once every three months or so, and they tell me they're reading on their Kindles now, so they're just coming in for things they can't get that way." She shook her head. "I hope they leave me standing."

I've often said that, if you turn a bookshop owner's heart inside out, what you get is their shop; it's a perfect display of who and what the person is. Joe and Joyce were on opposite ends of the organization continuum, but both embodied the kind of store we saw most often: a pleasantly unpretentious gathering of various types of titles, mostly paperbacks, stacked sideways on shelves by genre or author. The Wise Old Owl in Mississippi, the Book Barn in Tennessee, Book Traders in Missouri, and Chop Suey Books in Virginia fit this model.

But there are people who sell books because they're books, and then there are people who sell books because that's what they ended up selling. This second group is by far the smallest category, and they feel oddly out of place. Jack and I saw only three such shops on our road trip, all denoted by high prices and low lighting. I suppose that combination is meant to connote elegance, but to us it looked more like thievery. At one such store we spotted Bill Frist's *Healing America* on a shelf (signed first edition). Back in 2007, the Christian Appalachian Project brought cartons full of this book into Wise County and handed them out for free. And I suppose that, if a title never gets a second printing, then technically, yes, the first round is the first edition. But it felt creepy to us, who had made purses, birdhouses, planters, and other less useful things from a book flung for free into our region, to be staring at it for thirty-eight dollars in a shop two states over.

In another such store a few states later, the owner proudly showed us his one-thousand-dollar signed first edition of S. E. Hinton's *The Outsiders*. Jack voiced my thoughts as we left: "What does owning a thousand-dollar book have to do with people reading?" Not much, but it must be fun for the collector. We don't begrudge anyone that thrill; we just don't get the allure ourselves, and certainly no one in our economic pool would dive that deep.

We also encountered bookstores that seemed like anchors in their community, not only serving the region but encouraging it to grow. In Oxford, Mississippi, Square Books, with its two offshoot stores Off Square Books and Square Books, Jr., are all run by Richard Howorth, a tall, thin man who also happens to be town mayor. Square Books sells new titles and is a bibliophile's dream, boasting sweet little corners with armchairs tucked into them, a coffee bar upstairs, recessed shelves along stair landings, books signed by the great and good topping every display. Jack and I were impressed, bordering on cowed. Richard and his wife opened their first store in 1979, after each working in other bookshops.

We wandered into a coffee shop before leaving Oxford, a chain masquerading as independent, deep and comfy leather couches carefully coordinated to match its wooden tables and chairs. So earnestly ersatz was the place, I had the feeling the lad at the window, wearing an Ole Miss sweatshirt and typing away at his laptop, had conjured us all as characters in his novel. When anyone left the shop—the elderly men with the Dickensian Christmas scarves 'round their necks; the cute twentysomething couple, she wearing the white puffy ski jacket and alpine hat, he sporting school sweats and a pom-pom beanie; the woman with twin babies in the pram, one in pink, one in blue—we would all flatten back onto the pages the student generated. I told Jack to enjoy his coffee, because like Jostein Gaarder's Sophie, we would have to escape our destiny as literary pawns in the student's brain. Jack suggested we might need to take a break from driving, as I had clearly become overtired, but I still think Oxford, Mississippi, doesn't exist; it's the perfect projection from someone's mind of how a town should work to be utterly charming.

Similar to Square Books in function but certainly not in style was Burke's Books in Memphis, Tennessee. Owned by Cheryl and her husband, Burke's is twenty years strong and decorated in urban funk. Cheryl sells used books via several online sites as well as her bricks-and-mortar store. As she said, "We're not getting rich, but we're not getting killed by the Kindle, either." I told her my theory that e-readers took down the strong while letting smaller shops slip through the Net. She pondered a moment, then laughed. "I think that's exactly right. We'll still be here." She gave me a chin nod and tossed her jaw-length brown hair in defiance, the proud flash in her eyes as they met mine suggesting sisterhood.

Memphis is large enough to support five used book stores, and one new. We entered Booksellers at Laurelwood at high noon on December 24. The place was packed with shoppers. As we took in the sight of more than a hundred people buying up new, physical books, Jack said, "Just look at this. It's still possible."

I think there was a tear in his voice.

We stood in line with a couple of volumes, waiting fifteen minutes to reach the man at the register—who kept ringing his bell for help, more in hope than expectation. The poor guy was sweating by the time we reached him, his arms a blur of motion.

Jack smiled. "We run a used book store," he said. "If it's any consolation, we dream about having this many customers."

The man's tired eyes held a smile as he said, "I'll come work for you, then." Then he surprised us. As he rang up the books he said, "What's the name of your store in Virginia?" (He had seen Jack's ID for his debit card.)

"Tales of the Lonesome Pine Used Books, but people call it the Little Bookstore of Big Stone

Gap," Jack said. "My wife has a book coming out about it."

"Really?" he asked, and Jack gave him a five-second spiel. The man held out our bag and made eye contact with me, giving one of those between-booksellers chin nods. "Good for you," he said. "And good luck with your bookstore."

As we left Booksellers at Laurelwood, I mentioned my surprise that such a busy person would take the time to actually listen to a customer's casual remarks and ask questions. "That doesn't often happen at big stores like that." (Huge, it was. Cavernous, yet stuffed to coziness with books.)

Jack responded, "But it was owned by one person, not a corporation with a set of rules, so the employees get to be themselves instead of having the card-reading machine ask 'Was your server friendly today?' It all goes back to the idea that people who get to think for themselves at work are happier. Plus people who work in bookstores usually love books, so he was interested, and even with that string of traffic, he was able to be himself."

In fact, when we had to visit Walmart earlier that day because we needed a piece of electronic equipment and didn't know what small shop might sell it, we experienced culture shock. I forgot where we were and spoke to the cashier as though she and I were humans with something in common. She stared at me, answered politely, and rang us up faster, as if in fear. We were out of there in two minutes, our purchase in a plastic bag bearing a corporate logo.

"Was that . . . weird?" I asked Jack as we walked through the crowded Walmart parking lot.

"Not for Walmart; we're just not used to it anymore. If you stay away a while, what it really is shows up again."

Our trip even unearthed one clandestine bookseller—plus a few others that should have been. In the Ozarks, we caught up with my graduate school pal Rachel, now teaching in the region. She took us around several bookstores, and at a strip-mall place we met an unfriendly shop owner. One of his shelves sported a sign reading, PUT IT BACK WHERE YOU FOUND IT. IF YOU CAN'T ALPHABETIZE, WHY ARE YOU IN A BOOKSTORE IN THE FIRST PLACE?

Since he was the first curmudgeon of our trip, we found him utterly adorable, like zoo visitors gathered around the cage going "Oh, look! He's doing it again!" when a gorilla flings poo. But this innocent bemusement paid off. Warming to my husband, Mr. Personality told us about "the secret store." Apparently, if you are a good little customer and read all your classics, someone will let you in on an unmarked shop known to those in the know as the Book Jungle. Rachel had heard of the store before, but not where to find it, so she was fairly excited. We visited, and found some of the lowest prices the book world will ever see in that plywood shack lit by bare bulbs hanging from the ceiling. Likely they keep it a secret so the fire marshal doesn't inspect.

A couple of hours after the Book Jungle we stumbled onto Redeemed, the first Christian secondhand book store we'd seen. Our big question was, how would a Christian used book store decide what non-Christian books to accept in trade? They had a small classics section, in which *Madame Bovary* appeared, but not *Dracula*, *Brideshead Revisited*, or *Tom Jones*. Was this happenstance? Sarah Palin's books had pride of place in Politics, but Barack Obama's *The Audacity of Hope* rested on the shelf as well. I was impressed that they didn't lean toward the "God is a white, English-speaking male" theological camp, but Rachel and I agreed that a Christian bookstore in that part of the country might be hard to defend from its own clientele; how would one know what to stock?

Rachel had to head out that evening, but another ethnographic friend, Julie, came by for a few tunes back at the hotel lobby; the clerk said later it was one of her more fun nights on duty. The next day we headed across Missouri. For some reason the hotel breakfast had not stuck, so when we turned right at the tiny dot called Buffalo, I was hungry enough to concede to a fast-food breakfast. Fortunately, at that moment there hove into view a small café. Over eggs and hash browns, we asked Brandy, our server, if there were any bookstores in town, and she pointed the way we'd come.

"One block over."

We'd driven right past a place selling books and not seen it? I thought our eyes had attuned to ten-point type by now, but we backtracked—and realized why we hadn't noticed. An aluminum-and-plywood shack sat next to a desultory thrift store. Aimee's Books and More looked . . . cheap and cheerful from the outside, and we walked into your basic dormer on a concrete slab. One good prairie wind, and the whole house of books would collapse. I took a quick look around and found a cheap book that would do, planning to beat a hasty retreat.

At the register, the owner introduced herself as Debbie and asked where we were from. Jack told her, adding that we owned a bookstore.

Her face lit up. "I'm friends with about three hundred booksellers on Facebook," she said, and launched into her story. Debbie took her life savings and birthed a bookstore to give her grown daughter a job in town. When her daughter later found work at the local hotel, Mom stepped in to keep it going, since by then people were regularly coming by with trades, and so happy to have her there. You can't judge a bookstore by its cover.

Debbie was absolutely lovely, and her store fit that community like a hand in a glove, reaching out to everyone who crossed her path. And like us, she had a list of pinch hitters who considered the bookshop a cooperative effort. If Debbie needed to leave town, she got by with a little help from her friends.

Right after Debbie's little dormer we drove into Rolla, Missouri, and found a vibrant downtown complete with renovated sidewalks and the most beautiful bookstore we had visited to that point. Large windows with intricate brick-and-wood molding were accented by old-fashioned hand lettering above them, spelling out READER'S CORNER. Inside, dark wood shelves of neatly aligned books were decorated with unusual statuary, old typewriters, and suitcases, stretching to the high ceiling. At the back, two castle turrets stood straight and true above the children's section, teddy bears storming their towers while a rag doll with braids looked down, smiling embroidered smiles.

I couldn't speak. Jack took one look and headed straight for the guy behind the counter.

About an hour and a half later, we tore ourselves away from Larry Bowen, who probably had gotten embarrassed by our repeated assertions that he ran the prettiest used book store we'd ever seen, while Brittany, his shop assistant, photographed us chatting away. Larry related several funny stories about his adventures as a shop owner. One covered the ever-present push me/pull me of shop-local-versus-get-it-cheaper competition with online sellers. Larry had instituted a policy that anything Amazon sold, he would match at two dollars higher. This took into account his bricks-and-mortar expenses and the low budgets of a downturned economy's customers. It seemed a good compromise.

Not so fast. A customer who'd come in a few weeks earlier to get a donation for her church went away with fifty dollars in gift certificates. She reappeared and showed him a book on Amazon for $13.57. "Can you beat that price? I want to shop local," she said, smiling.

Larry sighed, swallowed, and pushed up his metaphorical shirt sleeves. "I can do $15.57."

Her face fell. "But you can't beat it? I need ten copies. The church board wants these for our next Bible study."

Larry smiled, and repeated, "I can do $15.57."

She frowned. "I don't think our board would authorize that extra expense. It would be twenty dollars more than Amazon, all told. No, I'm sorry, I just don't think that will do."

"What about the fifty-dollar donation I gave you last month?"

She looked suddenly sheepish. "Well . . . I mean, we do want to shop local. It's just that we need to be good money stewards."

Larry smiled again. "So do I. I need to keep my business viable in the community I want to continue serving."

Larry 10 × $15.57, Amazon 0.

One of the things we learned on this trip was that bookshops are networking, making alliances and allies. Larry told us that the four independent bookshops in St. Louis, Missouri, had hooked themselves together into the Independent Bookstore Alliance. Our first stop was one of these, Pudd'nhead Books. The children's manager was working the shop, and told me something interesting about when Amazon put out its now-infamous campaign over the holiday shopping season. In a nutshell, anyone who found a print ad from local retailers selling an item for less than the Big A could get the product for five dollars below that price if they purchased it from Amazon. And the ad sparked quite a reaction. People brought lists of books they wanted to local bookshops and said, in essence, "We were going to buy these on Amazon but after what they tried to do to local shops with that campaign, we'll shop with you instead." Backlash is America's greatest asset, and much of our history is actually built on it, for good or ill. Up the locavores!

Jack and I watched the lady at Pudd'nhead spend considerable time advising a family on a book purchase for a young child, again something that doesn't happen in the big-box stores. And she drew us a map to the other Alliance members.

At Left Bank Books, our spirits soared. They had a resident cat! Spike sat in an office at a laptop, presumably working on his novel. Staff member Danielle kindly left her desk (where she was clearly pretty busy) and spent fifteen minutes telling us about Spike and Left Bank, and hearing about our cats and shop. Left Bank has been in business forty-two years, and has used books downstairs, new upstairs.

I mentioned Amazon and Danielle gave a disdainful sniff. "We're not worried."

They didn't have reason to be; even in the Dead Days between Christmas and New Year, the place thrummed with people (many of whom were happy to greet Spike when he sauntered up the stairs after leaving us). Left Bank had the comfortable feeling of an overstuffed armchair, books everywhere, people everywhere, cat ambling among them all.

The second partnership we encountered came in Kentucky, where we stayed with old friends. Mary Hamilton is the author of *Kentucky Folktales* and is well known in her community for her storytelling and scholarship on the subject. She and her husband Charles Wright are the kind of people who live simply but not slightly. They took us to Poor Richard's Books, hooked in partnership but not ownership with a coffeehouse called Kentucky Coffeetree Café and an artisan shop called Completely Kentucky. Now this is cooperation; the businesses on either end (Richard's and Kentucky) bought the shop between them and put in the coffeehouse, then sold it as a going concern some six years later. The three shops also knocked door holes in their shared walls so you could walk between them. Since each has different opening hours, they have signs that announce: IF THIS DOOR IS CLOSED, THE SHOP YOU'RE TRYING TO GET TO THROUGH IT IS NOT OPEN. So simple. So elegant. So cooperative.

Lexington is large enough to support several bookstores, each specializing in slightly different subject matter. An all-new retailer called the Morris Book Shop had one of the nicest art deco schemes we'd seen, and yet another form of cooperation. The owner of Morris is good friends with the manager of Parnassus Books in Nashville, the shop that author Ann Patchett co-owns. Networks are wonderful things—and perhaps necessities for small bookstores. From Morris we ambled to Glover's Bookery, a rare and used book dealership with a resident Irish setter. Thea was the size of a small pony and gentler than a sleepy Quaker. She shared her toys with me—repeatedly—as the owner, John, and I chatted.

We met our first African-American bookseller in Lexington. Ron Davis bought the shop from its previous owner, for whom he had worked, and renamed it the Wild Fig Bookstore, "after a metaphor Gayl Jones, an author here in town, uses a lot. My wife, Crystal Wilkinson, is a writer, and she really admires Gayl, so that's how the store got its name."

Crystal's name was familiar to Charles and me as a founding Afrilachian poet, along with Nikki Finney and Frank X Walker. Wild Fig, as Ron explained, stocked new books but was primarily a shop for used, and he'd only brought in the new books because most of the best books had left the shop in the closing-out sale. He had a cracking art history section; when I commented on it, he grinned. "Yep. All my beautiful art books, the things that really mattered to me, that I'd bought with my discount while working here, they all went back in. It hurt, but I did what had to be done." We shared the smile of Those Who Sacrifice to Make It Happen before saying good-bye.

Ron wasn't the only owner to throw his life's blood into inventory. In Washington, D.C., I visited Idle Time Books, owned by a man named Jacques and his wife (and staffed by an affably talkative man named Paul the day I visited). It turns out the couple bought their building and lived upstairs while turning the downstairs into a bookstore. And they stocked their shop by selling his lifelong comic collection for cash to turn into inventory. Jacques/Jack? They say everyone has a doppelgänger. . . .

The funniest moment of the whole trip came in Indiana. We had some trouble locating a shop called Fulton Avenue Books, and when we pulled in, a man getting out of a large pickup gave us a funny—okay, unfriendly—look.

"What's his problem?" I asked, slipping my wallet into a shoulder bag as we walked toward the door.

"Urk," said Jack.

"Urk" is a not a sound I associate with Jack, so I looked up to see him pointing, wordless, at a sign: GENTLEMEN ONLY. MUST BE 18 TO ENTER. Well, who knew? This bookstore was actually a porn shop. Wow! That hadn't happened the whole trip. We got back in the car (quickly!) and drove toward the next address.

"When you think about it, we've visited more than thirty bookstores, so one of them had to be a duffer," Jack said as we sped away from Fulton Avenue Books to Bookmart.

Which was also a porn shop.

"No way," Jack said, staring at the sign.

Please note: my beloved is usually far more articulate than "urk" and "no way." His speechlessness is a sure sign of how deeply startled we were.

"Let's get out of this town," I said, and we floored it, leaving behind two more shops that shall never be explored by the Beck-Welch team.

Probably at least one was run by a sweet little old lady with a resident cat, who would have been knitting a sweater (the lady, not the cat). We left Pornsville at 70 mph, passing some incredibly large and beautiful newly built houses. In any economy, they would have stood out, but in recession times?

"This will be the porn king and his children," Jack said, and at that precise moment, an ornate sign overhead announced FUQUAY AVENUE.

Jack laughed so hard I thought he would asphyxiate.

The Booking Down the Road Tour ended back at our own dear little bookstore in Big Stone Gap, where we rested up and thought about what we'd seen, learned, and enjoyed. We covered 2,690 miles (on just four tanks of gas, thank you!) saw four old friends, made several new ones, and bought forty-two books. We ate at two restaurants that were chains and shopped in Walmart once, because we had no other choices. (Which is kind of chilling, when you think about it.)

What did we learn? That people who follow their own dreams and do what's in front of them—build, paint, renovate, stock, defy, buy, sell, and smile—are still standing, while those who wait for permission, or guarantees, or help from someone else, disappear fairly quietly into that good night. One small town we visited in Tennessee stands out as an example; not only was the bookstore we went there to visit closed down, but the pottery painting place that had replaced it was also shut for good. Meanwhile, the town's planners are pinning their hopes on reopening the old theater as an entertainment center. All the eggs, as it were, are in one grant-funded basket. What if some of that funding had been channeled to local businesses, as the now-rather-embittered merchants had asked? Likewise, the owners of a general store in a town not so far away had self-published a book about their area's infamous Scopes Trial, believing they would be supported by the local tourism industry. Instead they found themselves pretty much on their own in moving the stock.

Several of the booksellers we met had stories about their town's business associations proving to be what George Orwell might have called "doubleplusdishelpful." (If you haven't read his dystopian *1984* yet, that's the language of Big Brother's government—and what many of us found when we tried to turn our dreams into permit applications.)

On the road trip, Jack and I learned that a lot of very capable people who are comfortable in their own skins live in these United States, doing their day-to-day deeds while enjoying what life brings. And we learned that east or west, home looks much better than we thought. Settling back into the store, we implemented some of the cool things we had seen in various shops—hanging signs from the ceiling saying which books were where, putting wheels on shelves so they could be moved to create more floor space for events, and other practical touches.

We also started a network with many of the people we met, connecting on social media and via e-mails. And we thought about what we'd seen. Is small-town America closing? Well, in large measure, yes. But when it's not closing, it's because someone with a vision and a brain got busy. Often it was just an individual who did what seemed best—whether that was investing his life's savings into a beautiful downtown building and anchoring a shopping block, as Larry did; or Debbie's buying an aluminum dormer to put atop a concrete slab so her daughter could have a job in Buffalo; or Ron's reopening his employer's store as his own, with a new name and a new vision; or Joe's plastering flyers on all the cars in the Barnes & Noble parking lot. People followed their bliss, but they also worked hard, learned fast, and didn't take no for an answer. Perhaps that, more than anything else, is what keeps small towns open in America: the tenacity of people who believe in their own abilities.

CHAPTER 24

Bibliophiliacs Versus Book Snobs

We read books and tell stories to find each other.

—Wendy Welch

ONE DAY A LADY CAME in with an older woman in tow. The older woman clutched a baby doll. That should have been a clue, but apparently my brain had the day off. The lady, perhaps in her sixties, pointed to an easy chair near the Christian books. "Sit there and mind your baby and I'll be ready in a minute." The older woman perched on the chair and with a vacant smile began crooning to the doll.

Jack approached the younger woman as she browsed Christian nonfiction. "Can I help you find anything?"

"I'm looking for a book about—"

The older woman shot from her chair. "What are you looking for, dear? I'll help!" she shouted, dropping the doll and lurching forward.

"No, Mama, it's okay, sit back down." Her

daughter grasped the older woman's elbows and moved her backward—gently, as if in a waltz—until she reached the chair. "You might fall. Sit with your baby and I'll be ready in a minute."

Jack figured it out first. He turned to the mother. "That's a lovely child you have there. Would you like a cup of tea while you're waiting?"

"Not too hot," the browsing woman said, even as her eyes scanned the shelf in rapid strokes.

"Help you find something?" I asked *sotto voce* as Jack and the mom began a conversation with no meaning but lots of volume.

"I'm looking for the latest in that Amish series," she said, referencing a popular topic for Christian romance writers.

"Wrong section." I led her to the other side of the shelf. "Where you were was nonfiction. Are you looking for Beverly Lewis or Wanda Brunstetter?" Both write bestsellers in this genre.

Just then her eyes lit up, her hand swooped down, and she snatched a paperback to her chest. "This one!" she exclaimed in triumph, and her mother dropped her conversation with Jack and came loping over.

"Did you hurt yourself?" the older woman half asked, half scolded. "I told you not to run inside the school!"

"Okay, Mommy, please, sit down," the woman said. Mommy subsided into her chair and began undressing the doll.

"Do you have any Dean Koontz?" the woman turned to me, whispering.

"Yes," I said, and didn't move. My brain could not connect someone who read Christian romances set among the Amish with a request for horror; it seemed more like an odd rhetorical question.

The woman stared at me. "Um, miss, I'm kind of in a hurry. Mama won't wait long."

"Oh! Of course." I led the way, embarrassed, to the horror section, and stood there as she ran her finger down the row of titles stacked on the counter. Watching customers browse is a no-no—leave them to it and wait until they ask a question—but shopkeeper etiquette had flown out the window. Behind me, I heard Jack saying, "And here is your tea, madam."

The browsing woman's head flew up and she started to say something, but Jack's voice floated through the doorway in reassurance. "It's tap water in a paper cup. No worries."

The daughter gave a smile of radiant sunshine and bent to the Koontz titles again. She selected two as I continued to stare, unabashed. "These three, please," she said, holding out the romance and the horrors.

"Yes, ma'am." I shook myself and hurried to the other side of the room where the cash box and receipt book waited. The woman followed.

As I tallied and added tax, she said suddenly, "I guess you know Mama has dementia."

"I figured it was something like that," I said.

"Normally I get time to myself once a week when my daughter comes and sits with her, but her daughter's sick and stayed home from school so she couldn't come, and I'd been wanting to check this place out—" She indicated the bookstore with a furtive sweep of her hand. "Reading is such a refuge for me. When Mama naps I can lose myself." She giggled. "I go into another world, like Mama. So I figured I would just run out with her this once. She's not real steady on her feet, falls a lot." She glanced to where Jack stood next to her mother, chatting like a professional talk-show host as Mom sipped "tea" from the cup and simpered beneath his flirting.

The woman's eyes filled with sudden tears, but none fell.

"We're glad you came in," I said, meaning two different things, but not knowing how to say the second one. I tried again. "Come back anytime."

The woman picked up her titles and change, then gave me a conspiratorial smile. "Oh, I'll be back. I just love Dean Koontz. He takes my mind off things. After everything that happens to the people in his books, maybe my life's not so bad." She said that last sentence so fast and low, it was almost as if she hadn't said it at all. "Okay, Mama," she said in a louder voice. "Time to go. Got your baby?"

Out the door they went, Mama clutching her

daughter's arm and her doll as they descended our porch stairs in a rhythmic, slow step-shuffle-pause, step-shuffle-pause.

Jack looked at me. I looked at Jack. "I'll put the kettle on," he said.

We have learned that it doesn't do for a bookseller to make assumptions about who reads what. People read for information, for entertainment, for distraction, for status, for a plethora of other reasons. Whatever readers want, books—and the people who sell them—should be able to give it to them.

Honestly, the sense of perspective that a bookstore imposes is life-altering. Try moving a presidential biography ten years later, or the tell-all confessional of a Hollywood madam once her fifteen minutes of fame are up. The people writing for all of us, describing things in a timeless way, endure. The rest are quick flashes of burning-out stars. Their light can indeed burn bright and beautiful, but it's mercifully brief. Timeless writers endure because, in Alan Bennett's words from the play *The History Boys*, "The best moments in reading are when you come across something—a thought, a feeling, a way of looking at things—that you'd thought special, particular to you. And here it is, set down by someone else, a person you've never met, maybe even someone long dead. And it's as if a hand has come out, and taken yours."

Or, as Mr. Antolini told Holden Caulfield in *The Catcher in the Rye*, "Among other things, you'll find that you're not the first person who was ever confused and frightened and even sickened by human behavior. You're by no means alone on that score, you'll be excited and stimulated to know. Many, many men have been just as troubled morally and spiritually as you are right now. Happily, some of them kept records of their troubles. You'll learn from them—if you want to. Just as someday, if you have something to offer, someone will learn something from you. It's a beautiful reciprocal arrangement. And it isn't education. It's history. It's poetry."

In the words of Helene Hanff (who wrote *84, Charing Cross Road*) we cry, "Comrade!" when we meet someone we recognize in the pages of a book. Leading storytelling workshops, I often compared the well-told story—written or spoken—to a coloring book; there are guidelines, but you create the details for yourself. A television does most of the work for you; one need not even think, only watch. Some writers are like TVs, but the best ones offer you sovereignty.

Jack says watching a customer meet the right book is like seeing a child who thinks she's lost on the playground spot her mother. Every book, from the most serious to the weirdest, has a buyer. We once had some tome about the British royal family secretly being a group of reptilians masquerading as humans. (Do *not* get my Scottish husband started on this theme.) I don't know how it got in the shop, but it sat in—where else—science for a couple of years. Either we missed culling it, or Jack considered it too funny to give up.

In walked Tim (the man who launched our textbook-valuing career). A really nice guy who lives in New England, he's one of our semiannual regulars. The semiannuals come by mostly during summers and holidays, but also whenever they visit family in the area. Tim trolled the science section, gave a cry of delight, and held up the reptilian royalty book. "I've heard about this!" he exclaimed. I wouldn't have been surprised if he'd yelled, "Eureka!"

"Oh?" It was the most polite thing that came to mind, and probably beat my first impulse: *Then should I stop thinking of you as a nice guy and be afraid?*

"Yeah. My college roommate dated the geek who wrote its girlfriend." (It took me a minute to decipher that syntax.) "He was a loony bird, but she was nice. So how much is this?"

A book for everyone, and everyone will find the right book. Eventually. Tim had probably been in our shop twice a year for four years before he "reunited" with that creepy tome. The Scots have a saying: "What's fer ye 'l no gang by ye." (What's for you will not pass you by.) After five years in the business, I can say that this includes books.

CHAPTER 25
On Recommending Books

*Second-hand books are wild books,
homeless books; they have come together
in vast flocks of variegated feather, and
have a charm which the domesticated
volumes of the library lack. Besides, in this
random miscellaneous company we may
rub against some complete stranger who
will, with luck, turn into the best friend we
have in the world.*

—Virginia Woolf,
"Street Haunting: A London Adventure"

BOOKS ARE NOT JUST THINGS, but dynamic
artifacts, milestones showing where the road
took a sudden turn on our individual journeys—
our very individual journeys, since a book that
changed one person's life is another person's
dreaded English assignment. There's no rhyme or
reason to what impacts whom except the alchemy
of timing, temperament, and title.

The first shelf someone sees when entering our

bookstore is local fiction. Gracing its top, tall and silent, stand two marble bookends in the shape of human noses. Between these lies the section we call "Staff Picks."

Yeah, our senses of humor aren't very sophisticated.

Staff Picks is a nod to the awareness that people like to visit bookstores because someone will suggest things for them to read. Do you think Amazon and Half.com would be so aggressively making suggestions "just for you," or that Facebook would analyze your posts and fill the side of your screen with little pop-up promos if people didn't like such recommendations?

Getting to recommend books to people is one of the most rewarding parts of running a bookshop, but it's also a bit tricky. The timing has to be good; as I said before, someone in the middle of a story about their recent family loss doesn't need to be struck upside the head with a sales pitch. We don't suggest *Old Yeller* to a customer talking about her dog's death. There are basic tenets of human decency (and common sense) that all retailers must follow.

One evening pretty close to closing time, a woman entered our shop and stopped just inside the door. I didn't recognize her as a repeat customer, so I asked if she needed any help acclimating to where things were.

Her eyes remained stuck on the books in Staff

Picks as she said, "No, I think this will be fine."

"Excuse me?" I asked, since she had nothing in her hands, and the woman shook herself and turned to me.

"You close in fifteen minutes, according to your sign out front. I am in town with my husband; he's spending the weekend doing some contract work for the town. I will spend the next two days holed up in a hotel room, and I must have something to read or I'll go crazy. Who chose these books?" Her hand indicated the Staff Picks.

"Mostly me," I said, "although my husband may have chosen one or two."

The woman moved to our table and sat down. Extracting a twenty from her purse, she held it out to me. "Find me something to read this weekend," she said. "I'm in a historic novel frame of mind."

As I stared at the twenty, the woman's imperious expression relaxed into a smile. "Four of my all-time favorite books are in your Staff Picks," she said. "If you like it, I'll like it. Now get cracking; you close in twelve minutes."

It is fun to introduce other people to what you like. So, a book about running a bookstore simply must contain a Top Ten List of the author's favorites. And since I'm a fan of Christopher Guest films, my list goes to eleven.

Here, in pure self-indulgence and alphabetical order, is my own list of books I love to recommend to people who enjoy reading—along with my even more self-indulgent stories of what miles they marked on my personal journey. Like any bibliophile, I will talk about these titles anytime, anywhere, with anyone—and like any bookstore owner, I rarely get to with customers. So consider yourself trapped, get a cup of tea, and enjoy.

Charlotte's Web

E. B. White wrote what is arguably the greatest opening sentence in literature: *"Where's Papa going with that ax?" said Fern to her mother as they were setting the table for breakfast.* C'mon, admit it, you're hooked from that moment forward. A literate spider, a frightened pig, a little girl helping generations of young'uns come to terms with life's cruelties: magic happens. You learn to cry over the written page when you're seven, and you never stop.

Storyteller and children's author Carmen Deedy tells a personal tale about being a slow reader as a child, and how the first book she ever checked out of a library (*Charlotte's Web*) took three renewals to finish. "Finally, I marched back to the children's desk in a flood of tears and said, 'This is the saddest I've ever felt in my whole life! It's horrible! How can books do this to you? Give me another one!' And those words sealed my fate. I became a reader for life." Don't you know just how she feels?

Web wasn't the first book I ever checked out of

a library; that was *The Snowy Day* by Ezra Jack Keats, when I was three. My dad taught both my sister and me to read as preschoolers; he filled a paint bucket (hopefully scrubbed clean of toxins) with plastic letters. "Pull out W," he'd say, and I'd grasp this red spiky thing bigger than my hand and haul it into meaning. Letters formed words, words formed ideas, ideas formed stories, stories formed lives. As with generations of little girls and boys before me, *Charlotte's Web* was my earliest introduction to the reality that not all stories end happily, or fit neatly into a cozy world. It hurt, and it sealed my fate.

The English and Scottish Popular Ballads, Volumes 1–5

Before writing, singing moved information—truth, spin, dogma, lies, and funny things that happened at the castle. Francis James Child published a collection of his favorite ballads in the late 1800s; as my Scots husband points out, they are mostly Scottish even though England enjoys equal titular credit. (He's not a nationalist, just has his moments.) The poetic expressions found in these outpourings of human spirit remind us what's best and worst about ourselves.

One of the things I love about this collection is how it proves that there is so little new under the sun. The common themes of literature—love gone wrong, family dynamics, the wistful longing for a better life—are alive and well in ancient snapshots of what people wanted to hear then. It's still what we want to hear now: who loves whom; who killed whom and why; who overreached himself and fell down; who outran her humble beginnings to make good. In "Twa Sisters," sibling rivalry for a boy's love dooms them all; "Long Lankin," about the murder of a highborn baby, evokes stomach-churning disgust even as it asks some harsh questions about haves and have-nots; the upbeat "Comfort for the Comfortless" gives scorned lovers a new outlook. One of the world's first paranormal romances, "House Carpenter," still raises goose bumps on my skin when the fate of the doomed faithless wife and her not-who-he-appears lover is sung:

> *"Oh what are those hills, yon high, high hills,*
> *With flowers as white as snow"*
> *"Those are the hills of heaven, my love*
> *That you and I will never know."*
> *Then twice around went the gallant ship*
> *I'm sure it was not three*
> *His hoof broke that shining ship in half*
> *And they sank to the bottom of the sea*

Their archaic language makes the enduring quality of their themes stand out even more. These ballads are beautiful, creepy, stark, strong, and timeless.

The Grapes of Wrath

Pushing his literary lens in for close-ups of one family, then pulling back to explore a generation's terrible luck, John Steinbeck made people think. He made even those tucked up safe in warm houses seventy years later feel the fear and betrayal of being turned out from them. And he did it with such beautiful, beautiful language.

I read *Wrath* for the first time in high school. Up to then, I'd read classics when they were assigned, but everything else in the library like a voracious little vacuum cleaner. My reasoning was simple; adults were weird, so if they were pushing something, it probably wasn't nearly as good as the stuff they dismissed as "junk." I devoured Madeleine L'Engle, Paula Danziger, *Summer of My German Soldier*, and a whole bunch of lit lite for kids, but plowed my way through *The Scarlet Letter* with martyred sighs and CliffsNotes. Then Mr. Beekman, our eleventh-grade advanced placement American literature teacher, assigned *The Grapes of Wrath*.

The class was a survey starting with the 1600s, but for some reason, probably availability, I checked Steinbeck out of the library first. Finish and cross it off, then blast through the other titles so I could get back to reading the good stuff: that was the plan.

Do you remember high school, where social strata affect your life every day and the strong rule while the weak try to fly below the radar? And do you remember what *The Grapes of Wrath* is about? Talk about context creating meaning; this book, an adult treatise of the haves and have-nots caught in the unfairness of economics, takes on a different significance to a high schooler whose understanding of injustice is that pretty girls get asked to dance before sweet ones do. *Wrath* was a wake-up call with instant empathy; we all knew what "wrong" felt like, but had never seen it on such a large scale. There were worse things than what was happening to us, happening in the world, every day. That simple lesson some kids learn by the time they're five, sheltered old me discovered in high school. For the first time, the big picture formed in which small players moved, each having to make individual choices, even if there weren't any good ones.

At that age, injustices look easily changeable; if the adults only knew how silly they were acting, they'd stop. It was our duty, when we grew up, to act more sensibly and end this silly unfair nonsense. Anne Frank wrote something very similar in her diary, some forty years before Steinbeck expanded my sight line.

When I finished *Wrath*, I understood three new ideas: America, let alone the world, was bigger than I'd ever imagined, but still looked a lot like high school; there were other people who thought things should be fairer than they were, and I could join them in working to make life that way; and classic literature was awesome. Awesome in the classic sense: awe-inspiring and awful. Good-bye, teen pop lit, hello, Hemingway, Miller, even Chaucer and Voltaire once I got used to the language. What a wonderful, horrible, ambiguous world!

The Grapes of Wrath marked the end of childhood and the beginning of a lifelong passion I couldn't even put a name to then, although its slickest moniker has become "social justice." I thank Mr. Beekman (the lit teacher) for introducing me to it. But this story has a coda, because the book—or rather, the play—hit me again some twenty years later. A call went out from the theater department at a nearby college: volunteer musicians were sought for a production of *The Grapes of Wrath* to be staged during the fall term. A customer who knew our musical background brought it to my attention, and I raced to Jack with the flyer in my hand.

"This book changed my life! We have to do this!" I babbled, then fired an e-mail off to the theater faculty. That's how we met Dr. Gary Crum, executive director of an organization that recruited medical professionals to underserved areas (to wit, where we live). He played concertina, banjo, and harmonica, and also responded to the e-mail. Gary, Jack, and I had a blast creating the music for *Wrath*, in large part because Michael, Michael, and

Ben, the faculty members running the show, gave us a free hand to embed folk music throughout the production. It wasn't a musical; we just aided with mood and ambiance, plus scene openings and closings. It seemed like neo-heaven.

Michael is an unusually nurturing director, one who sees his job as getting the kids to understand more than to act. Most of them were just a couple of years older than I'd been when *Wrath* interrupted my cozy little life; watching them figure some things out as practices progressed rekindled hope that the next generation might make a few more changes than mine had managed. And on opening night, when Gary, Jack, and I stood up to sing, "I Ain't Got No Home in This World Anymore," twenty years of meekness, patience, and anger turned our voices into melodic steel. The theater students didn't so much perform as explode; they knew what the play was about. A student in the audience said later, "I cried four times. Y'all just changed my life."

I hope so, kid. For all of us, I hope so.

Green Shadows, White Whale

Actually, almost any collection of Ray Bradbury's stories would be among my favorites. In short spurts of fiction interspersed with essays and bits of memoir, *Shadows* details Bradbury's career as a young screenwriter working on *Moby Dick* under the dubious care of legendary director John

Huston. Bradbury has the most interesting way of revealing meaning by obscuring it; his characters wrap three times around human nature, but just as you believe yourself lost in a maze of descriptive symbolism, the angel choir sings and lights you home. Baby, could this guy write. And he mostly mined his own life.

Although it would be hard to choose a favorite of all Bradbury's stories, one stands out as a recurring theme in my life, its warning subtle yet clear. Bradbury wrote about a man (but it was him, on assignment with Huston) being in Dublin and hearing a street beggar playing her harp on one of the three famous bridges. He gave her money and complimented her incredible playing—and nearly wrecked everything, because he made her aware of what she was doing. Her fingers fumbled, she lost her nonchalant confidence, and it wasn't until he fled in horror at what he'd done that she regained a deft, unexamined touch. Bradbury learned then not to ask too many questions, a lesson that threads through his beautiful, bizarre story collections.

Sometimes people talk to writers and storytellers about "talent" and "charisma" and "learning the craft." Humans have always wanted to find the line, to bottle (and then sell) the difference between that little magic spark and a lot of bloody hard work to master an art form. I'm all for anyone learning new skills, and as Edison once said, "Opportunity is missed by most people because it arrives dressed in overalls and looks like work." Still, with those caveats in mind, perhaps it doesn't do to lean too far over when peering into the deep well of creativity. One of the muses might sneak up from behind and push you headlong down the shaft.

Homestead
Rosina Lippi (this little paperback's author) may not think the following anecdote cute, but I picked up a dog-eared copy of her work for ten pence at a library sale in Britain one day, on the basis that the cover looked interesting. If I didn't like it, it could go to the used book store in Milnathort and nary a word needed to be said about my extravagance. I curled up in an armchair and opened the book that weekend, when Jack was out for the day with a friend.

Falling in love is a sneaky business; you start reading, and then you look up and it's two hours past dinnertime and the light is failing in the room and the dog is whining insistently because you haven't let him out and your husband is home from his excursion wondering why you look as though you've been crying.

What a beautiful book this is. Patricia Hampl, another writer whose work I admire, wrote in her memoir *The Florist's Daughter*, "Nothing is

354

harder to grasp than a relentlessly modest life." Lippi grasped the lives of not just one but a dozen modest women in the mountains between Austria and Italy, living as quietly as circumstances and world wars would allow through the twentieth century. The book tells the story of successive generations of women in one tiny village—how they lived, died, loved, coped—in a removed fashion, with such gracious yet loving distance to the writing that you could almost wonder afterward why you cared.

Because you do care. Very much. Lippi makes her characters so real you can smell their milk, sweat, and perfume, and she does it with an economy of words bordering on magic. She depicts the changes that time, custom, even the coming of electricity make on the women and their way of life, simply by mentioning them in passing while talking about something else; it's as if the part she's ignoring is the aspect of their lives most sharply in focus.

Briefly, before returning to the States from Britain, I ran two book clubs for a library in England. Despite my best marketing efforts, one remained small, at one point dropping to just two other members: a young man of Pakistani descent and a British woman nearing retirement. Finding books that interested both would be tricky, I thought, but the pair seemed happy to take it in turns that we three should each suggest a book to read together. When my month came, I passed out copies of *Homestead*, apologizing to Hamza as I did so: "Perhaps it's more of a girl's book, but it does have some interesting social history to it, chronicles the wars and all."

Hamza read the book's jacket blurb, then shot me an old-fashioned look. "Is this *Steel Magnolias* set in some remote village?" he asked, and Irene, our other member, guffawed. It turned out she had already read the book and loved it, but despite my pleas that I would retract this and choose another before we went home, she insisted that we keep to the agreement and read it together.

"I do want Hamza to try it, but rather agree that it might be more female-centric and therefore inaccessible," she said. (She was a legal wizard and talked like that as a matter of course.) "But I remember enjoying it very much, and want to read it again."

Home they went, Lippi's slim volume tucked under an arm. Next month, Hamza was last to arrive, so late that Irene joked, "I believe he might be fed up with us. Perhaps we should have read something more testosterone-laden."

Just then Hamza breezed in, took his seat, and pulled out his copy. "See this book?" he growled, holding it by one corner and smashing his finger against the cover until his knuckle turned white. His face dissolved into a smile. "I loved it. The writing is gorgeous, but that's not all. I read it twice, once for me, and once translating it for my mum. She grew up in a mountain village in Pakistan, and the stories she told me were a lot like this, that whole passage-of-time, mother-daughter-aunt-sister holding-it-together feminine mystique stuff. My mum loved it, and she probably loved it differently than I did, but I cried my way through each chapter." He set the book down and fixed us with a baleful glare. "And if you repeat that to anyone, I'll deny it."

Yeah, that whole passage-of-time, mother-daughter-aunt-sister thing does me in, too. Huzzah for Rosina Lippi, telling a simple story with beautiful words that make such different people feel the same thing.

I Capture the Castle
Better known for creating *The 101 Dalmatians*, Dodie Smith also penned the first "teen novel." Literature professors ever since have been bemoaning either how little credit she receives for this contribution, or the fact that she made it in the first place. (Some lit profs look like real curmudgeons until you get to know them. And some really are.) *Castle* pioneered the genre that would detail the angst and anguish of being a young adult in love, telling the story from the ingenue's baffled-yet-brave point of view. *"I love. I have loved. I will love."* That has to be one of the greatest literary endings of all time. Smith's poetic

phrase gets quoted again and again without people realizing the original source.

I gave a copy of *Castle* to a friend's daughter when she turned thirteen. Mature for her age and able to see right through much of what passes for relationship advice among young women today, Maeve as child-becoming-woman reminded me of *Castle*'s narrator Cassandra. Questioning, probing, trying hard to believe in themselves and to face down the outside world without drying up inside, young women stumble forward in life, chins up, eyes wide open, hearts all too often lying vulnerably on their sleeves. Go, girls. Go forth and conquer! You have been, will be, and are loved.

Portraits of "The Whiteman"

Keith Basso isn't necessarily a well-known author outside folklore and anthropology circles, which is a shame because his book has so much to say about human relationships. Basso describes very different groups of people seeking human connections across invisible boundaries—or maybe, just maybe, he describes the ways in which these groups subtly keep those invisible barriers up with language and humor. That's one of the aspects I love about this book: he doesn't tell you what to think, just lays a whole lot of interesting facts and plausible observations out in the sun for you to have a look at.

Basso analyzes magnanimous behavior on one side viewed as condescension from the other, the classic relationship between the colonizer and the colonized, the dominant and the subservient. He does it by recording jokes. In a nutshell, Basso, as a young and green anthropologist, was engaged in some run-of-the-mill fieldwork in Cibecue, Arizona, among Western Apaches, and left his tape recorder behind, running. ("Did he do it on purpose?" will remain one of those great literature questions of the centuries, alongside "Does Faust love Gretchen?" and "Would Elizabeth have learned to love Mr. Darcy without first seeing his manor?") He captured a Native man acting like a white anthropologist in a humorous impromptu sketch: shaking hands with everyone, speaking too loudly, asking how much things cost, making personal inquiries about health and family matters. Listening to his covert recording later, Basso realized he'd gotten what Robert Burns called the greatest gift: "to see ourselves as others see us." So he started over with his fieldwork, and the result is this book.

The simultaneous humor and depth of its concepts are easy to grasp because we've experienced them, whether we gave them an anthropological name or not. How do we relate to people who are racially, ethnically, socially, educationally, idealistically, or economically different from us? Basso uses only one example, the "whiteman" and the Western Apaches. He is not trying to universalize power relationships, only to record a joking and speech tradition among a certain people group.

Still, his writing all but smacks you in the face. Perhaps the book's biggest effect is in the questions it does *not* ask: Can racism flow in two directions, or only from those with the most power toward those with the least? Is it possible that a larger group can covertly expect a smaller to learn its customs and social norms by pretending to be intellectually interested in the "quaint traditions" of the smaller? Just what does it mean to be white in America today? And, by proxy, what makes something funny when it happens between two people who don't share common biological ancestry, but who have grown up side by side, each believing the other did wrong? Just what is entitlement, really?

This is neither a simple book nor even a well-known one, but its concepts are ubiquitous in our lives and reading it challenges unexamined complicity with such ideas.

Raney
Clyde Edgerton's novelization of the first two years, two months, and two days of a Southern/ Northern mixed marriage has you laughing out loud even as it breaks your heart. Although his other novels are funnier and sometimes sweeter,

Edgerton gets into a young married girl's mind in a way that has readers checking again and again to make sure he really was a guy.

Wally Lamb accomplished the same feat in *She's Come Undone*, but *Raney* is so culturally spot-on, it makes Southern readers giggle even as we say, "Ouch!" He touches on racism, sexism, ageism, and the rude-stupid fight between North and South so very deftly through the eyes of one small, nonthreatening woman that you don't really realize how challenging it all is until you close the book on its last enigmatic paragraph.

Then the words follow you around as you go through your heretofore unexamined motions of daily Southern living, catching yourself in an action to wonder why you're behaving as you are. It is not nearly as passive as it deceptively seems, this *Raney* book. Neither are any of his others, particularly *Walking Across Egypt*. If you don't want to reexamine your cultural norms, don't get started on Edgerton. Yeah, he's funny, but a sting rests in the tale. It's just that you don't notice while you're reading because you've split a gut laughing.

A Tale of Two Cities

Of course anyone who spends two hours a week at something called Needlework Night is going to love a novel with the world's most famous knitter in it. Even people who have never read *A*

Tale of Two Cities know about "that lady who makes lists with her knitting," Thérèse Defarge. Madame Defarge kept a record of which aristocrats were accused of what crimes before the revolution began, and of gossip that might lead to where they were hiding afterward. Knitters can't help but reference her on a regular basis, along with that other famous women's needlework story, "A Jury of Her Peers" by Susan Glaspell. (That's the one where the women realize a wife murdered her husband after looking at her quilting, which contains clues the women discern but the investigating men miss.)

Still, *Two Cities* has much more than a vengeful knitter to recommend it. Scholars have been saying for decades that this book is unlike anything else Charles Dickens wrote. It is, for him, brief. Its themes are vast but the writing tight. Its predictability only adds to its appeal. *Two Cities* breaks just about every rule of good fiction, yet gets away with it. And it has a brilliant opening (you remember: best of times, worst of times) and tearjerker closing (far, far better thing I've done, etc.). They'll live forever.

I read it in high school, after *Grapes of Wrath* turned me on to the classics. I thought I knew what it was about. (Heck, in high school, didn't we all think we knew just about everything?) I read it again after taking Western Civilization in college, when the French Revolution was not a romantic nebulous concept but one in a series of fierce history lessons, proving just how fast the pendulum could swing between the powerful and the powerless. (English folksinger Vin Garbutt has a thought-provoking song on this theme: "When oppressed becomes oppressor, when the best comes the worst, when the meek become the mighty and the blest take on the curse . . ." You can look it up. It's not a cheery little number, so it doesn't get sung that often.)

The French Revolution is just one more example of how justice denied becomes the foundation for another generation of justice denied, in the same way that meanness begets meanness. Dickens knew that in this book, although critics still argue whether his other works delved to the same depth of the human condition. Yet in the middle of it all one flawed antihero becomes someone generations of students have learned to admire, if not imitate.

Lest this all seem too horribly earnest, however, let me repeat: *Two Cities* is a ripping good read.

Till We Have Faces
C. S. Lewis has written many classics, including the Chronicles of Narnia stories, the Perelandra trilogy, and *Mere Christianity*. Of them all, his personal favorite was *Faces*. It's the retelling of the Cupid and Psyche myth, and its explorations

of what love is and does are profound. He pulls no punches in examining the heights and depths of what we have decided to call love for God, for family, for country, and for fellow humans. And he can hit bloody hard.

My favorite part—although it struck me silent the first time I read it—is when Oraul, the narrator, finally gets to the council of gods where she can petition for the return of her beloved little sister, the Psyche character. But when she speaks to them, she finds that what she has been demanding all along is not Psyche's redemption from a "monster" husband, nor even her well-being, but that she, Oraul, be the primary source of love in Psyche's life. And that moment devastates her into this speech:

"When the time comes to you at which you will be forced at last to utter the speech which has lain at the center of your soul for years, which you have, all that time, idiot-like, been saying over and over, you'll not talk about joy of words. I saw well why the gods do not speak to us openly, nor let us answer. Till that word can be dug out of us, why should they hear the babble that we think we mean? How can they meet us face to face till we have faces?"

For anyone who loves to write, those words are a constant challenge. And for anyone who believes in accountability at the end of mortal life, what does this mean? Whose voices do we speak with if not our own, and why? How do we learn to become ourselves? And to whom do we owe fealty, devotion, love?

Vanity Fair

People are fascinating, and from the time Becky hurls the dictionary out the carriage window until she brings about the marriage of her enemy-friend, she demands attention. Women who have enjoyed complicated relationships with friends—or with themselves—will recognize, perhaps even celebrate, her character. After ensuring her "friend" Amelia's marriage to a man who has been slavishly devoted to her, Becky arranges in cold blood her own marriage to Amelia's rich brother. William Makepeace Thackeray brings to life the motivations and machinations of two very different women without moralizing, or even at times being very clear about what did or didn't take place. He leaves the reader to draw conclusions, never being too overt, too pushy in his nuanced presentation.

Thackeray subtitled his work *A Novel Without a Hero* and it has one of the most layered and enigmatic casts of characters—not to mention unsatisfying endings—in classicdom. Becky is such a confusing mass of motives, Amelia such an annoying lump of passivity, and the men so rampant and roughshod in their thoughts and actions that you want to chuck your hands in the air and pray for a good BBC adaptation—which there was, along with some pretty bad movies that gave the whole thing an alternate happy ending. Happiness isn't really the point of this book.

If you want to learn to write good characters without insulting your readers' intelligence, this is the novel to study. Populated as it is with schemers and dreamers, as well as brokenhearted losers spurred to action by pride and fear (mostly of poverty) it's hard to identify a hero, easy to find someone with whom to identify.

The title comes from yet another classic, John Bunyan's *Pilgrim's Progress*, where Vanity is a town with a never-ending street fair full of worldly delights to tempt Pilgrim from his path. It's also the name of a magazine, which kinda makes you wonder who thought that was a good selling point, or if they'd read either book.

So if people in the shop ask me for my all-time favorites, those are the books I am most likely to evangelize for, but I can't leave this list without adding two short stories by favorite authors.

"Xingu"

A word of advice: do not read this while drinking a carbonated beverage, because you will snort it up your nose laughing. Edith Wharton's 1911 short story about women having an intellectual club of culture is a hilarious study of pseudo-smarts on display. Mrs. Roby, the woman who doesn't quite fit in because she doesn't see why she should try to, could be the hero or the villain, depending on how you take this tale. Is she making fun of the other women or saving them when she introduces the mysterious topic of "Xingu" at the luncheon where the snobbish authoress disdains their company?

The language of the story is itself so stiff and thick it reminds one of the brocaded cushions and horsehair sofas on which the ladies sit in their perfect parlor, trying to score intellectual points off one another. We've all known such women: the Pillars of Society that are Mrs. Plinth and Mrs. Ballinger, the meek little Mrs. Leveret, the enthusiastic airhead Miss Glyde, and confident, self-possessed Mrs. Roby, who really isn't very nice but is very real—which is more than can be said for the other ladies.

" 'We have a standard,' said Mrs. Plinth, feeling herself suddenly secure on the vast expanse of a generalization: and Mrs. Leveret, thinking there must be room for more than one in so broad a statement, took courage to murmur: 'Oh, certainly; we have a standard.' "

Since when was modern writing ever so subtle, so sarcastic, so rapier-sharp-robed-in-velvet-brocade in depicting how women talk to each other? I like Ms. Wharton's other books, too—*Ethan Frome* left me in a week-long depressed daze—but I don't know that I have ever read anything funnier than "Xingu." Actually, I think it should be required reading for all academics once a year. Nothing helps communication like a little humility.

"The Garden Lodge"

Willa Cather published this masterpiece in 1905. Her protagonist Caroline Noble's nonaffair with a great opera singer precipitates an unexpected and unwelcome self-examination. Caroline's even-mindedness, her ability to manage everything about her life and those around her so beautifully, stems from childhood hardship and a passionate need to have no passions. She is as self-possessed as a statue—except she isn't. Inside her is the woman she's denied herself the possibility of being, and when for one brief moment this other Caroline appears, even her husband can't believe it's really her. Among the literary examinations of the mazes that make up women's hearts, with their twists of motive, secret passages and sudden reversals, I've never read one that rings so true as the story of Caroline Noble's stormy night in her garden lodge. Bruce Springsteen sang about the secret gardens in women's hearts almost a hundred years later, but it was Cather's story that first explored them with such a nuanced touch.

Do you know what is ironic, though? I don't get the same pleasure from Cather's other, bigger works: *O Pioneers!* or *My Ántonia*, which examine themes of passion and duty very like "The Garden Lodge." Exploring the same ideas in these novels, later and at greater length, didn't really reveal any better observations. She hit the mark in Caroline Noble's single sleepless summer night.

When I was working on this book about the bookstore, the monthly writing group that meets there reviewed most of my musings. The list of books I loved elicited a not entirely surprising comment from Jenny. Within our first months of meeting it became evident that we had very dissimilar tastes in fiction, so when she said, "I never could get into Edith Wharton," I just laughed. We had long ago accepted our different tastes. But of course the discussion turned to each person's personal favorites, and James named Robert Service (the Yukon bard who penned, among other famous narrative poems, "The Cremation of Sam McGee").

"Really?" I barked with a laugh before I could even think. "I hated his stuff in high school!"

"Well," huffed James, "if I recall correctly, you're the one who's always talking about a bookstore teaching you to never comment on anyone else's tastes. *And* you also said you hated *Moby-Dick*. I question the good sense of any person who could dislike such a great book."

Jenny jumped in. "Hey! I hate Melville, too!"

Mike rolled his eyes. Although he didn't say it, I could hear him thinking "women." Aloud, he said only, "I loved *Dracula*." (Mike has always been the diplomat in our group.)

"*Twilight* was better," Jenny said, but James and I could see the sparkle in her eye, and knew she was trying to get a rise out of even-tempered Mike, just this once.

"Okay," Mike challenged, with a wry smile. "Let's just lay this on the table. Everybody go around and name a book you hate." That was all we wrote; abandoning our evening plans, we tore into the subject with relish.

De gustibus non est disputandum (there's no disputing taste). Works that have changed the lives of some people reading this—possibly even for the better—are no doubt listed below. Huzzah, and we here at the Big Stone Gap Writing Group are very happy for you. Now, without apology or humility, recognizing that a book snob bobs not far below the surface of all literate hearts, we present our individual choices for the **Top Ten Classics That Shouldn't Be:**

Anna Karenina

As Mike, remembering "Intro to Russian Literature," commented on Leo Tolstoy's novel of aristocratic adultery, "It could be shorter. Three pages would do very well." None of the rest of us tried to save this one, although Jenny did murmur, "But I like Tolstoy overall."

So did the rest of us, just not li'l Annie.

Beowulf

Disarmament theme notwithstanding, this is such disDaneful writing. A monster terrorizes a village until a boatload of tough guys show up to take him out. That's not a literary classic; it's Showtime Feature Film of the Week. Even the fight scenes drag. No wonder the author(s) decided to remain anonymous.

James challenged my diatribe; he likes action and thrills, and when the group penned (just for fun, mind you) a medieval romance one year, each taking a chapter in turn, he made sure he got to write all the swordfights and assassination attempts.

"It's a guy thing," I smirked.

"Ahem," Jenny said. "I just adore Ken Follett."

We let that pass.

Clarissa

Jenny hates this book with the passion of a thousand flaming suns. "By a third of the way in, I was hoping she would kill herself. Living in a whorehouse without knowing it? She's so stupid she deserves to die. Die, bitch, die!" Thus spake the gentle Southern belle we have seen cry over little frozen birds in the snow. Again, no one tried to save this novel, one of the longest in the English language. Instead, we asked why Samuel Richardson wrote it in the first place. None of us knew for sure, but when someone snidely suggested he was getting paid by the word, we figured that had something to do with it.

The Jungle

We realize we're on shaky ground, as Upton Sinclair's work is often hailed as one of the Great American Novels, but the group was pretty unified on this one as well. The sad thing is, we might have appreciated Sinclair's opus if not for the many bad book reports we all heard in high school.

Mike spoke for all of us: "They stood in front of the class clutching their paper and read, '*The Jungle* is about a poor Lithuanian immigrant who . . .' Tell us something we don't know, already!" Like why grossing people out is considered artistic. (We also guffawed at the snarky comment James made, that a Great American Novel would naturally have a lot of hamburger in it, but perhaps Lewis needed an apple pie as well. A little sweetness would have helped us stomach all that red meat.)

Moby-Dick

I don't care what the guys say; this is my opinion and I'm sticking to it. Remember high school English, when your teachers taught you about economy of words, making meanings clear, using adverbs sparingly? Neither did Herman Melville. Way to stretch a metaphor, Herm. That whole allegorical epic of obsession and power thing—never seen that before! Using a leviathan for your symbol doesn't make it better, you know, just bigger. Size doesn't matter; it's what you do with it that counts. Of course, given the masculinity of your work, you probably didn't date enough to learn that, either. Don't call me, Ishmael.

The Pillars of the Earth

Mike might have put his finger on the pulse of what was wrong with this book when he said, "If the movie version of your book flows better than the book itself, you're in trouble."

Even Jenny agreed that this particular title might be "below the standard" of his espionage thrillers. Ken Follett's twelfth-century saga holds advice for aspiring historic fiction writers: never let the facts get in the way of a good story; never let anachronistic thoughts or behaviors bother you as a writer; always assume your reader is less well read than you; and if a coronation, or an assassination, or a war would be more conveniently located in a different part of the timeline than reality, no problem. After all, writers are allowed to play historian anytime they want to. Philippa Gregory paved that road to hell years ago, and now that schools and universities are so poorly funded, who's gonna know anyway?

Truth be told, Follett's masterpiece does have one thing going for it; in the paperback version, it is almost as thick as it is tall, and thus has a most satisfying heft when hurled across the backyard.

A Prayer for Owen Meany

Lonely is the voice of truth. I started in on this book that I love to hate with my usual combination of sarcasm and confidence: Say wha-a-a-a-a-at? A boy with a voice like strangling mice, a father who can't remember having sex, and taking out Mom with a baseball combine to make art? No, actually, they don't. They just make one convoluted mess written in elegiac prose. Couldn't you have found something else to do with your talent, Mr. Irving? I'd rather swallow broken glass than read *Owen Meany* again. And by the way, readers, don't look too closely or you might realize you're getting *The World According to Garp* with different characters.

Then I sat back, confident of collusion—and heard silence. James and Michael avoided my eyes, while Jenny fiddled with her pen. "I really love John Irving's writing," was all she said, and James, stroking Beulah on the chair beside him, gave a small nod. It seemed prudent to move on.

But so desperate was I for backup that after the group went home, I called one of my oldest friends, now living in Seattle, and told her the whole story. Cami and I encouraged each other through writing our first books, went on annual creativity retreats together, even owned the same model of laptop. She would understand. Reiterating my diatribe on *Meany*, I ended with the breathless laughter of one who knows she's talking to a soul mate.

After a brief pause, Cami's voice came, measured and even, across the miles. "I. Absolutely. Adore. *Owen. Meany.* How can anyone with an ounce of compassion in her soul hate *A Prayer for Owen Meany*? And you have the gall to call yourself a humanitarian?" *Click.*

Tropic of Cancer

Jenny and I were the only ones in the writing group who had read this book by Henry Miller, and we shared the same disdain. Look, you wanna read porn, read porn. You wanna read erotica, read erotica. You wanna read surreal sentences chopped into hard-to-follow sections, read Jonathan Safran Foer. But for crying out loud, don't bind them all together into a first novel and label it a classic.

Just because no one understands you doesn't mean you're an artist, and writing about sex doesn't automatically make you interesting.

The Virginian

In the succinct words of our poet James, "Nobody acts like that." The rest of us agreed with this perfect four-word dismissal of Owen Wister's "classic."

"Young Goodman Brown"

Jenny is of the firm opinion that this high school classic (aka "piece of crap") has made massive contributions to the demise of reading for pleasure among Advanced Placement American Literature students everywhere. Poor Nathaniel Hawthorne. There are pills for depression now. Perhaps teachers do consider this short story a way to help pupils wade into both history and literature, but the mind-numbed, crushed students think the rest of the term is going to look like "Brown." They think there aren't any better short stories out there. They think all Puritans were tormented schizophrenics. By the time *The Crucible* shows up, they see "Goodman" on the page, their eyes glaze over and they skim the CliffsNotes. They miss the joy of discovering that *The Scarlet Letter* is both interesting *and* about sex.

Let me reiterate: one reader's life-altering, truth-revealing milestone-marking classic is another reader's forced term paper. Live and let live. If you come to my establishment and ask for a copy of *A Prayer for Owen Meany*, I'm not going to refuse to sell it to you. (But I might also suggest you try a Rosina Lippi.)

CHAPTER 26

Citizen Jack

"A good man is a nobler object of contemplation than a great author."
—Ross Perot

FIVE YEARS AFTER WE OPENED our shop, Jack came in from collecting the mail one afternoon and said, "I think I'll become an American citizen." Then he began opening the day's book packages.

I can't say that I was gobsmacked, but it was a bit startling. "Why do you want to be a citizen?" I asked as he scrunched up the advertising circulars and tossed them into the bin.

Jack paused, then said, "I guess I didn't tell you this before, but last year, when I came back here from my Scottish tour, it was the first time it fel* like coming home instead of just returning to c home."

As I mentioned before, Jack leads annual to Scotland and Ireland for no more than *people, taking them to folklore and herit* and generally showing them a good time on the traditional music and general tourism scenes. The tour he was talking about would have been his fourth, in our sixth year of living in the States.

The tours were something he enjoyed doing, a way for him to stay connected with his friends on the music circuit back in the Old World. Secretly I'd always thought it a nice way for him to excise the homesickness that builds up when you live long-term outside your homeland.

"No, you didn't mention that before, but, really, wow, that's great if it's what you want to do. Become an American?"

Jack laughed. "Become an American citizen, anyway, someone who has a vote and a say in what happens next over here. And . . ." He paused, then sat down at the front room table. "You know how you and I often talk about the community that's gathered around the shop, the friends and the regular customers, and the way we've grown into the town. People come in and say how wonderful it is, all we do here, that we're a community center, a hub for activity.

"And I always say how grateful I am to have been made so welcome. Not in a smarmy, lovefest way, but just that people have made space for us. And the truth is—" He laughed. "The truth is, true. I think people believe it's Southern ness, just something to say. But I want to ck. By being a citizen, I can take a more active role in helping out about the town, stand for council someday, perhaps, but meantime just . . ." His hands lifted, then fell back to his lap. "Be a part of it all."

I kissed my husband's bald spot. "Okay. Let's start doing the paperwork."

Paperwork followed on paperwork—each piece accompanied by an application fee. We sent four hundred dollars, two hundred dollars, one hundred dollars, waited for phone calls, returned forms, waited, returned, waited, got notarized signatures, waited, waited, waited . . .

And one day a package came in the mail containing a glossy, thin booklet of one hundred questions, with accompanying CD. These were the quiz items from which Jack would have to answer ten, six of them correctly, before he could become a citizen. His written examination was scheduled for six weeks hence in Fairfax, Virginia.

I grilled Jack on the questions that night. He got ninety-six correct. I got ninety-one.

The night before the interview, Jack and I drove to a cut-rate hotel a few miles from the designated municipal building. Though we had tried hard to avoid it, we arrived at rush hour. We'd been country mice too long and I'd lost my driving nerve; we pulled into a restaurant and waited until the stream of steel faded into occasional head-lights as the sun set, then got back into the car and found our hotel.

The next day, I braved the morning commuter rush to drop Jack for his interview, and waited four hours at the hotel for him to call. Since the letter informing him of his schedule had suggested he would need only two hours, I was panicking by the time he rang.

"Everything okay?" I blurted into the phone.

"Tell you all about it when you get here," he said, and I threw the last of our things into the case and raced to fetch him. Was he being deported? Had he failed the exam? Aced it and been asked to perform special duties? What?

"They forgot me," he said as soon as he slid into the car, all smiles.

"They *what?*"

"I was sitting in the waiting room, and they called everyone who came in with me, and another group of people had started showing up, so I went up and asked at the desk, and she rooted around and looked concerned, then looked behind a desk and came up with a piece of paper from the floor. 'Mr. Beck? Your file fell. I'm so sorry. We'll do you next.'"

I couldn't help but laugh. "Only you, dear. Only you!"

Jack received a letter; he passed his oral and written examination, and it was now just a matter of waiting for notification of when the naturalization ceremony would take place. The government would be in touch.

We took the list of one hundred questions across to the Mutual and passed it around among Bo, David, Cotton, and the gang. Bo looked at the booklet suspiciously, flipping its pages.

"Are these the laws that govern us inside the mountains, or those people on the other side?" he asked, and the men eating around us grinned.

Five years ago, that question would have flummoxed Jack, but now he knew not only what they were saying, but what they weren't.

"Ah, Bo," Jack said with a laugh. "You and I know the government has never understood how to run the Coalfields, and we like it best when they stay on their side and let us get on with things."

The boys gave appreciative grins and Bo slapped Jack on the back with the booklet. "I don't believe I could answer a one of these"—his voice boomed through the diner—"but I'm glad you did! Welcome, brother! But," he added, dropping his tone confidentially so that only the six nearest tables could hear, "you were already our brother, weren'tcha?"

Back when we started the bookstore, the gates of central Appalachia's Coalfields had seemed as tightly shut as the vaults of Fort Knox. It was hard to remember those days, that morning in the Mutual.

The phone rang and caller ID listed it as coming from 000-000-0000.

"It's for you," I said, handing the unanswered

receiver to Jack. " 'Cause that has to be a govern-ment agency."

It was—homeland security. A background check to ensure Jack wasn't a member of the Communist Party or a terrorist cell. Neither of these is big in Big Stone.

The awaited letter arrived; the naturalization ceremony would be three weeks hence, in the federal courthouse in Abingdon. Since about our second year in operation, we'd been sending e-mail notices to customers who signed up for them, letting people know of upcoming events. On our next round, Jack included his citizenship status update. He got more than one hundred e-mails congratulating him, and several requests to know when and where the ceremony would take place, if guests could attend, and would there be a "Citizen Jack" party at the bookstore.

On the day of Jack's ceremony, a crowd carpooled to Abingdon: Erin (who organizes some of our special events and attends Needlework Nights); Becky and Tony; Virginia, one of our staunchest supporters, a county board of supervisors member, the organist at the Presbyterian church, and a past murder victim; guitarist Grace and her husband Bill, who had rounded up financial support for the Celtic Day that Jack started in the town three years before; Elissa, our friend and photographer; a friend from my college days, Abingdon's storyteller-in-residence Donnamarie; Fiona; Isabel; and our *Grapes of Wrath* music fellow traveler Gary and his wife, Millie.

It pleased us, as it also pleased the person in question, that one of these friends had been among those rejecting Jack for membership in the Kiwanis Club all those years ago. Times change, and people are basically good at heart; enough said.

As Jack—resplendent in kilt and sporran—accepted his certificate, the gang burst into cheers, waving American flags and clapping wildly. The judge conducting the ceremony looked up and smiled before reading the other fourteen names on his list.

Afterward, we went together for that most American of celebratory dinners: pizza. Around the table, Jack raised his glass of cola and thanked our friends for coming. "You made me a part of this community long before I joined it formally, and I thank you from the bottom of my heart."

People in the restaurant began to figure out what the unruly bunch with the American flags and red, white, and blue stuffed sequined eagle sitting on the table were celebrating (aided, no doubt, by our singing, "Happy Citizenship, Dear Jack, Happy Citizenship to you" when the pizzas arrived). Patrons started getting up and coming over to shake Jack's hand and wish him well.

Back at the bookstore, we held our monthly Let's

Talk on citizenship. Tony summed up for all of us when he said, "Fitting in is one thing. Belonging is another. And then there's contributing. I think Jack and Wendy have done all three."

In short, it was a day for knowing that some things are better when done within the gracious bounds of community and camaraderie. And it was, as much as any ceremony ever could be, the culmination of years of working to be a contributing part of our town. *Our* town.

CHAPTER 27

The Last Word

To be satisfied with a little, is the greatest wisdom; and he that increaseth his riches, increaseth his cares; but a contented mind is a hidden treasure.

—Akhenaten

BHUTAN IS AN INSIGHTFUL COUNTRY. This nation has a Gross National Happiness index. The index is calculated using several indicators: citizens' psychological well-being, education, and time use; the perceived value and sustainability of ecology, culture, and community vitality in the nation; public health; living standards; and whether citizens think they have good governance. This is how the Bhutanese measure the success of their collective lives.

It's a good measurement. Jack assesses our bookstore's performance each month, totting up Internet and shop sales. He compares these to the same time last year. Quarterly we sit down with a glass of wine and talk about what we liked, incidents remembered for good or ill, any rearranging of the stock we'd like to try, ideas for promotions or events or fixing a recurring problem.

In our first four years, sales figures climbed. During the worst of the recession, they skyrocketed as people stayed home, walked around town instead of driving, and bought cheaper methods of entertaining themselves. At the end of year four, our sales peaked. Year five, they were the same, with only a slight increase tangential to our starting to serve in-store soups and salads. We had reached a plateau, doing as well as the shop could be expected to in our region.

Year five was the moment. If we intended to expand our business, we needed to start a franchise in another county, double our Internet efforts, and/or pack up and move to a bigger location. Asheville had long been on our minds; we love nothing better than to visit North Carolina's Paris of the South. Kingsport, Tennessee, presented another possibility; we knew lots of people in that larger population area. Plus, we had investment capital this time. Opening a second store, or closing this one and moving to a larger city, would be so different: no more scratchy thrift-store chairs and endless pots of mac and cheese; we knew how to run a bookshop now.

We sat and stared at the graph Jack had drawn. Then Jack, as he is wont to do, asked the perfect question: "What do we want?"

That didn't take long to answer: "The way we live now." We had what we wanted. The shop makes enough money for us to live life with frugal grace. My college work provides health insurance; Jack's steadily growing tours cover the cost of his annual visit home and let him impart his love of Scots and Irish culture; our performing gives us busman's holidays more interesting than what we could dream up for ourselves. Food, shelter, heat, and light, not to mention bucketloads of entertainment better than anything we could buy, were ours from selling books.

We started the bookstore to live as we saw fit, solving our own problems, scheduling our own lives, no longer living as renters inside our skins. It's done that and more. The shop made us members of a community we entered as heartbroken, tired people. Tales of the Lonesome Pine gave us friends and fun. It offered perspective, and while we were busy trying to figure out how to run the shop, it quietly returned us to a balanced and honest way of living, neither smug nor grim.

Who could ask for more? Amid the jumble of listening to life plots and hefting boxes and stocking shelves and pricing books, underneath it all contentment flows like a little burbling mountain stream. Cat pee, guerrilla bargainers, fifty-pound boxes of Harlequin romances and all, we are having the time of our lives.

Glenn is a customer who attends several of our special events but shops with us rarely. He appeared just as we were closing one snowy December evening. Handing Jack a package, he lifted his hat to me in the twilight and marched back out with only two words flung over his shoulder: "Merry Christmas!"

Jack sat down at the table and unwrapped a bottle of exceptionally good lowland single-malt, his favorite that has to be special-ordered—and that we couldn't afford except on rare occasions. A note accompanied the gift. "Dear Jack and Wendy, I don't know what we did around here before you showed up! Found a treasure for one of our town's finest treasures. Enjoy!"

We are so very, very rich.

A good book has no ending.
—R. D. Cumming

ACKNOWLEDGMENTS

THE CUSTOMERS OF TALES OF the Lonesome Pine, past, present, and future: You make it so much fun to be so busy. Thanks!

The UVA-Wise CABs: Margie (this book's godmother), Cyndi, Ann (the academic's best friend and secret weapon), and Michael.

The Grammar Guerrilla Girls: You know who you are (in every sense of those words); you know how important what you do is; and you know how much we mean to each other.

The Needlework Night Babes: may your stitches never ravel and your needles point only to the truth.

The Big Stone Gap Writing Group: you saw it first (and pretty much last, and at every stage in between. Are you as sick of me as I am?!).

Pamela and Louise Malpas at Harold Ober: from the first phone call in that parking lot to the last edit, thank you! And to Michelle Montalbano: thank you for, among other things, the epigraph research and the Melville backup.

Nichole Argyres (let's not talk about *Meany*) and Laura Chasen at St. Martin's Press: thank you for making this book better every time you touched it and every time we talked. And thank you for liking it so much. You were right, Nichole; this was fun, fun, fun (mostly because you were so much fun to work with).

Team Emert: we see way too much of each other, but thanks for keeping the smiles going anyway.

The people of Coalfields Appalachia: we get the hype end of the media, the short end of the funding stick, the stereotypes, the extraction without infrastructure, and the platitudes. And we still belong to ourselves and to God's Country. The mountains hold things in, and they also keep things out. Here's to us!

Cassie, Kim, and the rest of the workaholics at SMP: thank you for thinking of the stuff no one else thinks of, with a style and panache that makes everyone else glad you thought of it.

Kathy Still: I think it's ironic that you're behind the scenes making it all better in this book, as you do in real life for so many.

Jessica Ketron and Elissa Powers: your combined genius crafted an author head shot I didn't want to burn.

Cami Ostman: all the years of "your turn/my turn" have been good. Here's to many more!

Carolyn Jourdan: for numerous wisdom swaps, online and off.

Tony and Anne and the congregation of BSG Presbyterian, plus the Quakers who meet in our bookstore: y'all are bastions of sanity and good manners, no matter what.

The booksellers we met and the friends we met up with on the "Booking Down the Road Trip": Brave, hardworking, always quirky, and usually right; that about sums you up.

My parents and sister: Yes, you are funny!

The owners and operators of mom-and-pop stores everywhere: Hang in there! We are the collective reason civilization hasn't self-destructed yet!

PAWS, In His Hands, and the rest of the rescuers who find homes for shelter animals: You do good, and you do right. (And please, world, spay and neuter your pets!)

The day jobbers: Diane, Keith, Gary and Millie, Susan, Norma, and Libz (and Chelsie the Twitter tutor).

The theatricals: Jerry Lou and Jimmy, Erin, Harry, Jenny, and the gang.

And Jack: it seems superfluous to thank you here because you were such a part of it all. Every day with you is a good one.

Center Point Large Print

600 Brooks Road / PO Box 1
Thorndike ME 04986-0001 USA

(207) 568-3717

US & Canada:
1 800 929-9108
www.centerpointlargeprint.com